ALL
MIGHTY

Horst-Eberhard Richter

ALL
MIGHTY

A Study of the
God Complex
in Western Man

**Translated from the German
by Jan van Heurck**

Hunter House Inc. Publishers, U.S.A.

Contents

PART FOUR
Case History:
An Object Lesson in Overcoming
the Myth of Omnipotence

Preface to the U.S. Edition

The theme of this book is the disastrous belief of our civilization that it is all-powerful, omnipotent. The book contends that the suppression of suffering, weakness and mortality in our societies is linked to a boundless megalomania, which threatens unwittingly to destroy the very conditions of our existence—both as living creatures and as social beings. Because of our boundless desire for power, more than one million dollars is spent each minute on armaments, while every day 40,000 children in poorer countries die in conditions of abject misery. Yet the nuclear age, with its dreadful risks, threatens the population of the leading industrial nations as well. As if blind to the consequences, the super-powers are producing increasingly powerful nuclear weapon systems, the use of which—whether intentional or, as might easily happen, accidental—could result only in mutual and global destruction.

Nuclear overarmament is closely linked to and symbolic of a process of virtually demented "psychological armament." The French physicist and Nobel Prize-winner Alfred Kastler has quite rightly issued the warming that without "psychological disarmament" all treaties on the reduction, or even abolition, of certain weapon systems or categories would be useless. For they would not prevent men from producing new and even more terrible weapons tomorrow, weapons which would lie outside the definitions of all treaties in existence today.

What we need, therefore, is a process of radical rethinking, as Albert Einstein tirelessly demanded. This book is concerned with those collective mechanisms which have hitherto obstructed this rethinking. And the book also attempts to indicate those areas from which a new consciousness could arise.

The citizens of the U.S.A.—the leading nation of our civilization—bear an especial responsibility in the present crisis. Therefore I am grateful to the publishers, Hunter House, for now making this book available to the American public. And I am glad this is happening at a time when important moral and political movements within American public life are showing signs of that beneficent rethinking which could yet rescue the imperiled future of our children and our children's children.

I think, for example, of the nuclear-freeze movement and of the peace commitment of the Catholic bishops, the National Council of Protestant Churches and various lay organizations. I myself have received considerable stimulus and encouragement from colleagues in the American branch of "Physicians for Social Responsibility," and I mention with gratitude the names of Robert Jay Lifton, John Mack, Helen Caldicott, Bernard Lowen, Eric Chivian and Judy Lipton.

My thanks also go to the publishers for the meticulous preparation of the American edition; to Miss Jan van Heurck for the sensitive translation, the Appendix to which will certainly be welcomed by the American reader as a valuable aid and guide; and to Dr. Richard Brenzo and Ms. Louanna Heuhsen for assisting me with shaping the English text.

Horst-Eberhard Richter
Giessen, August 1983

Introduction

This book represents my attempt to treat a problem which I first addressed in a book written some thirty years ago. Fortunately this first book was never published. The galleys and the page proofs had already been corrected when, overnight, the publishing house went bankrupt, and I did not submit the manuscript to any other publishers. My book was to have been called *Über den Schmerz* ("About Pain"). Not until later did I realize that in writing it I had been trying to find out for myself how suffering could be dealt with.

At that time I found myself in the same predicament as many other young people who, although emotionally shattered by the experience of war and imprisonment, had immediately set about rebuilding their lives as soon as external circumstances allowed. I created—or rather I searched for—a new family to replace the one I had lost in the war. At an age when others have already firmly established themselves professionally, I set out to learn a profession. Like most people of my generation, I had already been through the school of war, which had trained us to endure hunger, poverty, fatigue and unremitting effort, as well as to deal with crises, improvise spur-of-the-moment solutions and accept responsibility. As people say nowadays, I knew how to "cope" with life.

It is significant that when I returned to the bombed-out German city which had been my home and found that my family and almost all my friends were dead, I reacted by developing a psychosomatic illness. I felt— and indeed I have never completely rid myself of this feeling—that I ought to have died with my loved ones. Of course, neurotic conflicts originating in my childhood played a role in this fantasy and later, in the course of two series of psychoanalytic treatment, I learned, to some degree, to understand these conflicts. But my feelings involved something more than childhood neurosis. I could not come to terms with the fact that all of us— we Germans and the whole human race—had consented to travel together this road to self-destruction: that we had been capable of betraying our true human goals. And thus at a time when I was already rebuilding my life as if it were no more than a house demolished by some natural catastrophe—in other words, at a time when I was behaving in the way I had been taught to regard as right and proper—I felt that I had not learned anything at all.

After the long years I had spent in a climate of both physical and political confinement, it was easy to get used to the less oppressive climate of democracy. I simply took things as they came, adjusted to the changes in my world, continued to function and "pulled myself together" as I had been trained to do. This behavior made me feel like an old man too set in his ways to change, and at the same time like an immature child—like the child I had been when I had first become a soldier and been dragged into the war. I could not make heads or tails of what had happened to me in the course of the past few years, and so I could not seem to find an identity appropriate to a man of my age. People only four or five years younger seemed to me to belong to a completely new generation of carefree innocents. On the other hand, neither did I have much in common with those "old campaigners," hard-boiled by disillusionment. In their own way they had internalized the antimortality of wartime and had easily and without conflict found a place for themselves in the corrupt black-market milieu of the postwar years in Germany. I found very few people I could talk to about things that mattered—the things which I desperately needed to understand but could not make sense of on my own. Then I decided to try psychoanalysis, no doubt because, as a patient during the war, I had had the good fortune to meet Werner Hollmann, a student of Viktor von Weizsäcker, (I) and he had told me that psychoanalysis might help me to become better acquainted with myself and my feelings.

Gradually it dawned on me that my loss of contact with my emotional roots in a world which had vanished forever was due to something more than the repression caused by my own personal anxieties. I was well on the way to destroying myself by trying to live up to a false standard of normalcy, of what a human being ought to be—a standard which I shared with the society around me. I wanted to be strong and stable. Yet, at the same time, I did not want to forget the things which had been destroyed, i.e., the things which all of us had actively helped to destroy, within ourselves and around about us. I was unable to reconcile these seemingly incompatible urges. I was afraid that I would fall apart if I lowered my defenses and really "opened up," without reservation, to my feelings of helplessness and confusion. Yet that was exactly what I had to do in order to remain faithful to my own past and to the dead, as well as to preserve the emotional continuity of my life. I could not help being ashamed of our common past. But whenever I tried to implicate my dead friends and family in this collective shame, I felt as if I were betraying them. What I really needed was to have those who had been killed restored to life, so that we could have learned to deal with our memories together.

Then I would not have been forced to do it on my own and in a sense at the expense of the dead, rather than with their cooperation. But of course their death was irrevocable. The upshot of this conflict was that I tried to go on living in the same old way—the very way which had caused all our misery in the first place. Unfortunately this attempt to "grin and bear it" was reinforced by all those precepts and behavioral role models which had governed my life in the past, and which—so I had been taught—constituted the norm of how a "real man" ought to behave.

Since that time, the many years which I have spent trying to learn the art of suffering without sacrificing my emotional stability in the process have left their imprint—sometimes without my even being aware of it—on many of my scientific and scholarly projects. In my first printed (but unpublished) book, which grew out of my doctoral dissertation in philosophy, I traced the evolution of attitudes toward pain and suffering in the history of Western philosophy. Later, as a physician specializing in psychosomatic diseases, I spent years studying cardiac neurosis, a condition in which people experience cardiac symptoms such as palpitations, rapid pulse, fatigue and shortness of breath after mild exertion, in the absence of any organic disease of the heart. In collaboration with my colleagues at our clinic, (II) I investigated the phenomena of emotional fragility, fear of being alone and anxiety about death in persons afflicted with cardiac neurosis. These people also do not know how to suffer. Either they make tremendous efforts to create lives which, on the surface, appear absolutely idyllic, or they break down completely. They are unable to tolerate any discord between themselves and the world and people around them, as well as any intrapsychic conflict; they are incapable of dealing with negative feelings or of living with guilt. I treated many people afflicted with cardiac neurosis at a stage in my life when I too had much to learn about how to deal with suffering, and I hoped that we could learn together.

It was extremely difficult for me to stop conforming to the society around me. But at long last I came to understand that I could not really be free to gratify my need to belong until I had first learned to resist those pressures to "fit in" which, under the guise of promoting social solidarity, in effect represent ways to force people to adjust to hierarchical social structures—i.e., to make them submit to the principle of authority. I realized that man's sense of community is invariably corrupted whenever it is turned into the duty to exhibit "solidarity" with some particular group within a social system characterized by the competition between rival camps. The primary phenomenon of sympathy (III) involves a commiseration, a suffering-with and fellow feeling with all human life, an intimate bond between equals. Yet we are constantly besieged with the message that the only true solidarity lies in joining forces *with* some people and *against* others. Thus, the principle of sympathy is, in a sense, engulfed by the power principle, and "solidarity" becomes an instrument in the struggle for domination. We are all filed away into neat compartments or "in-groups," and the principle of "solidarity" is designed to increase the combat strength of these groups, all of whom want to enhance their power or at least defend it against other groups. Yet the root of the principle of solidarity lies in its indivisibility, and by its very nature it demands the mutual recognition of equality and the abolition of societal schisms based on the unequal distribution of power. Thus in reality we can gratify our need for social integration only if we carry it beyond those limitations imposed by the principle of power. This is why a person feels better about himself and more in harmony with his own humanity when he allies himself, both emotionally and in his day-to-day behavior, with individuals or groups who suffer oppression because they are alleged to be alien, inferior or evil, and who consequently become social outcasts or are only marginally tolerated by their society. For it is these very groups who represent the suffering to which our society must open its heart if it is to be protected against social intolerance in the future.

Unfortunately the power principle which dominates our society is reinforced by the patriarchal principles which we have traditionally instilled in the young—principles which young boys are expected to act upon immediately, and young girls to passively revere. Boys learn to regard suffering as a sign of weakness and thus as a quality which can appropriately be manifested only by girls; so they relinquish their suffering to the female. They are systematically taught to pattern themselves after a series of fairy-tale or comic-strip heroes and historical Supermen, the collective incarnation of grandeur, strength, victory and the will to power. These young males are subjected to a steady barrage of propaganda which encourages them to strive onward and upward, to attain a position of dominance and authority. At the same time, being placed under burdens which they cannot live up to, they are sorely tempted to feel envy, resentment and a desire for revenge. In the end, this training program leaves them highly susceptible to alluring new political schemes—schemes of which fascism merely represents the most archaic and barbarous example. In other words, by the primacy which it assigns to authoritarian principles, a normal middle-class upbringing goes a long way towards promoting that self-alienation which makes it possible for the politically powerful, whenever they choose, to sow discord among individuals or groups in violation of their own human nature, which is disposed towards sympathy and solidarity. Males, both as boys and as men, are systematically indoctrinated to regard themselves as good and worthwhile people only when they have repressed that emotional sensitivity which alone could provide them the strength to undertake the uncompromising defense of humanitarian values.

Thus it is essential that we acknowledge, and reintegrate into our lives, those manifestations of emotional fragility, weakness and suffering which are repressed, both psychically and socially, by the males of our patriarchal society—or more precisely, manifestations psychically repressed by males through the instrumentality of societal repression. Consequently, we can make appropriate attitudinal changes only if a simultaneous change takes place on the behavioral level, in the relations between the sexes and in general between those who hold positions of power in our society and those who do not. To be sure, we do have to *think* about our situation in new ways if we are able to realize how necessary it is that we eliminate artificially-structured relationships which make some people dependent on others. But unless the changes in our *thinking* are immediately converted into political *action,* all our theorizing could easily turn into a narcissistic fantasy obliging us to take no action whatsoever. At the moment, I can think of no more fitting terms in which to describe this phenomenon than those I employed in my book *Engagierte Analysen* ("Committed Analyses"), a collection of essays on interpersonal relations [74]: "If, when we *act*, we fail to apply what we *know*, in the end we cease to *know* how we should *act*. If we do nothing but theoretically criticize something when it is within our power to personally do something about it, in the end our default on the practical plane corrupts even our capacity for critical thought. Outward submission, the failure to fight back, dulls our emotions and blinds our cognitive faculties."

In some of my earlier writings I described various forms of social activity, intending to show how other people and I collaborated in the attempt to achieve this link between theory and social action through a socially oriented self-help procedure. Yet these descriptions, intended as mere accounts of facts, have been consistently misinterpreted, and the activities which I portrayed—child-parent work groups, initiatives to aid the socially disadvantaged, psychosocial work and study teams—have in fact been isolated and interpreted as would-be panaceas for the ills of

society. In particular, orthodox Marxists, i.e. materialists, who habitually
and unilaterally analyze psychical changes as the result of changes of
circumstances, have consistently misconstrued the accounts of my experiences with spontaneous group initiatives and have failed to appre-
ciate the modesty of my claims for the capacity of such groups to
effect social change. For although such down-to-earth, critical steps
towards reform are of crucial importance with regard to those limited
political goals they can achieve, I consider equally valuable the lessons we
can learn from them. They can supply us with significant guidelines for
the future, as well as with stimulation for further theoretical work. They
provide data for reflection both on our own inner reality and on the
realities of society. For frequently the discrepancy between theory and
practice creates a "credibility gap," leading to the kind of total passivity
and resignation which has overcome thousands of former members of the
student protest movement of the sixties.

However, in the present book I concentrate, more than in most of my
earlier writings, on theory, analysis and reflection, rather than on
practical applications. Apart from the medical case history in the final
section, I do not describe any projects of a practical nature. What I have
attempted to do here is to pick up the thread of those reflections which I
abandoned thirty years ago. I begin my discussion with an examination of
those same philosophers to whom I looked for help all those years ago, in
my effort to integrate and deal with a mass of unassimilated, inarticulate
suffering. This time, however, I approach the problem not merely from a
philosophical standpoint, but also as a psychoanalyst—a psychoanalyst
who presumes to ask questions and to think about the unconscious roots
and implications of philosophic thought. I do this less with a view to
"psychoanalyzing" individual philosophers or individual intellectual
motifs than with the hope of understanding the unconscious of that
Zeitgeist ("spirit of the age") which was expressed in the philosophies I
examine. This philosophical retrospective will be followed by an attempt,
based on the foregoing analysis of Western intellectual history, to draw
some general conclusions about the cultural attitudes of contemporary
Western man. The focus of the book will be that conflict which I outlined
at the beginning of these remarks in describing problems encountered in
my personal life—i.e., the conflict surrounding suffering and behavioral
role models. I will conclude by describing one of my experiences as a
psychoanalyst, an experience which suggested the central theme of this
book.

Notes to Introduction

(I) Viktor von Weizsäcker (1886–1957), a German professor, neurologist and pioneer in the field of psychosomatic medicine, believed that disease must be understood in terms of the personal characteristics and life history of the patient. Thus disease had both a physical or literal aspect, and a metaphorical aspect which pointed to other causes.—Tr.

(II) Dr. Richter, who has been associated with various German medical clinics since the 1950's, has, since 1962, been director of the Clinic of Psychosomatic Medicine at the University of Giessen.—Tr.

(III) V. Part III for discussion of the concept of sympathy, built on the principles of Max Scheler and others.—Tr.

PART ONE

The "God Complex"
A History
of the Myth
# of Man's Omnipotence

1

The Escape from the Middle Ages: Man Loses God and Desires to Become God Himself

When young children at a certain age of intellectual development have learned to distrust their parents, they sometimes react in a way which may seem puzzling but actually makes perfect sense if one assumes their point of view. At a time when, objectively speaking, they are totally dependent on parental care and protection, it throws them into a panic if they feel that they can no longer rely on this protection. Their sense of self has developed to the point that they understand quite well what it would mean to lose the care their parents afford them. Driven by anxiety, they try to assume complete control of their lives themselves. They refuse to adopt a passive role and let other people or events control them. They even refuse to submit to the demands of their own bodies. Instead they make a gargantuan effort to supervise and control everything around and inside them. At night they will not let themselves fall asleep, or will sleep only if a light is on and the door left open; for it is essential that nothing should happen without their knowledge. They feel that they must know about everything. Anything which happens "behind their backs" seems to them ominous and threatening. Moreover, they feel that no one has the right to do anything to them against their will. They even try to eliminate the element of chance by calculating and determining everything beforehand. When their parents ask them to do something, they frequently say "No!" simply to assert their own autonomy. Often they refuse to eat when they are supposed to, and wish to decide for themselves exactly when, what and how often they will eat. In fact they want to make their own decisions about everything. If their parents allow themselves to get trapped into a power struggle with such children, the parents usually lose. The more pressure is applied to make the children obey, the more rebellious they become. They resist any act of coercion, for they experience it as an attempted assault and feel that some catastrophe will befall them if they give in. They feel secure only if they themselves determine how they are

3

going to act, at any time or place, on the basis of their own observations and inclinations.

The people around them find the behavior of these children strange, baffling and annoying. The parents, who are directly implicated in the child's distrustful behavior, have usually had ambivalent feelings towards him from the very beginning. They counteract their impulses to reject him by exhibiting an overly scrupulous concern for his welfare. But it is precisely their deep-rooted feelings of ambivalence which have aroused the child's distrust in the first place and which continually reinforce or increase it. If I don't keep an eye on everything, the child thinks, they'll abandon me or destroy me. This constant state of inner tension and overly alert concentration invariably leads to a rapid and dramatic development of the child's perceptual faculties. Moreover, children of this kind soon become aware of highly complex chains of cause and effect. Their anxiety compels them to try to "second-guess" everyone and everything around them, for only if they know what will happen next can they calculate what action to take in order to forestall the calamity which they per-petually expect. Thus they are unable to fall asleep, because losing consciousness would make it completely impossible for them to defend themselves and would give absolute dominion to that evil world which, so they believe, they can fend off only if their ego, their conscious self, remains wide awake.

Of course, neither the parents nor their distrustful child is aware of the hidden ramifications of their relationship. None of them realizes that the child's fantasy that he is totally helpless and hence in mortal danger is driving him to take refuge in another fantasy—the narcissistic fantasy of his own omnipotence. To other people the child's behavior appears incomprehensible and even absurd. The disparity between the child's actual dependency and immaturity on the one hand, and his demand for sovereign authority on the other, is apparent to everyone around him, and people cannot help regarding his attitude as ridiculous. They are clearly aware that something is wrong with the child: that he is under a strain and doing himself harm because of his compulsive urge to supervise and control everything going on around him. However, as a rule they do not understand that the child's apparently illogical behavior actually conforms to a careful plan, based on the hidden logic of his emotions. The child must be understood in terms of his own special brand of logic if he is to receive the kind of help and therapy he needs. It would not help him in the least to convince him, by rational arguments, that his refusal to go to sleep and his obstinate refusal to eat when and what he is supposed to are harming his health. For the child is caught up in a tragic contradiction. His ego is trying to achieve security by means of careful calculation and supervision of the world, which it has reduced to the status of an object to be studied and controlled; and yet his unconscious, emotional motivations are beyond the reach of rational argumentation. Thus he is dominated by the conviction that the only way he can compensate for his helplessness and prevent his own destruction is by *over*compensation, by becoming omnipotent and omniscient. The only thing which can help him now is to develop a whole new *emotional* orientation towards the world.

*

It seems logical to assume that, during the transition from the Middle Ages to the modern era, psychological processes somewhat akin to those which I have just described as typical of the reactions of certain children must have taken place in the psyche of European man, and that all the nations of the West are still suffering from their aftereffects. For centuries medieval man had felt secure in his role as a child of God. This feeling of security had enabled him to forego the exact investigation of the physical universe; nor did he feel compelled to calculate and plan all the details of his life beforehand. One expression of this devout attitude, this submission to the will of God, was the doctrine of predestination as formulated by the patristic theologian St. Augustine. Augustine had declared that the fate of every human being was wholly predetermined by divine decree. Man was not intended to gain access to divine truth by the exercise of reason, but rather through faith. God would reveal truth only to those whose ethical conduct showed them worthy of such revelation. Thus what really counted was absolute obedience to God's will. Skepticism led nowhere; and neither did knowledge established through personal cognition.

But in a sense Augustine himself had pointed out the weak spot in this argument: a kind of seed which, over succeeding centuries, gradually grew into a loss of trust. For Augustine taught that no one could be certain whether, by the unfathomable decree of divine Providence, he had been numbered among those who would partake of salvation or those who must atone for original sin. It was difficult for people to acknowledge their absolute dependency on God when they could not count on receiving His grace. How could they blindly trust in God when there was no way of knowing whether He would mete out salvation or hideous punishment? Given this fact, was not man justified in placing greater reliance on the knowledge he could personally acquire by the exercise of his own intellect, which might enable him to better safeguard his position? Clearly Augustine felt a growing tension between the need for independent thought as a source of guidance and direction, and the inclination to submit blindly to the dictates of revealed truth. Thus he warned against the powerful urge to acquire knowledge: "For apart from this wicked lust of the flesh which resides in all sensual desire and all craving for pleasure and which destroys those who, far from Thy countenance, devote themselves to its service, there abides in the soul another craving which, to be sure ... does not desire to take delight in the flesh, but which *through* the flesh, in vain curiosity wills to learn idle and fruitless things, which are then painted, as with face-paint, with the name of knowledge and of science." Mere curiosity leads people to "search out all nature's mysteries, which were not created for our faculties, and seek after things the knowledge of which profits us nothing; notwithstanding all men feel this one desire: to know." [4]

On the other hand, in *The City of God* Augustine attributed a certain importance to intellectual judgment and to the principle of the freedom of the will. However, in matters of real significance, faith in revealed truth and in its governance within Church tradition was supposed to take precedence over intellectual cognition. As for freedom of the will, this had been imparted to mankind in Adam, but he had abused it and thus destroyed it before it could be passed down to his descendents. [5]

It appears that, during the Middle Ages, the feeling of being cared for and protected like a child by one's father, God, was steadily waning, while at the same time the need to exorcise a growing sense of uneasiness intensified the urge to acquire personal power over one's circumstances. Man's distrust of God was nourished not only by the fear of being found unacceptable in His eyes, but also by anxiety concerning the evil or punitive side of God's nature. Man's announcement of his refusal to go on blindly obeying took the form of an intensified demand for knowledge and the right of self-determination. However, this behavior simply enmeshed him more deeply in the same old dilemma, for now he had every reason to fear that his rebellion might truly call down on his head the wrath of God which, among other things, had roused his feelings of distrust in the first place. This situation inevitably gave rise to a self-activating, self-reinforcing vicious circle: Man's growing sense of insecurity relative to God forced him to compensate by a narcissistic attempt to provide for his own security. But each magnification of his personal power brought with it a magnification of the threat of divine retribution, and this threat in turn released new anxieties which, once again, made it necessary for man to take additional defensive measures to compensate for the change in the situation—although of course this compensation took the form of an *over*compensation. In other words, from the very outset the process of emerging from a state of total dependency and passivity included the tendency for a sudden, radical swing to the opposite extreme: *identification with the omniscience and omnipotence of God.* And in fact man's subsequent emotional development exhibits many features of a classical reaction described by psychoanalysis, involving the flight from narcissistic feelings of impotence into narcissistic feelings of omnipotence. We may have difficulty in perceiving the radical nature of this psychic reversal, because men of the modern era have evolved ever new theories, or rather rationalizations, to explain away their attempts to incorporate divine omnipotence through the mechanism of identification. The more of God's power man usurped, the more vehemently and ingeniously he convinced himself that this was not what he was really doing at all, and that in reality the only reason why he wanted to annex those of God's powers which were operative in nature was to acquire a greater awareness of God himself.

However, the medieval and Renaissance alchemists' quest for the "Philosophers' Stone," which supposedly possessed the power to heal all diseases, transform any substance into gold and confer on its possessor power over all spirits, revealed that, in reality, man had intended all along to seize God's infinite greatness and power for himself. Alchemy was a blatant manifestation of man's desire to appropriate all of God's miraculous powers, symbolized by one element—gold—which he wanted to be able to produce at will. Man's first attempts at the systematic investigation of nature were accompanied by overwhelming feelings of anxiety, which expressed themselves in a strange hybrid of intellectual reflection and archaic superstition of the kind which characterizes the mind during infancy. The human ego reified nature, turned it into an object of scientific study, thus creating for itself a new role: that of the detached intellectual observer. This role provided the ego with an elevated vantage point from which to analyze, supervise and control phenomena. But in the very act of attempting to create this attitude of objectivity and detachment, it became more deeply enmeshed than ever in fears derived from a magical mode of thinking. Nature became animated with hordes of demons (spiritual intelligences of various orders), which men hoped to strip of their power through sorcery. Neoplatonic and, above all, Jewish Kabbalistic notions fed into this magical mode of thought, whose proponents diligently occupied themselves with the interpretation of dreams and symbols, the art of divination and the mystical properties of numbers. There arose a whole complex of occult spirit-powers which allegedly influenced human lives. Moreover, each of those simple numbers being used in the mathematical studies of the burgeoning natural sciences turned out to be in possession of suprasensuous meanings and powers as well. Agrippa von Nettesheim, commonly know as Cornelius Agrippa, was, along with Johannes Reuchlin, the most renowned writer on theosophical and magical subjects at the beginning of the sixteenth century. He devoted some one hundred pages of his famous hermetic treatise, the *De occulta philosophia*, to the analysis of the occult powers of numbers and letters. [2]   During this era, there existed a comprehensive science of demonology, with extensive catalogues containing magic formulas, rituals, and instruction in the arts of divination and the concoction of magic potions and other substances designed to produce magical effects. There were little "do-it-yourself" manuals on the practice of geomancy (divination based on lines and figures derived from the random connection of dots on paper, or more generally, figures related to natural features of the landscape and magnetic and spiritual currents within the earth, including burial sites), pyromancy (divination by fire), hydromancy (divination by water), necromancy (divination by communication with the dead), ichthyomancy (divination with fish), and many other magic arts. It was a stimulating age, but also an age of upheaval. The first tentative efforts were being made to subject to critical scrutiny that image of the world, based on Church teachings, which in the past had been taken as absolute truth. These efforts were moderately successful and brought a slight increase in man's sense of security by increasing his confidence in his intellectual powers. However, this new security was far outweighed by the additional *insecurity* resulting from application of the scientific method, which compelled man to redouble his efforts to compensate for the loss of his role as the devout child of God, by magnifying, to truly grandiose proportions, the powers of his own ego. The "Philosophers' Stone," with its unlimited magical powers, reflected the spirit of the age, for it symbolized man's desire, or rather his compulsion, to appropriate God's omnipotence: If it was no longer possible to *have* God, at least it might be possible to *become* Him.

The medieval attitude toward life might be described as dominated by the figure of the sphere. Medieval man's image of the world was geocentric, with the heavenly bodies revolving around the earth. But in this circular universe, man was *below* the heavens, and the eye of God watched him from *above*. The universe was a closed circuit, as was the human life cycle, which began and ended in God. This circular, closed system was breached the moment the distrustful ego of man began looking beyond the circumscription of revealed truth for the answers to his questions. *The first attempts to think in terms of scientific causation introduced man to a linear* (as opposed to a cyclical) *perspective, the perspective of an infinite chain of cause and effect.* The theories of Copernicus confirmed that man occupied a peripheral position in a boundless universe. However, long before Copernicus—in the thirteenth century namely—the invention of the mechanical clock had revealed that European man was on the verge of abandoning his sense of finitude within a closed, cyclical existence and now preferred to view existence as a straight line stretching through time into infinity. As Lewis Mumford wrote in *Technics and Civilization,* the mechanical clock decisively altered man's relationship to eternity. [59]   After its invention, philosophers persistently employed the simile of the clock or watch to describe all organic processes (v. Chapter 2). Unlike the old sundial, the mechanical timepiece is not regulated by the circular progression of the day which emerges from the night and then sinks back into it again. Instead it just goes on ticking, as if it were moving along a straight line. With its measured beat it indicates that time, like the series of numbers, is infinite and marches forward forever; that it has no beginning or end any more than the scientific chain of cause and effect, or the thought processes of human beings who subscribe to the principle of scientific causation. For the pious Christian of the Middle Ages, life was an eternal circle, beginning and ending in God. At the end of the Middle Ages man began to experience with increasing poignancy the sensation that he was a traveller along an infinitely long highway.

The natural philosophers of late medieval scholasticism were the first to attempt to clarify the concept of infinity. However, it is significant to note that medieval man still conceived of his position in the universe as predominantly static and that he was thus prevented from evolving an exact account of physical motion. He had not yet learned to interpret velocity in terms of the time rate of motion in a given direction. Nor was he capable of understanding shifting velocities by means of the definition of instantaneous velocity. [50]   He could not yet conceive of the differential quotient or coefficient—in other words, the unit of the ratio between two infinitesimal, ever-shifting values of distance and time. After he had fallen—or perhaps simple walked—out of the finite, cyclical world of the Christian faith, man was forced to seek some meaning in the fact that he was now moving along a straight line which to all appearances was going to go on forever. Eventually he tried to solve the problem of meaning in terms of an equation: Simple forward motion along the line of time = *Progress,* perpetual evolution not only onward but *upward.* His faith in progress was reinforced by an unending stream of scientific and technological advances. The idea of retrogression seemed by nature incompatible with science and technology. Thus for a long time it proved possible to maintain the illusion that man's lot was steadily improving. Naturally this belief in progress was (and is) anything but the result of experience and careful reflection. Instead it was the product of desperation, a straw which people grasped at in their fear of a world absolutely devoid of purpose. Behind the modern ideology of progress there still lingers, in a latent form, the dream of the Philosophers' Stone. This dream has changed since the Renaissance only in the sense that now people hope for some kind of high-powered medical technology which will guarantee them perpetual youth and virtual immortality.

The seventeenth-century philosophy of Descartes was the most significant expression of man's epoch-making resolve to appropriate the absolute knowledge and power of the Almighty in order to regain the emotional equilibrium which he had lost when, at the close of the Middle Ages, he was bereft of his reassuring role as a child of God. *After forfeiting the protective care of God, modern man derived his sense of security from his individual self-conceit.* In psychoanalytic terms, what took place could be described as a narcissistic identification. The sense of sanctuary stemming from the guarantees of the giant, idealized figure of the parent (God) was replaced by the exaggerated self-regard of the individual ego. The prodigious power of the divine parent now reappears in another guise, in the form of man's boundless overestimation of his significance and capabilities. *The individual ego was turned into the image of God.* Consequently the supreme and central truth of the age was summed up in the famous dictum: *Cogito ergo sum,* "I think; therefore I am." [14]   What masquerades as a logical *deduction* is really an intuitive *judgment.* The self-assertive ego is positing its own primacy. Of course, in this case one can speak of a judgment only in the sense that ultimately the ego is responsible not only for conscious choices, but also for the unconscious defense mechanism which led it to this conviction of its pre-eminence. At least, this view is the logical consequence of the hypothesis that the hidden dynamics of European history paralleled those at work in the child described at the beginning of this chapter, who resorts to narcissistic overcompensation in the effort to overcome his fears.

In the seventeenth century men were still wrestling with an almost overwhelming fear—the fear of confessing that they were deliberately usurping God's power, and thereby calling down His wrath on their heads. Thus Descartes had to marshall all his ingenuity to demonstrate that this act of unbridled presumption on the part of the individual ego not only had the sanction of God, but in fact had been determined by divine decree. To prove the validity of this notion, he devised a seemingly plausible proof which, from the psychoanalytic standpoint, might be described as a classic example of rationalization. Descartes argued that God himself was the source of the idea that all knowledge could be deduced through an individual's own intellectual self-assurance: For the supreme clarity and precision which characterized individual self-consciousness could, he reasoned, have been imparted to man only by God. And because God was good, therefore all those conceptions of the individual mind which exhibited a similar clarity and precision must likewise be true; for a good God could not choose to mislead us. Even Descartes' famous demonstration of the existence of God was in reality nothing more than a rationalization, a denial of the reality of man's usurpation of God's power. This proof ran as follows: The idea of a perfect being must have some cause. Man is imperfect, and thus the cause of his conception of a perfect being must be God Himself. How could we conceive of a perfect being if this being did not actually exist and had not caused us to have this conception? "Having considered the immensity of the perfections represented to us by [the idea of God], we are compelled to confess that it could be instilled in us only by a being who comprehends all perfections, in other words by a God who truly is and exists. For not only is it evident by the natural light [of reason] that nothingness can-not give rise to anything whatever, and that that which is more perfect cannot be derived from that which is less perfect as its total and efficient cause, but also that it is impossible for us to have the idea or image of anything whatever unless there exists, within us or elsewhere, an original which actually possesses all the perfections so conceived." [14]

In reality this argument does not reflect trust in God, but rather trust in the infallibility of the individual intellect. If the process of intellectual inference were to lead to a different conclusion, God would, in a sense, be refuted. The logically thinking ego determines God's existence—or permits him to exist. Of course, in Descartes' time no one dared admit to such an act of presumption. Thus from the Renaissance to the Enlightenment, generations of philosophers labored to develop new arguments which would enable them to avoid confessing the truth: that men had ceased to rely on God and instead had chosen, through the mechanism of identification, to become divine and omnipotent themselves—they had undertaken to predict and avert all dangers by relying solely on their own resources.

In the philosophy of Descartes we see a particularly clear-cut case of man's radical reversal of attitude, from passive submission to a role of vigilant domination. The individual ego assumes the place of God. At the very moment when Galileo was conclusively establishing the illusory nature of the classical geocentric model of the universe, thus feeding man's fear of being abandoned, that same fear was driving man to take refuge in an inordinate faith in his own omnipotence. The human ego could no longer tolerate being enmeshed in that world of spirits and demons who had dominated the period of mysticism and magic. Thus the ego, in a sense, assimilated the whole potential of magic by denying the reality of everything which it had not verified and appropriated by its own intellectual power. The tempestuous investigation of nature, based on mathematical principles, which began with Descartes, Galileo and Leibniz, was from the very beginning characterized by an anxiety-ridden compulsion to know the causes of everything in order to avoid being overpowered by unknown forces. Man felt the need to find out all there was to know about the world around him and to establish dominion over it, for he no longer had any parental protector to afford him security. *Man's fear of abandonment by God turned into a fear of losing his absolute certitude, and thereby his ability to exercise intellectual dominion over the surrounding world.* Thus the steady stream of dazzling scientific discoveries and technological advances which began in the Renaissance and has continued down to the present day is rooted in psychological factors closely akin to those at work in the insecure, keyed-up, suspicious, obsessively curious and domineering tyrant-children who refuse to go to sleep and are incapable of adopting a passive role; who trust only in a world which they themselves can control—or *believe* they can control—by personal evaluation and action.

The moment when man stepped out of the Middle Ages and into the modern era, long celebrated as a sublime act of self-emancipation, was in reality a neurotic flight from a sense of narcissistic impotence into the illusion of narcissistic omnipotence. The psychological root of modern civilization, which appears so impressive on the surface, is in fact an infantile megalomania nourished by deep-lying, unmastered anxieties. Like the child who arbitrarily transforms himself into a self-deceptive copy of an omnipotent parent figure so that he can end his helpless dependence on his unreliable parents, Western civilization has, ever since the end of the Middle Ages, been exhibiting numerous symptoms of stress because of the excessive demands man has placed on his own powers. By identifying with God, man has simply evaded the responsibility of engaging in a protracted and painful confrontation with his problem: how to deal with his insecure relationship to God. But the exaggerated sense of self generated by this equation of the human ego with God has always been a mirage; and the sense of power based on the technological dominion over nature simply represents a denial of the true state of affairs, of man's infantile dependency on the natural world, without whose resources mankind could not survive. For this is the "catch" in the tactic of neurotic overcompensation: The anxiety arising from feelings of helplessness can be counteracted only by the uncritical overestimation of one's own powers, just as the state of passive vulnerability can be counteracted only by an overblown hyperactivity. Consequently—to his doom—man has become incapable of perceiving and accepting those natural dependencies which limit and define human existence. Unfortunately, an integral feature of this unconscious "impotence-omnipotence complex" is the extreme difficulty of perceiving the weakness underlying such a grandiose self-image. Once man lost the certitude of God's protection, and the ego had nothing to cling to but the conviction of its own power and the egocentric will to dominate nature, man had no choice but to deny the motivation, and the fact, of his delusory self-deification. From the outset, his spectacular scientific discoveries, mediated by the principle of scientific causation, reinforced this systemic denial of the truth; for unlike the recipes of medieval magic, scientific discoveries actually make it possible for us to understand many hitherto baffling natural phenomena. Intoxicated by the productivity of the scientific, mathematical method, Western man, like Descartes, was henceforth able to persuade himself that intellectual certitude ruled out the possibility of self-deception. Mathematical logic, he believed, could never mislead him. Nicolas de Malebranche (1638–1715), one of the most significant of those French philosophers who were the immediate intellectual successors to Descartes, declares that if one proceeds in accordance with *la raison*, with intellectual cognition, one has at one's command a self-sufficient principle, infinite in its capabilities, by which God himself is bound to abide: "Car Dieu ne peut agir que selon cette raison, il dépend d'elle dans un sens; il faut qu'il la consulte et qu'il la suive." [51]   ("For God cannot act but in accordance with this reason. In a sense he is dependent on it; he is compelled to take it into account and abide by its dictates.") There is an unspoken inference to be drawn from this proposition: namely the triumphant conclusion that man's ability to exercise "reason" affords him a self-sufficiency and power tantamount to those of God himself.

The propensity for superstition which lingered on, in a covert form, long after the end of the Middle Ages, is the source of man's illusion that the practical application of the mathematical laws of nature can confer on him the power to overcome his own finitude. Thus the unrealistic confidence placed in Kabbalistic and magical formulas and in rituals of conjuration, which were current at the time of Cornelius Agrippa, was simply transferred onto modern mathematics. When man perceives the continuous advances made in the mathematical investigation of the natural world, as well as the concomitant steady expansion of technological capabilities, he feels that he is gradually nearing his goal of possessing infinity, and of abolishing the limitations of human existence once and for all. Today we see striking evidence of man's inability to perceive the magical motivation underlying his creation of this fantasy-illusion. For at this moment, very few people appear capable of reacting rationally to the predictions being made by natural scientists themselves, that mankind is headed on a path towards collective self-annihilation, and that we will inevitably destroy ourselves if we automatically continue that expansionist policy—the attempt to exercise ever-growing dominion over nature—which we have followed in the past. People are unable to accept the idea that suddenly it is necessary for them to re-evaluate those scientific techniques which, up until now, have proved so effective in solving problems and have never ceased to enhance their feeling of self-confidence and well-being. It is a paradox closely linked to the unconscious dynamics of neurosis that the very moment when those quantitative methods of natural science which we have idealized for so long have clearly established that our demand for an ever more radical control of nature through science and technology must result in self-annihilation, should coincide with the moment in which it has become impossible for us to believe in these methods any longer. The disastrous truth is that man is afraid of admitting to himself that he still occupies that same position of infantile dependency, the awareness of which he has repressed since the Middle Ages. At least for the time being, his fear of admitting this truth outweighs his fear that he may destroy himself through a literally suicidal megalomania. This is the curse of that collective complex, characterized by repressed feelings of impotence and conscious feelings of omnipotence, which might be described as the "God complex," the modern myth of man's omnipotence.

2

Egocentrism and Its Masks
from Leibniz to Nietzsche

One feature of the narcissistic impotence-omnipotence complex which has left an indelible mark on the whole of the modern era is a radical *egocentrism*. We recall the typical reaction of the small child who, in his fear of being abandoned, attempts to acquire unconditional dominion over his surroundings. As a rule children of this type remain inveterate egocentrics. They have ceased to regard as trustworthy anything which comes from outside themselves, and thus they cannot grant anyone else the right to determine their fate. They can tolerate relationships with other people only if they themselves are able to assume the dominant role. If they were to submit, even to a limited degree, to the control of others, they would, in effect, be recreating that fear of dependency which they had found so intolerable in the first place. Thus all their efforts are directed towards manipulating their environment in such a way that they are able to at least maintain the illusion that their lives are totally under their own control.

Something analogous may have happened to European man during the Renaissance as a result of his identification with God. At this time egocentrism appears to have become deeply entrenched throughout Western society and has continued to characterize Western man down to the present day. This egocentrism is the product of man's introjection, or incorporation into his own person, of a Deity whom a long monotheistic tradition had taught man to regard as a unique and exalted being. *Man transformed himself into an image of this divine being and from that time on has regarded himself as a self-contained unit totally distinct from all other such units.*

Since the end of the sixteenth century, philosophers have labored to create metaphysical structures which confirm the individual in his belief that he is, in a sense, identical with the universe, or that he contains the totality of the universe in his own person. Renaissance natural philosophy established an equation between the essence of God and the world. Valentin Weigel* taught that we could *know* only what we ourselves *are*. Thus man was capable of apprehending the universe because he himself *was* in some sense the universe. Weigel and the early seventeenth-century German mystic Jakob Boehme saw man as possessing two aspects. On the one hand he represented, in corporeal form, the distillation of all material things and for this reason could grasp the whole of the material world. In the same way he also partook of the totality of the spiritual world and, being himself a "spark of divinity," could justly regard himself as the image or likeness of the divine being. In one of his didactic poems, Giordano Bruno elaborated on the concept of the monad. Each single elementary entity, each monad, constituted an individual manifestation of the divine being, a finite, existential form of the infinite essence. [19, 11]   A century later Leibniz adopted and modified Bruno's theory of monads. [48]   He too proceeded on the thesis that each elementary unit, each monad, was in itself a representation of the entire universe. Yet at the same time each monad was also an individual, i.e., something peculiar and distinct from all other monads. The diversity of the individual monads appeared to presuppose their qualitative imperfection. (I.e., if they had really represented the totality of the world, they would have possessed identical attributes and been absolutely simple.) Leibniz resolved this apparent contradiction by making the differences between the monads consist exclusively in the degree of clarity or distinctness with which each monad represented the universe. Thus no monad was *qualitatively* different from any other. Each one simply mirrored the universe with a distinctness or cloudiness peculiar to itself. God was the supreme monad within a vast hierarchical system of monads. Although each monad lived its own individual existence according to its own inherent potential, and was unable to interact with any other monad, it was nevertheless in harmony with all the others because of their identical content. A "pre-established harmony" reigned among all the monads.

Unlike other living beings, man was not merely an image of the created universe, but, by virtue of his intellect or spirit, was also the image of the Godhead itself, "capable of knowing the system of the universe and,

---

* Valentin Weigel (1535–1588), a German Protestant minister and theologian deeply influenced by Erasmus, Paracelsus, and the mystics, in turn influenced Jakob Boehme and Leibniz, as well as the development of German transcendental Idealism. He believed that spiritual truth transcended the boundaries of any particular church or faith and that the true church was made up of those who experienced direct illumination.—Tr.

at least to a degree, of imitating it by essaying [his] own architectural skill; for within its own domain, every mind is like a little divinity." [48]

In elucidating the concept of *pre-established harmony*, the philosophers of the seventeenth and eighteenth centuries made use of the famous simile of the timepieces, which in all probability originated with Geulincx.* This image suggests that all psychical and physical processes taking place in the universe are perfectly coordinated with each other like clocks (at times the word "watch" is used) which may have been set and wound up together and all "keep time" with each other, despite the fact that they are running independently. [48]   This clock imagery clearly betrays man's secret urge to strip God of his power, which is why the clock simile gave rise to so much controversy. For example, in the course of his famous epistolary debate with Leibniz, Samuel Clarke‡ rebuked his adversary as follows in his First Reply, dated 26 November 1715: "The notion of the world as being a great machine going on without the interposition of God, as a clock continues to go without the assistance of a clockmaker, tends (under the pretense of making God a *supra-mundane intelligence*) to exclude God's providence and God's government in reality out of the world. . . . And those men, who pretend that in an earthly government things may go on perfectly well without the king himself ordering or disposing of anything, may reasonably be suspected that they would like very well to set the king aside." According to this Deist or mechanist view of God and nature, man has ceased to need God. God had set the clocks running in the act of Creation. Now all the monads, all living creatures, go on functioning on their own, independent of God's influence.

The clock simile is significant in another respect. It portrays a world in which the individual, elementary beings or units have no contact. Each monad exists on its own. (As Leibniz says, monads "have no windows.")

---

*   Arnold Geulincx (1624-1669) was a Belgian-Dutch philosopher influenced by Descartes. His ethical theories anticipated those of Kant in that he held that ethical behavior could not be based on emotional factors such as fear of punishment or hope of reward. He also held the doctrine of occasionalism, stating that man was not the originator of his actions or perceptions but only an instrument of God, who used his body as an "occasion" or medium of divine action. Thus human motion and perception were those of God, not of man.—Tr.

‡   Samuel Clarke (1675-1729), an English philosopher, author of *Demonstration of the Existence and Attributes of God*, and a devoted friend and admirer of Newton, became embroiled in a theological debate with Leibniz when the latter attacked Newtonian principles on the grounds that they were undermining natural religion. The interchange of letters between the two men (1715-1716) was conducted through an intermediary.—The passage from Clarke is quoted from the *Leibniz-Clarke Correspondence*, Frone and London, Manchester University Press, 1956; Clarke's First Reply, 26 November 1715.—Tr.

The harmony of the monads with the universe and each other does not presuppose any mutual interaction, any *relationship* between them. The individual units give nothing to, and derive nothing from, one another. From the outset each monad contains totality, completeness, within itself in a latent form. Thus, in Leibniz's view, it is the task of the individual monad to know itself and thereby to further clarify its initially cloudy or somewhat indistinct reflection or representation of the universe. Thus the individual possesses the intrinsic capability of self-actualization or self-completion. The cooperation or assistance of others is not required.

In his book *Über den Prozess der Zivilisation* (1939; English translation *The Civilizing Process*), the sociologist Norbert Elias [16]   quite correctly pointed out that since the Renaissance, the societies of Europe have been defined by a view of man as an isolated being who is segregated by his own inner nature from everything outside himself. As Elias demonstrates, the philosophical and sociological tradition of the West contains virtually no system of thought which takes as its starting point the existence of large numbers of interdependent people. "It appears that from this time on, center stage of man's universe was to be occupied by each single human being, as an individual who was, in the final analysis, completely independent of all others." (Introduction to the 1968 edition, Part VIII.) In terms of this initial premise, society presents itself as an agglomeration of totally isolated people "whose true essence is sealed up inside them, and who thus, at best, communicate only an external and superficial way." (Ibid., Part VIII.) The result of all this was the concept of the individual as the "outsider," as a being who existed *outside* society, and the concept of society as something which existed *outside* the individual. [16]

Ultimately this conviction that the individual ego is totally self-contained, cut off from the outside world, in conjunction with the notion that the inner self houses a representation of the entire universe, can be understood only in the light of the historical process of man's narcissistic identification with God. The human ego, threatened with the prospect of becoming completely helpless and forlorn, saved itself by unconsciously equating itself with God and succumbing to the delusion that it had succeeded in appropriating his omnipotence and perfection. *Thus every man became*, in a sense, *his own God*. The monotheistic religious tradition in the West perpetuated itself in the form of a new monotheism, the single-minded self-apotheosis of the individual ego. For in the modern era, there no longer existed a community of gods whom man could mirror by conceiving of himself as a member of a group, part of an interrelated corporate body. There was only one way in which the monotheistic ideal could be transferred to the individual human: in the form of a grandiose self-image. Each person became a closed-off, self-contained monad. His personal identification with God turned him into an isolated ego with no inner bond to other human beings and things, rather than into a member of a community dependent upon communication among all its members.

Norbert Elias describes the concept of the *homo clausus*, the individual "self in a shell," as the cornerstone of the European intellectual tradition since the Renaissance. (Introduction to the 1968 edition of *The Civilizing Process*, VIII–IX.) Elias points out that this same basic concept is still operative, for example, in Kant's view of the subject of cognition which is never able to break through to the true nature of the "thing-in-itself" *(Ding an sich)*, as well as in the individualistic features of modern existentialist philosophy. (Ibid.)

Rash as it may appear to attempt to establish a link between the intellectual-historical processes we have examined and concepts drawn from the modern psychoanalytic investigation of narcissism, there nevertheless exists some cause to apply psychoanalytic interpretive categories to the task of elucidating social-psychological phenomena. For it seems essential that we gain a clearer understanding of those irrational emotional factors which led to the development, in Western man, of an inveterate egocentrism which, from that day to this, has largely determined the way we think about ourselves. It has, by an apparently irresistible process, led to the evolution of a society based on the principle of rivalry, in which the only way to resolve conflicts arising from the collision between various special-interest groups is to resort to overt violence or to a covert violence which remains almost invisible because it forms such an integral part of our social structure. The infantile idealization of a single, unique divine being may conceivably lie at the root of that exaggerated veneration of the individual self (the hypercathexis of the self) which has become a kind of obsession, an *idée fixe*, of Western culture. In the medieval community the individual had been only one among a flock of children who, first and foremost, looked up to God as an all-powerful father figure. In other words their point of view was primarily vertical. The idea of a *horizontal* community, a direct relationship between human beings as such, which did not involve the mediation of God, never became a basic principle of medieval society. Ultimately even the hierarchical organization of the Church helped to enforce the isolation of the individual members of the Christian flock, and this same hierarchical principle was carried over into the structure of the family. The subordination of women to men and of children to parents became a social norm which it was taboo to violate, and this inner divisiveness and unequal distribution of power destroyed all chance that people might band together to achieve a collective emancipation. A person's self-image was determined not along a horizontal plane, by the membership in a group of people approximately equal in status, but rather by his place in a vertical structure of relationships between subordinates and superiors. Ultimately everyone was totally dependent on, and helpless before, the only being who possessed true freedom of will, and whose disposition to confer grace or to inflict punishment for original sin could not even be predicted beforehand, much less be influenced by human effort. According to psychoanalytic principles, the degree of self-regard assumed in a narcissistic identification is always directly proportional to the status of the self before the identification took place. In other words, the more profound the ego's initial experience of its own smallness—that is, its remoteness from the magnitude of the idealized image of the parent—the higher this ego must build itself up through the defensive maneuver of identification with the parent figure. For the ego or self is forced to turn itself into a carbon copy of the authority figure it desires to become through the identification. Acting, as it does, under an unconscious compulsion, it can effect the identification only by assuming the same proportions as the idealized figure appeared to possess when the self was observing it from below. Thus it would appear that medieval society failed to produce human beings capable of a genuine sense of community with their fellows. Instead it sent into the future a swarm of unconfessed egocentrics and megalomaniacs whose descendants, in succeeding centuries, were faced again and again with the task of channelling, or inventing stopgap measures to curb, the destructive potential of their own egocentrism in order to prevent the collective self-annihilation of the entire human race. It is my intention, in the following pages, to examine more closely the philosophical arguments which they devised and employed for this purpose.

By its very nature, the flight from feelings of helplessness and impotence into grandiose feelings of omnipotence represents a radical reversal in attitude, rather than a gradual evolution. Yet those developments in the history of ideas which accompanied and followed this dramatic psychic transformation did take place gradually. To be sure, Descartes' victorious campaign to establish the authority of the individual intellect as the standard of measure for all things did blaze a trail for others to follow; but some time passed before the rest of society caught up with this revolutionary step. Moreover, as has already been indicated, both Descartes himself and his philosophical successors made every effort to conceal the fact that, on the theoretical plane, they had already completed the self-elevation of the individual to the rank of divinity. In reality God was rendered superfluous by the idea that man's own internal resources provided the individual with an adequate source of guidance and the means of guaranteeing his own security. Yet Descartes continually felt the need to reassure God that in fact no one could take a step without him. For—so Descartes said in his effort to appease both God and the Church—in reality God was the source and foundation of the authority of the individual mind. (Cf. earlier discussion of God as the warranty, by virtue of his goodness and unwillingness to lead man astray, of the correspondence between man's ideas and the objects of cognition.) All ideas whose validity was verified by the self-conceit of the sovereign self had—of course—been instilled in man by God. Finally, Descartes even actively availed himself of God when he postulated that God's instrumentality was required every time man, in cognition and action, made the transition from ideal to material reality. For without God's assistance, how could man possibly exit from the world of the mind to enter the dimension of time and space, and then return to the mind again? Like Descartes, Spinoza, who immediately followed him, regarded it as axiomatic that God revealed himself in every act of authentic cognition.

*

Thus the intellectual's achievement of intellectual autonomy began with a denial that he had in fact achieved such autonomy. To be sure, from the seventeenth century on, the individual refused to concede to God the absolute and unconditional power to control events. Man himself wanted to supervise and control everything that happened in the interior world of his psyche as well as in the physical world around him. There is no question but that he had taken the first step towards assuming personal dominion over both psychic and physical processes. He wanted, in a sense, to take out of God's hands those laws of nature which in the past had been the exclusive prerogative of divinity. Yet at the same time he tried to persuade himself that he was not withdrawing from God or relinquishing his role as the ward of a divine guardian, but merely wished to set forth the fullness of divine truth. Spinoza taught that man's efforts to achieve the mathematical and scientific cognition of the world were an expression of his love for God. Moreover, the Dutch philosopher regarded his metaphysical system, with its geometrical structure, as an indirect reflection of divine truth. At the very moment when the individual self was setting out to usurp absolute sovereignty, it was still telling itself that in reality it was more obedient than ever to the will of God.

However, eventually people began to perceive the difficulty involved in the ongoing process of narcissistic identification: How could they continue to lay claim to more and more divine power and at the same time continue to pretend that they were receiving God's care and sanction? Inventions and discoveries in many fields testified to the intensity of man's craving to seize possession of the planet. His self-esteem expanded rapidly as more and more wonderful scientific discoveries resulted from the effort to facilitate maritime navigation in the course of economic and colonial expansion. The inventions of the compass, gunpowder and the art of printing forged a new faith in man's creative powers and potentialities. The telescope disclosed the mysteries of the heavens. The English philosopher Francis Bacon taught that knowledge of the physical universe was necessary to facilitate man's dominion over the world. *Knowledge was power*, the only kind of power that lasted. It was essential that nature finally be made subservient to the human mind, and it was the task of the sciences to enforce her obedience. Part Two of Bacon's great projected series of works, the *Instauratio Magna* or *The Great Renewal of Learning*—known in English as *The New Organon (Novum Organum, 1620)*—bears the subtitle *De Regno Hominis*, "Concerning the Kingdom [or Dominion] of Man." To be sure, at the same time that Bacon was writing about the dominion of man, he continued to show a zealous regard for religion. But what kind of religion did he have in mind? It allowed great latitude to the egotistical principle of personal advantage. God was made an accomplice in the individual's struggle to achieve prosperity and success. Bacon, who had been trained as a lawyer, had something in common with Machiavelli in that both men emphasized the expediency of performing occasional, carefully delimited immoral acts. In Bacon the concept of the perfection or perfectibility of the world is already a thing of the past. He views the world as substantially evil, so that if a person wants to be successful, he cannot avoid resorting to underhanded methods. In his essay "Of Fortune" (Essay 40, dated 1597, of the *Essays or Counsells, Civill and Morall*), Bacon did not mince words in formulating his principle of egotism. There was, he said, no swifter way to achieve prosperity than as the result of the mistakes or even the deaths of other people. In his discussion he quoted the Latin of a Greek proverb, *Serpens nisi Serpentem comederit non fit Draco*, "No snake can become a dragon unless he devours other snakes," an older version of our modern phrase "It's a dog-eat-dog world." [6]

This new image of man, in which the primary human characteristic is egotism, is also reflected in the practical philosophy of Bacon's fellow-countryman Thomas Hobbes. Hobbes taught that the state of nature consists in the "war of all against all." This thesis is expounded in the famous sentence from Part I, Chapter 13 of the *Leviathan:* "Hereby it is manifest, that during the time men live without a common power to keep them all in awe, they are in that condition which is called war; and such a war, as is of every man, against every man." [38]   The contractual foundation of the state (the "commonwealth") serves merely to establish a balance among the vested interests of its individual members. Man is by nature solitary, and there is no such thing as an innate human need to live within a social group. This need is purely derivative, representing, so to speak, a strategy for reconciling the self-seeking inclinations of competing individuals. In the philosophy of Hobbes the state became a useful invention by which to adequately gratify the egotism of all men, while at the same time placing limits on that egotism. The great commonwealth was to be founded on a scientific basis, in much the same way that one would go about constructing a machine.

Hobbes was an outspoken advocate of individual freedom of thought in matters involving religion, and an outspoken opponent of any religious body which laid claim to political power. As a means to curb competition among individuals, all of whom were fighting for their own egotistical interests, Hobbes supported a principle which has tended to become a social-psychological predicate or prop of all authoritarian and totalitarian societies. In Hobbes' absolutist theory of the state, the authority of all members of the commonwealth was to be concentrated in a single representative individual, and the will of all the people united in the single will of the sovereign. [38]   (Cf. Part I, Chapter 16 of the *Leviathan:* "A multitude of men are made *one* person, when they are by one man, or one person, represented; so that it be done with the consent of every one of the multitude in particular. For it is the *unity* of the representer, not the *unity* of the represented, that maketh the person *one*. And it is the representer that beareth the person, and but one person: and *unity* cannot be otherwise understood in multitude.") This concept became the theoretical foundation of absolute monarchy. In terms of social psychology, the concept involves the surrender, by individuals, of a portion of their egotistical ambitions, which they transfer to the absolute sovereign. They are indemnified for this loss by the exercise of a mechanism described by psychoanalysis as projective identification, which enables them to continue identifying with their sovereign by projecting their own desires and impulses onto him. However, the sovereign is also the legislator who defines all norms and obligations, and thus at the same time he assumes, in the eyes of his subjects, the function of an externalized Superego (i.e., a superego existing outside the intrapsychic apparatus). Everyone is recompensed for the restrictions imposed on the gratification of his narcissistic drives by his participation in the omnipotence of the absolute monarch, which quite literally approaches that of a god. But such omnipotence can manifest itself only by the external expansion of its authority. Imperialism or territorial expansionism is invariably "preprogrammed" into this model of the state. The snake which wants to become a huge dragon must never cease to devour other snakes. An egotistical obsession with omnipotence is the driving force underlying this model society, and the same obsession is bound to reproduce itself on all levels of the society. Thus within a state constructed according to Hobbes' blueprint, there can never be total peace, and every peace is more or less the respite between two wars. The hyperbolic narcissistic expectations of individuals can never be completely accommodated *within* the system merely by a redistribution of power which turns over the lion's share of authority to the sovereign representative of the people. For in order to pacify his followers, the sovereign must continually strive for the unlimited *outward* expansion of his power.

The practical philosophy of Hobbes, which was based exclusively on the principle of egotism, not only caused quite a stir among his contemporaries, but continued to make its influence felt until well into the eighteenth century. The absorption of divine omnipotence by the egotistical, megalomaniacal individual was creating social problems of ever-increasing scope and complexity. How could the aim of providing for the general welfare be reconciled with man's new self-image, based on individual egotism?

Lord Shaftesbury* disputed Hobbes' pessimistic view that by its very nature, existence must consist of a war of all against all. He advanced the thesis that no inherent contradiction existed between morality and amour-propre, or between altruism and egotism. Building on concepts

* Anthony Ashley Cooper, third earl of Shaftesbury (1671-1713), an English philosopher educated under the direction of John Locke, wrote many philosophical essays, most of which are contained in the collection *Characteristics of Men, Manners, Opinions, Times* (1711).—Tr.

derieved from classical antiquity, he theorized that man possessed a natural moral sense and that if he simply developed his natural propensities to the full, he would automatically contribute to the common good; for only among the less cultivated, less highly evolved members of society (this was in part a class concept), did a genuine conflict exist between altruism and self-interest. Among those on a higher plane of human evolution it was possible to effect harmony between altruistic and egotistical aspirations, for like egotism, altruism was an innate human characteristic. Thus the man who had fully developed his own nature was the ethical man *per se*. The individual did not become a moral being by adapting his own inherent needs to universal norms or by sacrificing these needs altogether, but rather by fully actualizing the natural inclinations dormant within him. Thus in order to attain the highest degree of moral perfection, one had only to become the kind of person one really wanted to be. [97, 104]

However, it is no accident that Shaftesbury's philosophy drew a distinction between highly cultivated and less highly cultivated people, or that it suggested that the ability to harmonize the gratification of personal desire with moral perfection was the prerogative of an exclusive group. This exclusive group was typified by the "virtuoso," who recalls the *uomo universale,* the universal man of the Renaissance. [97]   He is the man of many skills and all-embracing education, a scientific, political and aesthetic individual of the highest moral character. In theory, Shaftesbury was propounding the idea that everyone was capable of fully developing his natural potential in this way; but in reality, he was perpetuating a divisive, elitist ideal. His philosophy reflected his own self-image, the image of an optimist and aristocrat, scion of one of the most powerful families in England. Essentially Shaftesbury's "optimism" was based on his denial of the fact that the grandiose ideals he preached were completely beyond the reach of the average man. It is characteristic of Shaftesbury that, in his philosophy of the state, he placed little trust in the civic-mindedness or public spirit of the average citizen. He opposed popular sovereignty on the grounds that the people were too unpredictable and would abuse their freedom. It was the task of statesmen to reason with the people and persuade them to do the right thing. At this point, we perceive the logical inconsistency between Shaftesbury's political thought and his optimistic moral philosophy, which equated moral perfection with acting according to one's natural impulses. After all, why should it be necessary to place restrictions on the liberty of the people if all people possess an innate sense of social solidarity?

Nevertheless, Shaftesbury was one of the few thinkers of his age who made any attempt to dispute Hobbes' view that society was composed of self-seeking individualists whose only natural interest was conflict and rivalry with their fellows. Shaftesbury remained alone in his assertion that man was by nature a social animal and that he ought to rely on his innate feelings of "partnership with human kind," (*Characteristics*, Vol. I, 72), "social feeling" and "common sense"—by which last he meant a concern for the common good rather than what we commonly understand by the term.

In the later history of moral philosophy, man's faith in such natural or innate social feelings steadily waned. The consensus was that ethical behavior could *not*, as Shaftesbury had claimed, be based on the natural inclinations of individuals, but only on the subordination of the individual will to universal norms. It appeared unrealistic to rely on the efficacy of some basic altruistic instinct whose very existence was hypothetical. The skeptical anthropology of Hobbes, based on the theory that man's instinctual urges were purely egotistical, seemed far more plausible. Thus again and again we find thinkers posing the same question: How can individuals be brought to renounce the unconditional gratification of their natural, egotistical desires in order to ensure the welfare of all? Eventually the notion of strategic compromise, advocated by Hobbes, was abandoned, and the attempt was made to discover an absolute principle as a guide to moral conduct.

The most famous result of this attempt is the moral law advanced by Kant, the categorical imperative:

"Act in such a way that you could will the maxim of your conduct to become a universal law." [44]

Many Europeans still regard this cornerstone of Kant's philosophy of practical reason as sacrosanct, as the indisputable guiding principle of all moral conduct. But for this very reason, it would seem to make sense to take a look at the categorical imperative in the light of the other intellectual historical documents we have reviewed and to try to understand its psychological ramifications.

In his *Critique of Practical Reason* Kant repeatedly asserts the impossibility of basing moral conduct on *emotional* motives. The fact that conduct based on emotional motives might happen to conform to the moral law is not, in his view, enough to qualify it as moral conduct; for no act which bears a merely casual relationship to duty is entitled to be regarded as a moral act. The only act which so qualifies is one performed *directly out of a sense of duty*, out of simple regard for the moral law. In the realm of ethics, man ought to rely exclusively on his practical reason, ignoring all other motivations or inducements. *"Duty and obligation are the only names which we must give to our relation to the moral law."* [44]

Again and again Kant reveals his utter distrust of natural feelings and inclinations. He believed that natural inclinations stemmed from physical causes and must always lead to a conflict with duty. In his view, a genuine moral disposition consisted in obeying the moral law purely out of a sense of duty, "not from spontaneous inclination, or from an urge to perform that which has not been commanded and which one would gladly have undertaken of one's own accord." Even acts involving great self-sacrifice might be regarded as noble and sublime only if they were performed out of the pure regard for duty, and not because of some "emotional transport." Kant defined virtue as "moral disposition in conflict." Self-control or self-coercion was integral to all moral disposition and represented "that within us which compels us to do what we do not particularly want to do." [44]

At this point the question presents itself: Whence is man to derive the incentive for moral conduct if emotions and inclinations are not permitted to play a role? Who provides the motivation for ethical action when allegedly such action is contrary to all natural impulse? Kant's reply is that the true motivation of practical reason "is nothing other than the moral law itself." However, it is difficult to imagine how an abstract principle of this kind could serve as an incentive to action. Later, it was the perceptive Schopenhauer who voiced his doubts concerning Kant's argument that the moral law is totally divorced from any kind of egotistical interests and drives. Schopenhauer reached just the opposite conclusion. He suggested that we examine the moral law from the vantage point of the recipient or beneficiary of the moral action. If we did this, we would realize that the ideal world would be one composed exclusively of people who obeyed the categorical imperative and thus invariably performed deeds beneficial to ourselves. [85]   Schopenhauer cites Paragraph 30 of Kant's *Doctrine of Virtue (Metaphysische Anfangsgründe der Tugendlehere*)*, Part II of *The Metaphysics of Morals (Die Metaphysik der Sitten,* 1797): "For every man desires to receive help. But if he were to breathe a word about the fact that it is not his principle to help others, everyone would be justified in refusing to lend him aid. Thus the principle of self-interest is in conflict with itself." In the

---

*   This work has also been translated into English under the title *Metaphysical Principles of Virtue,* Indianapolis, 1964.—Tr.

Critique of Practical Reason Kant writes: "I cannot will that there should be a universal law sanctioning the telling of lies, for in this case no one would believe anything I said, or would pay me back in the same coin." Kant's argument, "Do not do unto others what you would not have them do unto you!" does in fact suggest that there are surreptitious advantages to be gained from obedience to the moral law. Thus it is possible to observe the moral law from an ulterior motive—namely out of personal *egotism*, with a view to showing others how one would like to be treated oneself. Schopenhauer makes the sarcastic comment: "The direction for disclosing the true moral law given in Kant's supreme principle is based on the tacit assumption that I am capable of willing only that which will result in the greatest benefit to myself. In determining a maxim to be observed by all men, I cannot help but perceive that I will not always be the active initiator of moral action, but will at times play a passive role, as the object of the actions of others; and with this in mind, my egotism compels me to decide in favor of justice and the love of my fellow man."

Thus it is undeniable that the Kantian concept of ethics can be interpreted as an instrument of individual egotism. In view of the profit to be reaped by the individual beneficiary of actions performed by others who respect the moral law, one's own adherence to the moral law might be merely a strategic compromise, a sacrifice inspired by self-seeking motives. From this standpoint—notwithstanding the fact that Kant regarded himself as the antagonist of the practical philosophy of Hobbes—Kantian ethics appear to be saying much the same thing that Hobbes did. In other words, his system can be interpreted as a strategic compromise designed to reconcile the uncoordinated interests of self-seeking individuals—what we would call a policy of "enlightened self-interest." Of course, this strategic aspect of Kant's theories cannot be deduced directly from Kant's own formulations. On the contrary, the idea of a reconciliation between inclination and duty could not be farther from Kant's mind. No doubt he is *consciously* aware only of the role of duty in his theory. Inclination is demolished by his argument and is to play no role whatever in moral behavior. What by rights *ought* not to be, *cannot* be. In Kantian ethics moral conduct is characterized exclusively by concepts such as duty, obedience, self-sacrifice, intellectual discipline, obligation, self-coercion, the categorical imperative. These concepts are central to a system whose basic tenor is that of compulsive asceticism. The hallmarks of Kant's thought are rigor, pedantry and an almost morbid scrupulosity. Thus it may seem to border on sacrilege to suggest that the categorical imperative bears some relation to emotional needs. However, psychoanalytic findings about the dynamics of compulsion indicate that this very overemphasis on constraint, discipline, obligation and obedience is symptomatic of the existence of strong instinctual drives, against which the ego is attempting to defend itself. In psychoanalytic terms, the aggressive tone of Kant's incessant invective against instinct in the *Critique of Practical Reason* reveals his need to launch a counterattack against repressed instinctual impulse. Kant's ethics exhibit that joyless anankasm characteristic of obsessive-compulsive neurotic character disorders. Ultimately Kant's compulsive, exaggerated suppression of instinct led to his conception of a formalistic, purely abstract moral law completely remote from life.

If we choose to regard Kant's ethics as representative of the intellectual climate of an entire historical period, we might conclude that preceding and during this period man's egocentric attitudes had been steadily expanding and that this swelling tide of egocentrism was experienced as threatening, so that, inevitably, man's feeling of unease led to an attempt to stem the tide by denying it altogether, in the manner typical of persons suffering from compulsive neurosis, or compulsive neurotic reaction formation. In other words, we might look on the thesis of Kant as a defense mechanism, as the other side of the coin of that awakening "will to power" whose true character would, in the end, be remorselessly laid bare by Friedrich Nietzsche.

Examination of the psychological aspects of Kant's ethics discloses something beyond those undercurrents of egocentrism and a utilitarian concern with personal advantage, which were pointed out by Schopenhauer. We also find patent examples of *narcissistic and grandiose ideas*. But in this case we do not see the human ego or self engaging in an unmediated act of self-deification. Instead *the moral law* is depicted as a *person tantamount to a divinity*, which is transfigured and adored with clearly emotional fervor. The moral law, which at times is actually described as holy, appears as an abstract surrogate for a sublime, infallible, sovereign being. Kant states that the highest dignity or rank is to be imputed to the moral law, and speaks of its "solemn majesty." [44]   Moreover, in characterizing the psychical relationship of the individual to this hallowed principle, he employs conceptual categories commonly used to describe a dependent or subservient relationship between one human being and another. For example, he expressly compares the regard due to the law with the attitude proper towards a "person of incomparable worth."

This reverent glorification of the moral law turns it into a representation of God. As we have already noted, in Kant's theory the human ego is required to abide by a multitude of compulsive prohibitions and admonitions. However, the self also receives a narcissistic validation of its own worth from the moral law. After all, the compulsion to obey the categorical imperative derives ultimately from an act of legislation on the part of the individual's own reasoning faculty. Thus, practical reason becomes a vehicle for self-magnification. For in the end—so the theory goes—man possesses the freedom of self-determination in relation to the moral law. By exhibiting regard for the law, man exhibits regard for himself. To honor the dignity of the law means, at the same time, to honor the dignity of man, to honor one's own dignity. Thus adherence to the highest moral principle brings with it a personal elevation in rank, a high degree of indirect, narcissistic gratification. The radiance and glory of that abstract authority figure, the Moral Law, is reflected as from a mirror, and shines back on those who obey it.

Essentially the internal inconsistency of Kant's ethics remains unresolved. The purely formal, abstract moral law appears intangible and immutable on its throne high above its opposite, emotional desire. Thus human beings remained trapped in an inner conflict which they ultimately proved unable to master. The individual attempted to unite, in his own person, the concepts of insignificance and supreme eminence, freedom and compulsion, power and impotence; but in vain. No single individual could resolve the tension between the rigorous adherence to duty and obligation on the one hand, and, on the other, the notion that as an autonomous individual, he was supremely free. Thus it seems only logical that this antinomy should have been perpetuated in the structure of society as well. Duty and inclination, autonomy and compulsion were separated and assigned to different institutions. Authoritarian ethics could be pursued only within the framework of an authoritarian concept of society: "Man is an animal who needs a master if he is to live among others of his species. For there is no question but that he abuses his freedom with respect to others of his kind. And although, as a rational being, he may desire a law which imposes limits on the freedom of all, nevertheless, whenever he can get away with it, his own self-seeking, animalistic inclinations seduce him to exempt himself from [obeying] this law. Thus he needs a master who will subdue his personal will and compel him to obey a universally valid will, so that all men may be free." [45]

After Kant had made statements like this, from his *Idea for a Universal History from a Cosmopolitan Point of View*,* it was an easy matter for the authoritarian state of Prussia to mold Kant's theory of ethics into a tool for the exercise of authoritarian power. *The authority of the State placed itself on the throne of the moral law* and taught its subjects to repeat Kant's prayerful paean or laudation to Duty from Part I, Book I, Chapter 3 of the *Critique of Practical Reason:* "Duty! Thou great and exalted Name who dost contain nought which is pleasing or ingratiating, but demandest submission..." [44]   It is small wonder that, down to the present day, Kant has been cited as the star witness by all conservative advocates of the law-and-order state, who, viewing the world from the top of the social hierarchy, continually press for the increase of duty and obligation, discipline, self-control and respect for authority.

In light of the social-psychological deliberations expounded here, Kant's position, which in certain respects is perpetuated by Fichte and Hegel, might be interpreted as an innovative step in man's campaign to master what I have called the impotence-omnipotence complex. Kant's views reflect the attempt to conceive of the God within the self as an intellectual or spiritual principle, rather than, as had often been the case in the past, primarily as the embodiment of supreme power and might. God became equivalent to reason, to an idea which left nature behind or, more precisely, down *below*. Moreover, the individual participated in this process of spiritualization or dematerialization. At this point man's underlying fantasy ceased to be the desire to reign supreme within the world of nature, and became the desire to spiritualize nature and himself, thus giving himself wings with which to soar to divine heights. Fichte developed a new variation on the theme of self-aggrandizement when he claimed that the Ego not only posited itself, but at the same time also posited that which was not itself. (I.e., the Ego was the condition of all objectifiability while itself transcending objectification.) This Ego is a spiritual-intellectual entity. No world exists independently of consciousness. Fichte eliminated the concept of the "thing-in-itself" (the ultimate noumenal reality unfathomable by human cognition, but constituting the basis of moral, aesthetic and metaphysical truth), on which Kant had expended so much effort, as a cause of thought, and instead held that the intelligence-in-itself was the reality. Consciousness was capable of apprehending only what it contained within itself.

*   An English translation of this essay appears in *Kant's Political Writings*, Cambridge (Eng.) University Press, 1970.—Tr.

Philosophy represented the self-cognition of reason, and reason was the conditioning factor in all life. In Fichte's account consciousness ascended step by step. On the highest level the Ego apprehended itself as untrammelled, self-determining subjectivity, and all data were dissolved into pure activity. Thought and being became one, and as Fichte expressly declares, intellectual *contemplation* simultaneously becomes *action,* an action performed on ourselves: I am the subject of my act as well as its object. That which thinks and that which is thought are not two things, but are absolutely one. [106]   In Hegel's thought, intelligible concepts become categories of reality, the definite forms of all life. Hegel frequently uses the words "Idea" or "God" instead of "mind" (or "spirit").

Thus in the German transcendental idealist tradition, the identification with God is effected by a fusion of God and self within the mind. In this case, the narcissistic delusions of grandeur have a *spiritualistic* emphasis. What we have here is the concept of the omnipotence of *thoughts*. But Fichte and Hegel were far from being mere self-absorbed eccentrics totally indifferent to practical reality. Fichte in particular felt compelled to attempt to remodel the world according to his own views. However, the collision of these views with concrete social realities revealed, even more clearly than the social application of Kantian ethics, that the dissolution of egocentric claims to worldly power and authority, preached by the "spiritualized" system of transcendental idealism, existed only on paper. Thus in his political philosophy Fichte advocated an authoritarian system of government which exercised rigorous control over the lives of citizens. In his so-called socialistic "closed commercial state," the government was supposed to exercise absolute control over production and trade, tell citizens what duties they were expected to perform and ensure that these duties were carried out. On *a priori* grounds the individual was expected to sacrifice his "own personal welfare" to the "life of society as a whole." [24]

But Fichte did not content himself with providing an abstract blueprint of an ideal *social* order based, to a large extent, on a totalitarian, authoritarian *political* order. He went much further and laid the philosophical foundations for a new variety of narcissistic megalomania which was to have particularly disastrous political consequences (in the form, naturally, of Hitler's National Socialism). Fichte taught his contemporaries to express and to gratify their individual egotism in the form of a *nationalistic* egotism. He urged the German people to take charge of the whole world. To be sure, he made no explicit appeal to the narcissistic and inordinate cravings of his fellow-citizens but instead posed his program in the loftiest terms, employing an argument which the proponents of nationalistic imperialism invariably employ in the effort to lend legitimacy to their policies. The argument is that one's nation has, in a sense, a higher destiny to rule over other nations in order to lead them towards some grand and worthy goal. In Fichte's philosophy, the claim was that the Germans represented "the national medium [for the realization] of Christian principles." [106]   Fichte's *Patriotism and Its Opposite* (1807) and *Addresses to the German Nation* (1808) contain statements like the following: "If the German fails to assume the scientific governance of the world, then, at the conclusion of all manner of vexation and travail, the non-European nations, the tribes of North America, will do so, and will bring to an end the existing order of things." [22]   "There is no doubt that to possess [national] character is synonymous with being German." [23]   "Thus at the same time it must be apparent that only the German—the original human being, not the one who has perished within some arbitrary social structure—truly possesses a people and can justly rely on it, and that he alone is capable of genuine and rational love for his nation." [23]   Only the Germans were capable of creating the truly Christian state, and it was the mission entrusted to them by history to do so. This concept of nationalistic imperialism is a direct extension of Fichte's authoritarian political theory. Thus man's appropriation of divine power through identification with God is reflected not only in the form of individualistic delusions of grandeur, but also in the political theories of expansionist nationalism. Moreover, Fichte also laid the foundation of the racism which would be even more clearly articulated by Nietzsche.

Thus behind the sublime noumenal realm revered by the German Idealists there lurked a repressed world of latent violence in which the true realities were power and the exercise of force. This contradiction was never really overcome by the Idealists; their systematic attempt to eliminate it through logical or dialectical argument served only to establish it more firmly. Moreover, as I have already indicated, viewed in psychoanalytic terms, Kant's moralism of duty, which today is still widely regarded as the most high-minded expression of human nobility, looks more like a compulsive-neurotic reaction formation, an act of theoretical glorification screening an archaic egotism which has not been consciously mastered.

*

Perhaps Nietzsche's main contribution was his uninhibited revelation of this dark, instinctual, violence-ridden aspect of German Idealism, which its exponents had attempted to wave away with the magic wand of philosophy until, in the end, it became clear that merely ignoring the thing was not enough to make it vanish. Nietzsche not only blatantly confesses, he openly celebrates man's usurpation of God's power through the mechanism of identification: *God is dead, long live the Superman!* Nietzsche's Superman no longer recognizes the existence of any being superior to himself—neither a personal God, nor the sacred majesty of a moral law, nor a metaphysical intelligence, nor a universal mind or World Soul. The Superman lays claim to unlimited power. Nietzsche taught that the will to power was the strongest of human instincts and merited unqualified affirmation. "Are you a new force and a new law? A prime motion? A wheel rolling of itself? Can you compel stars to orbit about you?" [61]   The old standards of good and evil, the moral world order, was a thing of the past. Anything which enhanced power was good, anything which weakened it bad. The important thing was not whether our perceptions were true, but whether they enhanced our power. "The victorious concept of 'force,' which our physicists used to create God and the world, needs something more in order to be complete: We must attribute to this force an intrinsic will which I call the 'will to power'— that is, an insatiable desire to beget power, or to employ and exercise power, taking the form of a creative drive, and so on." [65]

The Superman enjoys the exercise of his unlimited despotism. For him his own power represents the absolute value. Neither the laws nor principles of logic nor those of ethics can impose any restrictions on this consummate power. Insofar as one can speak of morality at all, it is "master morality," the right and duty of the strong to rule over the weak and to abolish "slave morality." "Master morality" arises out of a "triumphant self-affirmation" (literally, a "triumphant Yea-saying of the self to itself"). [63]

The Superman is the "meaning of the earth." [61]   He is the perfect model of the human species. The herd animals, literally the "many-too-many," exist only so that the Superman may rise up from among them, a unique flash of lightning from heaven. In *Thus Spake Zarathustra* nothing happens to the Superman that he does not himself desire: "I am Zarathustra the godless one; I myself cook up every [morsel of] chance in *my* pot. And only when it is well done do I bid it welcome and permit it to serve as *my* food. And verily, many a chance came to me with an imperious air; but my will addressed it even more imperiously, and chance sank to its knees in entreaty." One cannot conceive a more graphic and suggestive expression of the fantasy of absolute freedom and self-determination.

Accordingly, the Superman loves himself. For Nietzsche-Zarathustra the love of one's fellow man is, in the end, merely the manifestation of a failure of self-love: "One man goes to his neighbor because he is seeking himself, another because he would like to lose himself. Your bad love for yourselves turns your solitude into a prison." The Superman does not need his "fellow man," for he is so strong that he no longer needs the support of anything outside himself. He feels nothing but a contemptuous pity when he sees people who, by wasting their abilities, or through some "idiocy of chance," fail to live up to their potential. "This is my kind of 'compassion,'" Nietzsche says mockingly, "even if there is no sufferer *with* whom I suffer." [65]

To elucidate Christian "slave morality," Nietzsche evolved the theory of *ressentiment,* which later was elaborated—with a difference—by Max Scheler.* [80]   This theory, extensively treated in Nietzsche's *The Genealogy of Morals and Beyond Good and Evil,* is briefly outlined in Nietzsche's posthumous notes: "The trend of moral evolution: Every person desires that no theory or evaluation of things should be regarded as valid unless it enables him to 'come off looking good.' The result: the basic propensity of the weak and mediocre in all ages to weaken the strong, to drag them down—their principal weapon being the moral judgment. The conduct of the strong man towards the weaker man is stigmatized, and the superior lot of the strong is the object of catcalls and abuse." [65]

Nietzsche wrote countless variations on this theme, generally couched in terms of caustic scorn. For example: "There is nothing surprising in the fact that lambs bear a grudge against the great birds of

---

* Max Ferdinand Scheler (1874-1928), a German phenomenological philosopher who has profoundly influenced fields such as psychology, sociology, and theory of religion, is of central importance to this book and is treated more extensively in later chapters. There is an English translation of his work *Ressentiment,* New York, Free Press at Glencoe, 1961. In this book he "turns the tables" on Nietzsche, who attributed the spirit of *ressentiment* to the "weak," i.e., those who believed in objective moral values, or who invented them because of their envy of the strong. Scheler, with his keen attention to axiology, did not believe in ethical relativism and held that there was such a thing as objective moral value. Thus he attributes *ressentiment* not to those who hold to a moral world order, but rather to those who reject it because of their fear of being measured, and found wanting, by an objective criterion of value.—Tr.

prey. But this is no reason to blame the great birds of prey for carrying off little lambs. And if the lambs tell each other, 'These birds of prey are evil; and those who least resemble a bird of prey, who in fact are the very opposite of a bird of prey, namely a lamb—are they not good?', one certainly cannot find fault with them for setting up such an ideal, even if the birds of prey regard them with a mocking eye and perhaps say to each other: 'We are not in the least annoyed with these good lambs, and indeed we even love them; for nothing is tastier than a tender lamb.' To demand of strength that it not show an increase in strength, that it not evince a will to conquer, to overpower, to become master, and a thirst for enemies and victories and obstacles to be overcome, is as absurd as to demand of weakness that it show an increase in strength." [63]

In reality, Nietzsche believed, the weak dreamed of the intoxication of sweet revenge on the strong, but because their weakness prevented them from achieving this revenge, they talked themselves and everyone else into believing that they loved their enemies. Nietzsche found this mendacity insufferable and loathsome, and was repelled by the sight of the failures, the stunted, shrivelled, embittered and sickly people who clung to Christian "slave morality."

Nietzsche's Superman represents the most complete (if visionary) realization of postmedieval man's dream of annexing the divine omnipotence. Uncompromising, and unfettered by feelings of constraint or guilt, the Superman raises himself above his fellows and enjoys the purely narcissistic exercise of his limitless strength. No external power imposes any bounds upon him. He is, as Nietzsche states at one point, "a wheel rolling of itself." Nothing *happens* to him any more. He himself *makes* himself what he is. Thus chance, contingency, becomes a food he cooks for himself, or a slave on bended knee before the power of his will, entreating his favor.

The Superman, being the offspring of a monotheistic religion which, in the exclusivity of its concept of divinity, served as a prototype for the narcissistic fantasies of the Western ego, can in fact exist only in the singular. This is why the Supermen are said to represent happy coincidences who signal to one another across the centuries. Thus although more than one may exist, they are separated by centuries. None of them impinges on the omnipotence of another.

Nietzsche makes every effort to invest the Superman with an aura of romantic genius. He depicts him in poetic terms as a fully-developed individual, as a redemptive exception, as the man who justifies man. He describes his perfection, beauty and refinement. But Nietzsche is unable to maintain this perspective. Again and again his cynicism breaks the spell. One actually senses his fear that this ideal being of his might somehow be suspected of having some weakness, of exhibiting gentleness or consideration for others. This fear leads to a compulsive, repetitive, stereotypical, hyperbolic emphasis on just the opposite traits. Thus the Superman's godlike refinement is quickly screened behind a grotesque mask of terrorism and bestiality. Nietzsche pours a kind of frantic desperation into the defense of his antisocial countermorality, thus revealing at every step that he has fallen prey to that same *ressentiment* which he accuses the "slavish" Christians of feeling. (Of course, in Nietzsche's case the resentment is of the weak and tender rather than the strong.) Moreover, Nietzsche himself is by no means an embodiment of those ideals he preaches. The desperation with which he clings to the concept of a violent super-masculinity, a crass *machismo*, clearly reveals his dread of the opposite traits, the dread of being pitiable, helpless and forlorn.

When he celebrates "the exultant monster" who murders, rapes, tortures and commits arson with the "blameless conscience of the predator" and departs "in high spirits and with an untroubled mind," [63]   Nietzsche's frenzied glorification of naked barbarism betrays his secret fear, his desire to eradicate in himself something which he feels is threatening to overwhelm him. His is the old fear of absolute dependency, for which he is driven to overcompensate through a narcissistic mechanism. Tenderness, sympathy and passivity must be eradicated once and for all. Only the most extreme form of expansionistic egotism can prevent a relapse into gentleness and weakness. Man would once again become small and weak and be left at the mercy of God, just as he had been in the Middle Ages, if he failed to root out of himself all those feelings which made him potentially susceptible to this reversion. Only a radical contrast to his former weakness—a contrast embodied in the ideal of terroristic barbarism—appeared capable of preventing a total capitulation to the enemy. There was no choice but to take refuge in a ruthless, aggressive policy of expansionism. The only way to prevent the eruption of repressed sensibility and vulnerablity was by the radical perversion of these feelings, by turning them into their polar opposite—a murderous terrorism.

The psychological processes evident in Nietzsche's thought are a paradigm of the way in which primordial feelings of impotence and dependency, which are denied or disguised in the manner of all "complexes" and never consciously dealt with much less overcome, can result in a complete identification of the self with God and a claim to divine omnipotence—despite the fact that the flawed and inauthentic character of this omnipotence is unmistakable. An experience of dependency which has given rise to feelings of despair, and by which the person has become arrested in the form of a terrifying fantasy that he is going to be destroyed and violated, is represented by the ego or conscious mind and triggers a shift from a passive to an active stance. Only by becoming a raging predator can one finally imagine oneself to be free from all coercion and threats. Thus what emerges in the end is not the image, in human form, of that God whom one had so profoundly feared and envied, but rather the image of the wild, hate-filled, murderous beast.*

Nietzsche accuses those with a Christian "slave mentality" of being moved, by envy of the strong, to glorify their own weakness and to "touch it up" so that it appears far more impressive than it really is. Yet Nietzsche himself, who is as incapable of accepting his weakness as the slavish Christians allegedly are, also resorts to denial and to a mechanism of overcompensation. He derides those who succeed in accepting their insignificance—albeit by making use of an act of self-deception—by consoling themselves with the pretense that power is not worth having in the first place, much as the famous fox comforted himself for his failure to reach the grapes by persuading himself that they were sour. Nietzsche himself far outstrips those who are guilty of this kind of self-deception, for he employs a narcissistic delusion as a sort of magic wand to charm away his own insignificance. He persuades himself that he actually *is* the man he would merely *like* to be. Falling prey to a classic narcissistic delusion, he confuses himself with his own antitype, with that grandiose figure who is the exact opposite of what Nietzsche fears he may be and, in reality, is. The obverse of the coin—that weak side of his nature which he repressed by means of a narcissistic overcompensation—is disclosed in the concluding stanzas of his melancholy poem "Left Alone" ("Vereinsamt"):

> Now you stand pale,
> condemned to winter wayfaring,
> like smoke that forever seeks to rise
> to colder skies.

---

* The personal histories of at least some members of modern West German terrorist groups suggest that much the same emotional dynamics, resulting in the same reaction, are operative in the terrorists, as those which determine Nietzsche's psychic profile.—Author.

Fly, bird, rasp out your song,
the desert notes of the bird of waste places!
You fool, conceal
your bleeding heart in ice and scorn!

The rooks shriek and seek
the town with whirring wings.
Soon it will snow—
Woe to him who has no home!

This poem is the lament of the narcissist in his hopeless isolation, whose "bleeding heart" longs for a home and a secure shelter. But he no longer believes that a home still exists for him, or that anyone will hearken to his cry for help. He fears that he will bleed to death from his longing, and thus he takes refuge within an armor-plated narcissism. Henceforth he must wield the weapons of ice, scorn and loathing to shield himself from his own feelings, which he believes are bound to destroy him. This unconscious, overcompensatory reaction formation* drives him to aim a never-ending stream of cynical jibes at the wretched herd animals: the weak, the sickly, the insignificant. For him there remains nothing but a "winter wayfaring," a flight into colder and colder skies. This image of ascent is an exact representation of that process of escalation which inevitably results from the escape into narcissistic delusions of grandeur and omnipotence. The only way to defend oneself against one's passive, repressed desires and emotions is to yield to the unceasing urge to press forward and to build even higher the wall of resistance to everything that one has repressed—and finally, by entering a deathly, icy, barren waste of solitude:

The wastelands wax: woe to him who harbors inner wastelands!
Stone grates on stone, the wasteland strangles and engulfs.
Atrocious death gazes glowing and tawny,
chewing away. His chewing is his life. [64]

---

* The psychoanalytic term "reaction formation" designates a defense mechanism against ambivalent feelings, in which the person represses or renders unconscious one of his ambivalent emotions by overemphasizing the other. Thus one may repress an urge to inflict pain by going out of one's way to be kind; the repressed emotion still persists on the unconscious level.—Tr.

Nietzsche's monumental portrait of the Superman was painted in those years when Western civilization was undergoing rapid industrialization and Western societies were turning into mass societies. Many people sensed that the opportunities for realizing the ideal of individualism on a grand scale were dwindling in this new world where living conditions were determined by industrial productivity. This threat that mankind might soon degenerate into the kind of herd animal depicted by Nietzsche turned his *Thus Spake Zarathustra* (1883–1885) into a best seller which worked on people like a drug. Multitudes clung to the notion of the "Superman," trying to hold fast the individualistic ideal he represented, at a time when the possibilities of realizing this ideal appeared to be vanishing, never to return. The extraordinary and never-abating popularity enjoyed by *Zarathustra* and Nietzsche's other works clearly demonstrates that generation after generation has felt (and continues to feel) that his philosophy is relevant to their situation. Moreover, it also reveals that they identify with the emotional dynamics of overcompensation underlying this philosophy. Participation in Nietzsche's vision of the Superman affords people, at least in fantasy, a certain compensation for the diminished significance of the individual in the dawning age of the mass man, bureaucracy and the conversion of man into a useful commodity. But, by describing his vision of the superordination of the ego, Nietzsche did more than simply provide the individual daydreamer with an illusory defense against the spectre of his own future status as a herd animal reduced to a state of ever-increasing helplessness. For, little as he may have intended it to do so, Nietzsche's philosophy also paved the way for one of the most abominable political movements in modern history.

For it was not the romantic, misty-eyed and muddle-headed Alfred Rosenberg, the official Nazi Party philosopher, who drew up the blueprint for Fascist racist attitudes; it was Nietzsche. Nietzsche's narcissistic and megalomaniacal notions not only generated the figure of the Superman, the omnipotent individual, but also the vision of a master race whose destiny it was to preserve mankind from decadence and corruption by the base influence of the slave races. The "blond beast" who, since the days of antiquity, has had to resist "all European and non-European specimens of thralldom, and in particular all members of the pre-Aryan population," is pictured "rising up in the wake of all the aristocratic races." In enraptured tones Nietzsche sings the praises of the "blond Teutonic beast," the "prowling beast of prey, greedy for victory and spoils." He is enchanted by the traits of the "aristocratic" races—

traits which in the past had been denounced as barbarian: "indifference and scorn for their safety, life, comfort, physical welfare," and a "terrible delight and abysmal joy in all destruction, in all the voluptuous pleasures of cruelty and victory." The blond, long-headed Aryans were, Nietzsche claimed, the true conqueror race, the master race. Yet at the moment the subject, pre-Aryan, short-headed and dark-haired races appeared to be gaining the upper hand. Moreover, these pre-Aryan people were probably responsible for the modern trend towards democritization and the "bias in favor of the *commune,* the most primitive form of society, now shared by all the socialists of Europe." But "everything which has been done on earth to damage 'the aristocrats,' 'the mighty,' 'the lords,' 'the powerful,' is as nothing compared to what the Jews . . . , with a terrifying consistency, have dared to do; namely to invert the aristocratic value equation—good = noble = beautiful = happy = beloved of heaven—and to which they have held fast with the teeth of the most abysmal hatred, the hatred of impotence." [63]

"The profound and icy suspicion aroused by the German the moment he rises to a position of power—a suspicion being manifested again today—is a vestige of that indelible horror with which for centuries Europe looked on at the raging of the blond Teutonic beast, despite the fact that it can hardly be claimed that any similarity in mental attitudes, much less a blood relationship, exists between the ancient Germanic tribes and the modern Germans." There may well be reason to fear the blond beast, "but who would not a hundred times rather be afraid, if at the same time he had cause to marvel, than to have no need for fear, but never succeed in escaping the loathsome sight of failures, of stunted, degraded, tainted beings?" [63]

Doubtless Nietzsche never envisioned that one day a lower-middle-class clique, banding around a dark-haired man, would feel themselves called upon to obey the clarion call which could, with some little effort, be heard between the lines of the passages just cited from *The Genealogy of Morals.* The summons they heard was that addressed to the descendents of the "blond Teutonic beast," enjoining them to undertake a task of high courage: to prove their predatory aristocracy by subjugating the allegedly inferior pre-Aryan and non-Aryan peoples so that they could breed a new and more exalted human race, a race of masters. It is a strange and disquieting fact that the delusory nature of Nietzsche's Superman philosophy became apparent only as a result of the grand-scale attempt of the Fascists to put his concept to a practical test.

3

Utopia,
or the Injured Individual's Quest
for Salvation:
Marx, Freud, Marcuse

It seems characteristic or our times that the two men whose thought holds
most sway over the modern mind made no claim to be philosophers in the
classical sense of the term. Both Marx and Freud regarded themselves as
scientists. Unlike their philosopher forebears, they did not wish their
thought to extend beyond the compass of reality. Instead, one of them
chose to study the immediacies of the historical process, the other the
immediacies of psychological development, with a view not only to
understanding, but to intervening in and changing them.

   Poles apart as Marx and Freud may be in most respects, they are
alike in their espousal of an attitude which has become characteristic of
modern man in general. Both take as their starting point the *damaged* or
injured human being. In his own way Nietzsche had done the same thing,
for his grandiose philosophy of the Superman is at bottom nothing but
the arbitrary and brutal celebration of the countertype to the weak, the
wretched, the injured. However, in Nietzsche recognition of the
essentially broken nature of man remained repressed and unavowed. Only
those discoveries later made by Freud enable us today to understand the
important role of "the Insulted and Injured" in Nietzsche's thought.
Nietzsche was still able to appeal to the widespread hope of various
groups that it was possible, by making an all-out effort, to escape the
confinements of the age of the mass man and to arbitrarily establish a
preserve of omnipotence.

   However, unlike Nietzsche, both Marx and Freud *explicitly* take the
alienated or neurotic man as the starting point for their thought, which
centers around the question of how this man's injuries can be overcome.
The human self reflected in both Marx and Freud experiences itself
primarily as oppressed or sick, and is seeking a political or therapeutic

way of ending its suffering. For unlike the thinkers of the past, neither Marx nor Freud believed that it was possible to give meaningful aid to the injured self merely by coming up with a new philosophical point of view. Thinking could not change reality, and unlike Nietzsche and others, Freud and Marx could see no way in which man could *think* himself out of and beyond the miseries of reality. They saw that a new method was needed to abolish the affliction of psychological alienation, or stunted emotional growth or mental illness. But this method could not be haphazard, it had to be absolutely reliable. And it could be regarded as reliable only if it could be validated scientifically. Thus, both Marxists and psychoanalysts regard their schools of thought as scientific disciplines. One of them teaches man how to interpret human history as a dialectical process, and what kind of political action to take in order to achieve certain historical goals, whereas the other teaches man how to interpret his interior, psychological history and how, by learning to understand himself, he can earn a new measure of emotional freedom.

Despite the fact that, as I have stated, Marx and Freud are poles apart in that one concentrates on economic and political realities, and the other on the intrapsychic reality, the two men agree on one point: Both are convinced that the injuries man has suffered were inflicted in the course of an *historical* process. For they take it as their basic premise that man's present deteriorated condition is not his natural state. Man could be much more than he is now—so they reason—if he had not been afflicted by prevailing social or psychic conditions which alienated him or made him sick. Both men, in vastly different ways, awakened great hopes in their fellow men, hopes based on the logical connection between the elucidation of the *cause* of a phenomenon, and the practical conclusions, based on the knowledge of this cause, as to what can be done to *change* the situation.

Marx explains man's alienation as the consequence of economic conditions engendered by capitalism. As a result of these conditions, Marx says, work has ceased to be a natural expression of human life and is being turned into something destructive of individuality—something which converts man into the slave of objects and ultimately converts man himself into an object, into "impotent human merchandise." Freud seeks those influences damaging to man primarily in the individual history of the sufferer. The individual's psychological development can be disrupted by his failure to master certain conflicts. But unlike Marx, Freud does not describe these conflicts as the expression of societal processes but rather as the result of an *internal* struggle, on the part of an individual who has not yet achieved emotional maturity, with the people who have been closest to him. Ignoring Freud's own final conclusions on this subject, many people have misinterpreted his views and mistakenly believed that he regarded inadequate methods of child-rearing, and other forms of avoidable social trauma, as primary causes of neurosis. Thus the general public tends to have an erroneous, oversimplified notion of Freud's views, and many people have drawn an inappropriate analogy between Marx's description of the oppression of man by capitalism in society at large, as macrocosm, and Freud's description of the repression of instinct imposed on the child by the adults who bring him up. In reality, although Freud initially attributed great significance, for the etiology of neurosis, to the influence of factors external to the afflicted person, he later assigned such factors a much less prominent role.

The great fascination of Marx and Freud can be attributed to the fact that—in part justifiably, in part unjustifiably—they have been viewed as the bearers of a messianic promise; they supposedly knew how man could repair the damage he had suffered and fully realize that greatness and freedom for which he was by nature intended. In reality Marx gave us only a few hints as to what man would be like after his liberation by Communism. And Freud expressed himself with great caution concerning the prospects that psychoanalysis might prove an effective therapy for mankind's ills. However, apart from these two, no other thinkers of the late nineteenth and early twentieth centuries proved remotely capable of marshalling man's vanishing faith in the doctrine of salvation through the grandiose self-actualization of the individual, and of showing him how to attain this long-cherished goal. If—so people reasoned—one simply followed Marx's proposals for the creation of a Socialist, and later a Communist state; or if one spent several years undergoing psychoanalysis in an all-out attempt to master the problems rooted in the unconscious mind, one might, in the end, still have some chance of realizing that state of narcissistic omnipotence which man had been striving to attain since the Middle Ages.

Marx left only the sketchiest indications of what man could expect from life after the alienation engendered by the capitalist system had been done away with. Concerning Communism he said: "It is the *true* resolution of the conflict between man and nature and between man and man, the true resolution of the strife between existence and essence, between objectivity and self-affirmation, between freedom and necessity, between the individual and the species. It is the solution to the riddle of history and knows that it is the solution." [54]   Today, Marx claims,

man has been transformed into a "monstrous cripple." Our goal must be
the development of the whole human being, the universal or well-
rounded man who has ceased to be a mere commodity and who is no
longer crippled by that specialization imposed by the division of labor.
Originally "man was a hunter, or a fisherman, or a shepherd, or a
discriminating critic, and he has had to remain so in order not to lose his
means of livelihood. But in the Communist society, no one will be
confined to one exclusive sphere of activity but can educate himself and
branch out in any direction he chooses, and where society as a whole will
regulate production, thus making it possible for me to do one thing today
and something else tomorrow. I can hunt in the morning, fish in the
afternoon, tend livestock in the evening, and be a critic after dinner,
whenever it pleases me to do so, without ever having to become a hunter, a
fisherman, a herdsman or a critic." [55]

Although, apart from these statements, Marx does not go into any
concrete detail about the future of man in a Communist society, he does
make it clear that the individual will be free of many constraints. Man
will no longer be cut into pieces by the division of labor. Nor will he any
longer be treated as an object, a producer or consumer of merchandise and
a piece of merchandise himself. Thus, Marx reasons, it is impossible for
man to be liberated if he continues to view himself as he does today, when
he has become a "mentally and physically dehumanized being . . . a self-
aware and self-moving commodity." Only Communism can reveal the
image of a man whose growth is no longer limited in any way and who
for the first time has the chance to achieve true selfhood, to become truly
himself.

Thus, the goal of Marxism is the creation of the authentic man, the
liberated individual who has fully developed all his capabilities as a
human being. Interpreters of Marxist psychology, including Erich
Fromm and Herbert Marcuse, are in basic agreement in their view that
Marx's ultimate goal was in fact oriented towards the individual. The very
fact that Marx said so little about the life of man in the utopian
Communist society of the future, and the fact that what he did say is so
vague, has given free rein to our imagination and opened up a vista of
infinite possibilities. In Marx's society of the future, many of the things
which oppress man today would no longer exist, and thus the individual
might be capable of developing in directions which are inconceivable to
us now. So Sève writes: "To be sure, it is true that when men think of the
great deeds of liberation performed in the past—and frequently in the
present as well—they tend to regard as the greatest those deeds which

relieve the most elementary needs—the liberation from hunger, from threats to personal safety, from oppression and bestial violence. Yet already we are seeing indications that an act of liberation of a far higher order awaits us at a higher stage of evolution: the liberation from anarchic and stunted psychological growth. Moreover, this liberation will no longer be confined to a small minority, but will be for all mankind. In other words, if it is true that Communism will abolish the governance of *men* by means of the management of *things*, then clearly by the same token Communism will shift our priorities from the production of things to the personal development of human beings. This is the true meaning of Marx's and Engels' contention concerning that leap out of the realm of necessity and into the realm of freedom which Communism will enable man to perform, and which will constitute 'The full development of man's dominion over the forces of nature, both over so-called [physical] nature and over his own nature.'" [92]

As I have indicated, Marx was very vague about the details of how man might develop in a non-oppressive civilization. Herbert Marcuse stepped in to fill this gap, chiefly in his book *Eros and Civilization*, in which he employed psychoanalytic concepts in drawing his portrait of the undreamed-of potentialities of the pleasure principle:

> Under optimum conditions, the prevalence, in mature civilizations, of material and intellectual wealth would be such as to allow the painless gratification of needs, while domination would no longer systematically forestall such gratification. In this case, the quantum of instinctual energy still to be diverted into necessary labor (in turn completely mechanized and rationalized) would be so small that a large area of repressive constraints and modifications, no longer sustained by external forces, would collapse. Consequently, an antagonistic relation between pleasure principle and reality principle would be altered in favor of the former. Eros, the life instincts, would be released to an unprecedented degree. [53]*

Freud's depiction of a mankind healed by psychoanalytic insight is far less resounding in its claims. Jaspers was wrong when he accused Freudian psychoanalysis of presenting itself as "*the* science of man *per se* and the bringer of our salvation." [41]   The salvation described by

* [53] Page 153 of chapter "Phantasy and Utopia" from *Eros and Civilization: A Philosophical Inquiry into Freud*, Boston, Beacon Press, 1971.—Tr.

Freud consists, quite simply, in working through and dealing with childhood repressions, a process which facilitates the subsequent development of the ego. In other words, it consists in an increased measure of emotional freedom acquired by eliminating compulsive behavior or automatisms of which the person has hitherto been unconscious, and which he has failed to understand. The increased available energy to be derived from this process makes it possible for a person to attain a relatively higher degree of self-determination, and thus of emotional health as well. But Freud never expressed an idealized, grandiose conception of emotional health. He does not describe the ideal of narcissistic omnipotence as an obtainable goal, but purely as a nostalgic fantasy on the part of parents who are trying to protect their children from all the hardships of life:

> Thus a compulsion exists to attribute to the child all perfections, although sober observation [of the child] would give one no cause to do so, and to conceal and overlook all the child's faults—a process associated with the denial of his sexuality. However, there is also a tendency [on the part of parents] when dealing with the child, to ignore all those civilized attainments which they have inculcated in themselves in violation of their own narcissistic inclinations, and to renew, in the child, those demands for special privileges which they renounced long ago. The child is supposed to have a better life than his parents; he is not supposed to be subject to those exigencies which the parents have learned hold sway over human life. Disease, death, the renunciation of pleasure, the restrictions imposed on the individual will, are not supposed to exist for the child; he is intended to be exempt from the laws of nature as well as those of society, and he is actually supposed to become, once again, the true center and core of the creation. His Majesty the Baby, just as the parents once thought themselves to be. [25]

Freud sees no rational purpose in abolishing, once they have been imposed, those limitations which experience and "reality testing" have set on the child's narcissism. For Freud regards feelings of ambivalence and the conflicts engendered by the natural schism between Ego and Id as permanent features of human nature; moreover, all his life he remained highly skeptical about the possibility of eliminating the various forms of societal coercion. In the last years of his life he continually warned his students against an uncritical overestimation of the potentialities of psychoanalysis to heal emotional illness. [39] Thus his views of the degree of psychological freedom attainable through therapy were far less optimistic than those expressed in the passages from Marx cited above. Freud did not suggest that man might one day engage in a great variety of unrestricted, outer-directed activities. He believed that a more realistic possibility of achieving gratification was a life style in which a person made himself, to a large extent, independent of the pressures exerted by the world around him. Thus he extolled the advantages of emotional and intellectual activity in which one "seeks gratification in interior, psychical events." Freud considered this "narcissistic approach to life" the most advantageous because he did not believe that the social environment of the individual could be fundamentally altered so as to become more hospitable to human beings. He explained his belief that it was a mistake to try to transform the world "instead of building another world in which the most intolerable features [of the old] have been erased and replaced by others more conformable to one's desires. As a rule anyone who, in a spirit of desperation and revolt, chooses the [former] road to happiness will achieve nothing; reality is too strong for him. He will become a madman who most often will find no one to assist him in implementing his deluded schemes." [30]

But the vast body of disciples who soon attached themselves to Freud did not share his cautious appraisal of the potentialities of psychoanalytic therapy, and indeed, they appeared to have deep-seated needs to reject his modest views on the matter. A widespread fantasy developed that all human anxieties and inhibitions resulted from sexual repression, from which the individual could free himself through psychoanalytic treatment, and which could be eliminated from society as a whole by reforming sexual mores and by better sex education. In his book *Reason and Anti-Reason in Our Time* (English translation Yale University Press, 1952), Karl Jaspers accused Freud, as well as Marx, of proposing dangerous messianic doctrines which were actually totalitarian in character; but in Freud's case this charge is wholly unjustified. For despite the fact that his followers all over the world made exaggerated claims about the capacity of psychoanalysis to effect transformation in both the private and public spheres, at no time did Freud himself credit psychoanalysis with miraculous powers to heal individuals or to revolutionize society. However, the tendency towards the uncritical overestimation of the potential influence of psychoanalytic therapy reveals the extent of man's frustration and of his longing for a cure for all his ills. People simply could not refrain from turning Freud's teachings

into a sacred cow by projecting onto them all their own dammed-up
fantasies of greatness and omnipotence.

*

Naturally it was only a matter of time before people realized the
possibility of combining the ideas of Marx and Freud, of melding their
basic approaches to form a complex socio-psychological theory for the
renovation of society and man. Psychoanalysts of stature, like Siegfried
Bernfeld, Wilhelm Reich and Otto Fenichel adopted Marxist ideas. This
development began in the twenties and was ushered in by Bernfeld when
he asked the fundamental question: "Is psychoanalysis, as a science,
compatible with socialism as a science—i.e., Marxism—or are the two
mutually exclusive?" He himself answered his question as follows: "The
method of psychoanalysis, the goal of its search, and the emphasis of its
investigations, conform to the Marxist approach to its material, the only
difference being that the object of psychoanalytic study is the history of
the psyche, whereas that of Marxism is the history of society. The
relationship between the two disciplines is not casual but inevitable, for
the life of the psyche and the life of society are dialectical processes, and
true knowledge consists in the conscious recognition of their dialectical
nature." [8]

Soon attempts were being made to incorporate Marxist elements
into psychoanalytic theory, as well as, conversely, to equip Marxism with
a dialectical-materialist psychology based on psychoanalysis. One
example of such attempts was Otto Fenichel's study, "Über die
Psychoanalyse als Keim einer zukünftigen dialektisch-materialistischen
Psychologie," 1934 ["On Psychoanalysis as the Seed of a Future
Dialectical-Materialistic Psychology"]. [21]   Wilhelm Reich went
further in his efforts to link Marx and Freud, in the sense that he used the
teachings of both men as the basis for a new science known as *sex
economy*. Reich claimed that the scientific function of psychoanalysis was
to facilitate "the understanding of the structure and dynamics of ideology,
not its historical ground. Through its incorporation of psychoanalytic
insights, sociology achieves a higher plane and is much better able to
master reality because finally it has a way of understanding the *structure*
of man. Only a narrow-minded politician would reproach structural
psychology, based on character analysis, for its incapacity to immediately
come up with sensible suggestions for the resolution of practical issues."
"The genuine psychologist will value the [psychoanalytic] analysis of

sexuality in children, which represents a major achievement in the scientific revolution."

Then Reich goes on to say: "From all this it is obvious that the social science of sex economy, which is based on the sociological foundation laid by Marx and the psychological foundation laid by Freud, is at the same time both a science of mass psychology and a science of sexual sociology." "Psychoanalysis discloses in detail the workings and mechanisms of sexual oppression and repression and their pathological consequences. The social science of sex economy goes on to ask the question: What is the sociological cause for the suppression of sexuality by society and its repression by the individual?" [71]

Reich regards the family as, so to speak, the transition point between Marx and Freud, for it is the family which reproduces and passes on the authoritarian structure of society. The function of the family is the "manufacture of the vassal who has adapted to the authoritarian order and who tolerates it despite his distress and degradation. To instruct him in the rudiments of this vassalage, the child is passed through the miniature authoritarian state of the family, to whose structure the child must adapt if he is to be capable, later on, of fitting into the framework of society at large." "The link between the socioeconomic and sexual structure; of society, on the one hand, and the reproduction of this structure, on the other, is forged in the first four or five years of life, within the authoritarian family." [71]

Moreover, Wilhelm Reich worked more intensively than any other analyst to achieve a union between psychoanalysis and practical socialist action. Seceding from the Freudian school of analysis, he founded the "Sex-Pol Group" (short for "Sex Politics Group") in the attempt to organize an international movement in support of a sex-affirmative culture.

However, orthodox Marxists were less inclined to open their doors to psychoanalysis than Reich and some other analysts were to open theirs to Marxism. By the same token, the majority of psychoanalysts were determined to resist any interbreeding of Marxist concepts with psychoanalytic theory and methodology. Aleksandr Luria, who had earlier founded a psychoanalytic group in Kazan in the Soviet Union, as well as W. Jurinetz [43] and J. Sapir [79] condemned Freudian psychoanalysis as "bourgeois aestheticism" and as the "philosophy of disintegration." In the same book Hans Jörg Sandkühler summed up orthodox Marxist criticism of psychoanalysis as follows:

According to the Marxists, psychoanalysis is a product of late-period bourgeois thinking, an idealistic, non-materialistic theory of subjectivity lacking any perspective on the class issue. It is accused of carelessly transferring to the masses conclusions extrapolated from the study of individuals, and thus degenerating from a science into a world-view. Its emphasis on biology is said to be responsible for its lack of historical consciousness. Its concept that man's psychic nature is ambivalent with respect to libido and aggression is described as pre-rational and mythological. It is accused of turning into an intellectual absolute insights derived from the study of the family in the late-period [i.e., modified and government-controlled] capitalistic society. And finally, it is said to reflect the dying world of capitalism, which has come to appear meaningless to the bourgeois consciousness, in the guise of *unconscious* material dominated by 'pansexualism.' [78]

The German Communist Party excommunicated the "Freudo-Marxists" on the grounds that they were revisionists. Much the same behavior was evinced by their ideological adversaries, the members of the International Psychoanalytic Association, who cancelled the membership of Bernfeld and Reich.

But these acts of mutual rejection during the 1930's did not prevent the resurgence, thirty years later, of the attempt to achieve a synthesis of Marx and Freud. It is only natural that such attempts should have been made, for more and more constraints and controls were being imposed on the individual in our modern technologized mass society, and as a result man's perception of his social thralldom was becoming more and more closely linked with a feeling of psychical thralldom. Marx and Freud have provided us with the most comprehensive and intriguing theories regarding man's lack of freedom—on the one hand the lack of societal, on the other of psychical freedom. Thus it was indeed natural that people should look to them for guidance in their distress. The more man associates his inner emotional impediments with forms of social intimidation and constraint, the more vehemently he clamors for some clarification of the interaction between his inner and outer worlds, and for a strategy which would enable him to eliminate those interrelated factors, in both worlds, which are disrupting his life.

With some modifications and in his own highly original fashion, Herbert Marcuse has adopted the basic premise of the old Freudo-Marxists. As virtually everyone is aware, the ideas which he expressed in

1957 in his book *Eros and Civilization* (in the German version the title was later changed to "Society and the Structure of Instinct") profoundly influenced the European student campus rebellions of the sixties, and to a somewhat lesser extent, the American campus rebellions as well. Marcuse combined various elements of Marxist and Freudian teaching to form a comprehensive theory of human repression. By somewhat indiscriminately lumping together all those social and psychological conflicts which were clamoring to be dealt with, he nourished the hope that an immediate revolutionary assault on all repressive forces and authorities might, as it were at a single blow, usher in the reign of pleasure and freedom. Unlike Marx and Freud, he was a sort of Pied Piper who seduced people with a rosy, alluring picture of a future Utopia untroubled by physical want and the constraints of authority. In his ideal world, work becomes play. Life is spent in contemplation and the pursuit of beauty. The guiding principle is the ideal of a higher order of existence associated with the figures of Orpheus and Narcissus—an order without oppression in which art, freedom and civilization are united forever. [53]   The production principle—the "work ethic"—is overcome. Having left this ethic behind, man's concern will be the universal gratification of fundamental human needs and the freedom from guilt and anxiety, both external and internal, instinctual as well as "rational." Thus Marcuse waxes ecstatic in his depiction of a utopian, idyllic world—in effect a gentler, more aesthetic and more erotic variation of Nietzsche's image of the Superman. The tangled web of societal conflicts and the variegated nature and deep, unconscious roots of psychological problems are glossed over, or engulfed in a paradisiac vision of the millennium, which seems close enough to reach out and touch. The struggle we are enjoined to undertake against oppressive societal forces assumes magical aspects. Concepts like revolution and the "Great Refusal" sound like archetypal magic formulas which appear to dispense man from the toil of analyzing concrete situations and of devising plans for dealing with a wide variety of vastly different problems. The world around us is transformed into the setting for a great drama in which the descendants of the gods of antiquity, or a series of incarnations of archaic, archetypal images, are assembled in an epic confrontation. Eros, Orpheus, Narcissus and Prometheus, the pleasure principle and the reality principle, are locked in mortal combat. The world of Marx and Freud has undergone a process of aesthetic transmutation and mystification so that it is easy to understand why, during the initial phase of the campus rebellions—the *Sturm-und-Drang* phase when people were still in the first throes of enthusiasm—the rebels could easily be aroused by a man like Marcuse. At that time hundreds of thousands of young people who had only a superficial knowledge of Freud and who, for the most part, had never read a word of Marx saw themselves as the champions of both Freudian and Marxist concepts. In reality, as Marcuse himself later concluded, the campus rebellions actually represented a kind of adolescent revolt in which the despair of the younger generation drove them to identify with ideas expressive of those same societal conflicts in which they themselves were at that age personally embroiled.

In any case, it appears that, following in Nietzsche's wake, Herbert Marcuse *has, for the time being, carried to its ultimate limit the philosophy of narcissistic omnipotence.* Marcuse's Superman, unlike Nietzsche's, does not regard himself as a master ruling over a race of slaves, but rather as an average citizen in a whole society of supermen who spend their time and energy in play, in the creation and enjoyment of art, and in the expression of a new, liberated form of eroticism. Nevertheless, some correspondence exists between the eroticism of Marcuse's man of the future and that of Nietzsche's Superman; for in both cases the eroticism appears to involve primarily the love of self. Marcuse celebrates Narcissus as one of the two archetypes of the "Great Refusal." Marcuse takes as the starting-point for his discussion of narcissism a passage from Freud's *Civilization and Its Discontents* in which Freud states: "In the beginning the self contains everything; later it draws a distinction between itself and the external world. Thus nowadays our feeling of self is merely the shrivelled stump of a comprehensive, indeed an all-embracing emotion corresponding to the more intimate bond which once existed between the self and the world around it."

This primary sense of self can be perpetuated, Marcuse says, in the form of infinitude and the bond with the universe as a whole. From this concept Marcuse derives the notion that narcissism, in this broader sense of the term, represents a basic connection to reality capable of creating a comprehensive existential order. In other words, he claims, narcissism might conceivably contain the germ of a different species of reality principle. One cannot help feeling that this theory reflects, in its most recent and, for the time being, ultimate disguise, the old dream of the godlike individual who occupies the center of the universe. Once again the attempt is being made to direct man's flight from the helplessness of childhood into an image of infinite, narcissistic grandeur which would mean the ultimate conquest of all anxiety, stress and repression. According to Marcuse, the revolution he envisions would create an individual free of the painful restrictions now imposed on the fulfillment of his needs; an individual who could spend his time freely in the pursuit of pleasure and play and whose grandiose self could soar to as yet undreamed-of heights. It may occur to us to wonder why so many former members of the student protest movement of little more than a decade ago, like Americans who a short time ago were dreaming of entering the Peace Corps or VISTA and basking in the aura of "Camelot" emanating from the Kennedy brothers and the ardor of crusades for civil rights, today exhibit such nostalgia when they think back to those vanished days. One reason may be that they, like the rest of us, now realize how difficult it would be to recreate that intoxicating feeling that Utopia was just around the corner.

4

Man Sells His Soul
to Save His Face, or
the Surrender of the Inner Life
to Salvage the Illusion
of Omnipotence: Behaviorism

In the past, and in the present as well, people have built on the ideas of Freud and Marcuse narcissistic dreams of salvation centered around a richly-developed subjectivity, a sense of the inner life. Megalomaniacal delusions have found expression in the ideal of the grandiose self free of all anxiety and repression. For several decades there has existed a school of thought opposed to this introspective, narcissistic vision of man, which has been unobtrusively but tenaciously gaining ground: the philosophy of behaviorism. The true founder of behaviorism was J.B. Watson, who in 1913 pubished his study "Psychology as the Behaviorist Views It" as a kind of manifesto of the new psychology. [99]

The behaviorists may, with some justice, be regarded as the most faithful successors of Descartes, or those who have applied his theories with the greatest degree of logical consistency. For Descartes insisted that only that of which we have clear and distinct knowledge can be regarded as truth, and the behaviorists have been uncompromising in their demand that this standard be applied to the study of man himself. The behaviorists believe that only a scientific method based on mathematical principles—the method which Descartes claimed was the most reliable instrument for understanding and mastering the physicial world—can provide us with valid information about ourselves. Any elements in man that cannot be observed and measured from the outside and explained in terms of external causes are considered obscure and unreliable. In other words, the whole of man's interior, psychic world, including thoughts, feelings and sensations, must be excluded as an object of study, for it cannot be grasped by "objective" methods. The era of self-scrutiny has run its course and been replaced by the observation of external behavior, which, it is claimed, represents the only admissible form of scientific procedure. B.F. Skinner, a leading proponent of behaviorism, teaches that behaviorism "does not *reduce* feelings to bodily states; it simply argues that bodily states are and always have been what are felt. It does not *reduce* thought processes to behavior; it simply analyzes the behavior previously explained by the invention of thought processes." [94]   (p. 265 of *About Behaviorism*)

The endless tedious quest for the inner causes of things is completely useless, and in Skinner's view represents one of the greatest disasters which has befallen man in the history of human thought. He demands "the most drastic change ever proposed in our way of thinking about man. It is almost literally a matter of turning the explanation of behavior inside out." (Ibid., p. 276) He explains radical behaviorism as the theoretical foundation on which to "build a world in which he [man] will feel freer than ever before and achieve greater things." (Ibid., p. 264)

But what kind of person is Skinner talking about? He is talking about the perfect image of the technological world which modern man has erected all around him. The person is merely a component of this world outside him, which swallows him up. The self becomes a repertoire of behaviors which can be understood only if they are observed and analyzed from the outside. The person becomes identical with the organism, the material substratum of behavior. Its mysteries will be completely resolved by the study of physiology: "What an organism does will eventually be seen to be due to what it is, at the moment it behaves. And the physiologist will one day give us all the details. He will also tell us how it has arrived at that condition as a result of its previous exposure to the environment as a member of the species and as an individual." [94]   (Ibid., p. 274)

Naturally those who are not at the moment actively engaged in the pursuit of behavioral science will continue to evince some interest in man's inner life. But this concern with inner data contributes nothing to bringing about positive changes in society. Instead it should be indulged in the sphere of private life, in idle chitchat and sentimental effusions, or by writing or reading autobiographies, novels or dramas.

Inevitably this kind of attitude leads to an ideal image of man as a smoothly-functioning machine within a society which, in its turn, is conceived as a perfectly functioning system composed of many coordinated subsystems. The theory of the individual based on the behavioral sciences is being supplemented by a behavioral-science communications theory which interprets human social relations as analogous to the functioning of mechanical-electrical control or communications systems, i.e., cybernetic systems such as computers. Computer science provides models enabling us to reduce everything which transpires between human beings to an exchange of signals between "senders" and "receivers." A group of people—for example a family—is turned into a "system" analogous to a self-regulating cybernetic system. Communications researchers who work with systems analysis admit that their approach has much more to do with mathematics than with traditional psychology. It is quite consistent with their basic approach that in their book *Pragmatics of Human Communication,* Paul Watzlawick, Janet H. Beavin and Donald D. Jackson should foresee the possibility that "human behavior may one day find its adequate expression in mathematical symbolism." [100]   (Chapter 1, "The Frame of Reference," p. 22)

Thus we see that as the world becomes increasingly dominated by technology, the old narcissistic desires for omnipotence are undergoing a corresponding metamorphosis. This metamorphosis closely parallels the shifting relationship between man and technology. People view themselves and each other the same way they view the artificial environment which they themselves have manufactured. This impoverishment of our image of man, resulting from the blocking-out or depreciation of the inner, psychical life, is the price many people pay in exchange for their fantasy that it is possible to turn man into a perfect machine. Artificial insemination and test-tube babies are already a reality, and the day no longer seems very far off when man will be able to manipulate the genetic inheritance through "biological engineering." Such capabilities are inevitably attended by plans to exercise control over those factors in man which are not genetically determined and in which the processes of evolution still retain some "growing room," with the aim of creating certain kinds of behavior by controlling the learning process, and of eliminating inappropriate behavior by subsequent reconditioning. We even possess the mathematical and technological apparatus by which to train people in the art of proper communication. Moreover, society as a whole can be organized in accordance with carefully-computed concepts, thus creating the optimum conditions for appropriate behavior on the part of individuals and of the entire social group.

By pursuing the model of behavioral science—so the theory goes— man could ultimately acquire the freedom and power to breed a new human race and to control the behavior of individuals, as well as social relations, by means of his own computations. Thus, at least in this respect, he would in fact have arrived at the goal of godlike power and autonomy, although only within the confines of a one-dimensional, technological world. Moreover, he could achieve this goal only at the price of repressing the overwhelming sense of being "bottled up inside," which would afflict all men once they determined to look at and judge each other and themselves only from the outside.

Behaviorism represents the most radical expression of that impulse, experienced by the young child who feels emotionally insecure, to assume total control of the world which is causing the anxiety. The self is no longer content to sit by passively and allow things to be done to it or to happen inside it. The pathic mode of existence, the mode of experiencing and feeling and suffering, has been done away with. Life now consists of nothing but *behavior* and physiological *functioning*. The ego or self, which desired to end its helpless suffering, has finally devised a philosophy in which—to borrow a concept from Viktor von Weizsäcker—death no longer stains life with the hue of suffering. The behaviorist view represents the apogee of the denial of fear and weakness. Only in the hostile invective they direct against the "mentalists"—those who attribute central importance to dealing with man's inner mental and emotional world—do the proponents of "radical behaviorism," B.F. Skinner among them, reveal the emotional strain induced by their effort to persuade themselves that only the exterior surface of life is real.

There is far more at stake here than a mere theoretical debate. For it is conceivable that human beings in general might undergo a gradual alienation from their inner lives and a blunting of their emotional sensibilities so pronounced in its effects that in the end man would be completely out of touch with his emotions and would in fact experience himself almost exclusively "from the outside," as a receiver or sender of signals, or as a machine whose ultimate desire was to compute all data relating to himself and others so that nothing whatever would be unaccounted for or left to chance. But those to whom this impoverishment and emptying-out of man's inner world appears synonymous with total self-alienation will do everything in their power to combat the behaviorist movement. For these people believe that if we are to salvage our human identity, we have no choice but to stand up for a truth expressed by Viktor von Weizsäcker: We cannot "speak the truth about organisms and life without bearing witness that life is not merely a process but also something which is suffered. It is not only self-determining and active. Its very existence is something which befalls it, and thus it is also passive." [103]

5

The Logic of the Head
(Descartes, Spinoza)
Defeats the Logic of the Heart
(Pascal)

Our initial premise was that the development of man since the Middle Ages has been characterized by a striving to escape his sense of being forsaken. He has done this by taking refuge in a feeling of absolute security in his own powers and by seeking to exchange a childlike helplessness and insignificance for invincible strength and greatness. Examining representative samples of postmedieval philosophy, we saw the quest of the human ego to ratify its potency and to create a "grandiose self." The central focus of our inquiry was to trace the various manifestations of man's egocentric will to power and his rivalry with God. In looking at what I have called the "impotence-omnipotence complex," we have thus far concentrated primarily on only one side of the coin—namely the craving for omnipotence. But what about the other, hidden side of the coin, that of repressed impotence? Only in Nietzsche's case did we analyze in any detail the dynamics of the relationship between the sense of impotence, which is warded off by the ego's defense mechanisms, and the overcompensatory resort to megalomania, or the exaggerated sense of one's power and importance. In Nietzsche the intimate link between façade and interior, or the visible and the hidden sides of the coin, was so blatant that it could not be overlooked.

However, Nietzsche is certainly not the only thinker of recent centuries who illustrates the tension between the desperate, egocentric attempt at self-validation and the repression of all traces of passivity, fragility and weakness. On the contrary, this tension has repeatedly left its mark on the history of philosophy, as well as on other aspects of life. After all, it is integral to the nature of defense mechanisms that the emotional impulses which the ego is warding off attempt, in their turn, to resist this suppression, and periodically break through the ego's defenses, manifesting their presence in one way or another. Consequently, in our reexamination of the past we must also take a close look at the repressed, pathic world of receptive suffering and endured emotion, for historical changes have taken place in this sphere too, and it is important that we understand these changes if we are to acquire a clearer understanding of our present situation. For we are not simply confronting the problem of how to come to terms with our failure to fulfill our egocentric desires for personal aggrandizement. Now that our efforts to compensate—or rather overcompensate—for our distress have foundered, we also have another, equally important problem to think about: the problem of discovering what emotional resources we possess, and under what conditions they will function in our struggle to regain our emotional equilibrium—this time on a more solid foundation.

*

At the end of the Middle Ages, when people were no longer certain of *having* God and instead decided to *be* God themselves, they became obsessed with the idea of knowing everything and doing everything for themselves so that they would no longer have to feel dependent. This moment represented an historical turning-point, a moment of decision in which man chose the principle of activity over that of passivity. From that time on, people have felt that there was something wrong with being passive. They have felt that they had to perform careful calculations so that they could predict, and thus control, the future. Man's relationship to his body, and to sensations and impulses of bodily origin, became fraught with difficulty because they necessitated his adopting a passive role. His desperate attempt to be active and never passive gave rise to the compulsion to detach himself from his body and its needs. At the very least he could flatter himself that he had the same absolute power to compute and control bodily sensations, impulses and feelings that he possessed over those processes of nature external to himself. Having fled from an intolerable state of passivity, and feelings that he was as helpless as a child, he now became the slave of a compulsion to be constantly active, and fell prey to an illusion of his own divine omniscience and omnipotence. This transformation led to that isolation of the body from the thinking and calculating self, or intensification of the subject-object dichotomy, which became the intellectual assumption of modern medicine and made possible its scientific and technological approach to disease. The first step in this direction was man's attempt to "objectivize" the body. He began to look at and analyze the body as an external structure on a par with all the other objects of the natural world.

This approach automatically led man to discard a belief which he had never questioned in the past—namely that the *heart* was the seat of the soul. Once again it was Descartes, whose rationalistic philosophy, to some extent, laid the intellectual cornerstone of the new age, who demolished the ancient concept that the heart played a central role in the human psyche. Descartes claimed that the principal seat of the soul was the *brain,* or rather the pineal body or gland (more precisely the *epiphysis cerebri*), an appendage of the brain which appears to be the remnant of an ancestral sense organ. In his treatise *On the Passions of the Soul,* published in 1649, Descartes provided detailed physiological evidence for his revolutionary hypothesis that neither the soul in general, nor the passions, derived primarily from the heart. This conclusion implied far more than that Descartes was discarding an ancient psycho-physiological view of the nature of man. It was also representative of the shift in man's whole relationship to himself and the world. The important thing was not that the heart ceased to be, from a physio-psychological standpoint, the central organ of the body. The crucial thing was that the devaluation of the heart effected, on the symbolical plane, the same transformation which was at the same time taking place in cultural attitudes: For it marked the onset of a prejudice against emotion and in favor of pure cerebration, which was to determine man's "mind-set" during the coming centuries. The emotional part of the human psyche was consigned to a peripheral sphere and came to be regarded by many people as nothing more than something which tended to disrupt intellectual functioning. At this point it seems appropriate to embark on a brief digression outlining the history of ideas from antiquity to the Enlightenment, concerning the relationship between the heart and the soul.

Empedocles (c. 495–c. 433 B.C.) had taught that "the blood which flows around the heart gives man the power of thought." [17]   Later the Greek atomists (Democritus and Leucippus) attributed thought to the brain, concupiscence to the liver, and wrath or choler to the heart. Plato designated the area between the neck and the diaphragm as the seat of courage, ambition, and irascibility or passion. He regarded the heart as a sort of guardroom which, as he wrote in the *Timaeus* (Paragraph 38 on the mortal parts of the soul), was supposed to raise the alarm in the event that any "wanton mischief was afoot directed against the whole man, whether stemming from an outside source or from internal appetites." [70]   Aristotle retained the view that the heart was the locus of "choler" or "irascibility" ("bile"). He regarded hotbloodedness and the wrathful desire for revenge as merely two aspects of the same reaction. [3]

With the coming of Christianity, the concept of the heart was expanded so that it became the center of the soul, the true seat of the inner life. For the time being its physiological aspects were disregarded. The heart was said to be the true foundation of men's relationship to God in faith. In the book of Deuteronomy we find the famous injunction: "And thou shalt love the Lord thy God *with all thine heart*, and with all thy soul, and with all thy might. And these words, which I command thee this day, shall be *in thine heart*" (Dt. 6:5-6). According to the Gospel of Luke, just before Christ recounts the parable of the Good Samaritan, a lawyer asks him what he must do to inherit eternal life, and Christ asks him to repeat this precept of Moses from Deuteronomy (see Lk 10:25 ff.)

However, in the Christian era people continued to speak of the heart as the seat of the passions, as well as the locus of faith. For example, it was the seat of hatred: "Thou shalt not hate thy brother in thine heart" (Lev 19:17). But Christians evinced a growing tendency to interpret the heart as the true core of the person, as the fundamental region of the soul. The *cor inquietum* of St. Augustine (the "restless heart" of man which cannot rest until it rests in God), and the *cor gentile* or "noble heart" of Dante, refer to the *essence* of the person, the substratum of his soul. A man's nature is determined by the nature of his heart. He is as his heart is. In the heart all pretense, all the playacting we put on for others and ourselves, is stripped away. Thus by this view the heart marks the boundary between the *surface* and the *depths* of the psyche: People can seem very different on the outside, or can pretend to be very different, from what they really are in their hearts. The theosophical mystic Jakob Boehme indignantly said of his contemporaries: "Alas, nowadays people are Christians only in name and word; their *hearts* are worse than when they were pagans!" [9]

Side by side with this central concept there developed a wide variety of bizarre notions concerning soul-body relations and the role of the heart as an organ. The following description by the sixteenth-century physician-philosopher Agrippa von Nettesheim, often known as Cornelius Agrippa, suggests what these magical, speculative theories were like:

For in its descent [the soul] first clothes itself in a celestial and airy envelope which is generally known as the ethereal vehicle of the soul, and by others is called the chariot of the soul. By this agency, upon the command of God who is the center of the universe, it is first infused into the midpoint of the *heart*, which is the center of the human body, and from thence spreads through all the parts and members of its body, by uniting its vehicle with the natural heat, and through this heat with the spirit engendered from the *heart*. Through this spirit it immerses itself in the [bodily] humours and through them cleaves to the [bodily] members so that it is equally close to all, despite the fact that it extends itself through one into the other, just as the heat of the fire is closely conjoined to the air and the water despite the fact that it is conducted to the water through the air. In this way it is evident how, through its imperishable envelope, namely the ethereal vehicle, the immortal soul is able to confine itself within the impermeable and mortal body. However, if the substances which mediate this union are dissolved by some disease or mishap, or cease to function, the soul withdraws from the various unitary agents and flows back into the *heart* which first received it. But if the spirit of the *heart* deserts [the body] and the heat is extinguished, the soul leaves the *heart* as well. The man dies, and the soul flies away with its ethereal vehicle, followed by the guardian spirits and demons, who lead her before the Judge, whereupon, in accordance with the sentence pronounced upon them, God conducts the good soul into his glory, but a wrathful demon drags away the evil souls to be punished. [1]   (Italics mine)

> From Book III of the *De occulta philosophia, Ch. XXXVII, "Concerning the Human Soul and By What Means It Is Joined to the Body"*

Agrippa's contemporary Paracelsus regarded heart and soul as one. In his *Philosophia Sagax* (the *Sagacious Philosophy of the Great Astronomy,* Book II, Chapter 7, "Concerning the Origin and Birth of the Soul and Its Essence," etc.) he wrote:

Now further mark you well, concerning the seat and lodgement of the soul, that it is seated in the *heart,* in the center of the man, and consumes the spirits assigned to it, which have knowledge of good and evil, and is seated in the man at the place where is that life against which death wages war, that is in the heart, and the soul is the heart in man of which Scripture says: Thou shalt love God with all thine heart. For the reason of this is: The soul resides in the man and has its seat in the heart. And if the love of God is to come from our whole heart, then everything repugnant or rebellious to God must depart from the soul, and whatever is not divine must be done away with, so that the soul may be wholly pure and unstained by, and perfectly separated from all else, that it may be pure and undefiled, and clean in its whole being. Now that is how a human being should be, when the soul within him is without stain and is pure in all its faculties and in all its temper. Then the soul is entirely single, the body new in God like a king whose heart is held in God's hand. But this is the king, a heart of such purity which makes a perfect man, and is like our Father in heaven: But hearts which are defiled are not kings; that is, they are not held in the hand of God. Thus the soul abides in the heart so that it has no hand or foot to be chopped off, but rather the whole life [of the person] must be taken; then the soul belongs to Him who gave it, just as a man to whom there befalls the death of the body duly belongs to the worms. [66]

Thus the heart as an organ came to be equated with the soul. The self experienced its emotional states as a seamless unity of spiritual impulse and corporeal sensation. As a rule the word "heart" designated the whole person as he was directly experienced, the innermost core of the person in which no distinction was drawn between his mental and physical aspects. Thus the heart was ultimately equated with the character. A man is as his heart is. But the individual does not merely possess his own particular heart, pure and impure, loving or pious or cold. Through the heart the self experiences not only what it *is*, but also what it *ought to be*. There exists an order of things which can be known only through the emotions, not with the intellect. The person experiences directly—that is, *feels*—what is good and evil. Thus the heart becomes an important source—perhaps even the decisive source—of guidance in making value judgments.

It was the mystical philosopher Pascal who introduced the famous concept of the *logique du coeur*, or the "logic of the heart." Pascal was born after Descartes and clearly was influenced by him. In no way did he resemble the stereotype of the romantic dreamer; he was, in fact, a well-known mathematician. But unlike Descartes, he was a fervent champion of the idea that the heart, i.e., feeling, played a significant role in giving man a sense of direction, a rule of life, for his conduct in the world as well as in his relationship to God. "It is not the reason but the heart which experiences God. Faith consists in this, that God is felt in the heart and not by the reason." [68]   (Paragraph 278)

Pascal never dreamed of suggesting that man should revert to a blind, emotional irrationalism. But he perceived the danger of placing absolute trust in one single criterion or source of guidance: the criterion of intellectual proof and empirical science. He did not believe that reason (*ratio* or *raison*) was a reliable guide to value. He also sensed that the decision to rely purely on the resources of reason brought with it the danger that life might turn into a treadmill leading nowhere, and that man might lose all ability to set meaningful goals.

"We apprehend truth not through reason (*raison*) alone, but also with the heart. It is in this latter way that we apprehend first principles, and it is in vain that rational thought (*raisonnement*), which does not partake thereof, seeks to impugn them. Those skeptics who have only this as their goal, here expand their labors in vain." (Paragraph 282)

"The heart has its reasons that the reason knows not of. We feel this on a thousand occasions." (Paragraph 277)

"The heart has its own order. The mind also has its order, which resides in principles and proofs. The order of the heart is different. We cannot prove that we ought to be loved, simply by expounding the reasons for love; it would be absurd to think so." (Paragraph 283)

Pascal counters Descartes' principle, "I think, therefore I am!" with a different principle: *"There can be no doubt that at least man knows that he is and that there is something he loves."* [68]

Thus man ought not to rely solely on thought, on cogitation (Descartes' *cogitare*). At the same time, and to an even greater extent, he ought to be governed by *feeling*—not in the sense that he blindly act upon emotional impulses, no matter what their nature, but rather in the sense that he obey the *logique du coeur*. Clearly Pascal was deeply troubled by the insecurity and lack of direction which he perceived in the men of his time, and which had resulted from man's "jailbreak" from the world of medieval faith. He perceived those processes which I have characterized and interpreted as the flight from feelings of infantile impotence into feelings of narcissistic omnipotence. Now that man had overcome that total dependency, resembling that of a minor child, which had determined his lot in the Middle Ages, how was he to find a place for himself between nothingness and infinity, between puny insignificance and colossal presumption?

"Here is this man, created to know the universe, to be the judge of all things, to govern an entire nation ... And yet in the end he is only a man, in other words capable of little and of much, of everything or nothing: he is neither an angel nor a brute, but a human being."

Thus the question was: How can the individual fully develop his powers, but at the same time accept his human limitations? How else was this possible if not by guiding his life by the "logic of the heart"? If he abandoned himself to the intellect alone, would he not inevitably be led to extremes, to the presumptuous claim to dominion over the whole world, and to a megalomaniacal, egocentric despotism?

"There are no limits to things; laws attempt to set limits, but the mind cannot endure this." And yet:

"The greatness of man is great in that he recognizes his misery. The tree knows nothing of its misery." (Paragraph 397)

One of the fascinating things about Pascal is his virtually prophetic powers, the clairvoyance with which he addressed conflicts which were only beginning to make themselves felt in his day. He warned against that impetuous, headlong flight which resulted in man's identification with God and arrogation of divine omnipotence. Pascal's premonitory aphorisms hint at all the dangerous consequences, which materialized after his own day, of the narcissistic "impotence-omnipotence complex." Having lost his former standard or sense of proportion, man's problem was to find a new standard. Pascal believed that man could not bear to be "the mean between Nothing and Everything." (Paragraph 72) He could not bear to know neither the origin of things nor their end. This uncertainty plunged him into "eternal despair." (Paragraph 72) He was bewildered by the contradiction of being "an All in comparison with Nothing" and at the same time "a Nothing in comparison with the Infinite." (Ibid.) He had to accept being a "Something," but was unable to do so. As a result he fell prey to presumption and arrogantly chose to become infinite himself: "Having neglected to reflect upon these Infinities, men have arrogantly set about investigating nature as if they were cut to the same measure that she is. It is strange that they should have desired to understand the origin of things and thence to derive the knowledge of all else, exhibiting a presumption as infinite as their object. For there is no doubt of the fact that no one can form this resolve without a presumption or capacity as infinite as nature herself." (Paragraph 72)

"Let us then be clear about our true proportion; we are something and we are not everything." (Paragraph 72)

In his own words Pascal has, in essence, described the very problem which we have described here, in terms of psychoanalytic concepts, as the problem of postmedieval man's attempt to find a new guideline to live by. The anxiety and despair which followed upon the loss of his secure relationship with God drove man to seek a sense of security elsewhere, and the only security seemed to lie in the ability of the ego to compute every detail of every phenomenon in order to exercise absolute personal control

over the world. Essentially Pascal is describing that same makeshift
expedient employed by the child who overcompensates for feelings of
helplessness by refusing to let anyone else control his life, and who
resolves to rely only on what he himself knows to be true, and to do only
what he himself chooses. The question, in Pascal's day, was whether—
and if so, how—it was possible to halt man's panic-stricken flight from
his feelings of insecurity. Could man find a "mean between Nothing and
Everything"? Were human beings capable of curbing their urge to pursue
to its ultimate, boundless conclusions their hope of mastering nature by
studying it in terms of the scientific principle of causation? Pascal
believed that men must not lose sight of their limitations and ought to
devote more attention to man himself, instead of occupying themselves
exclusively with abstract science and the newly-discovered powers it
conferred. Pascal has left us a vivid account of his personal experience
which reveals the importance he attributed to the study of man as a means
of restoring a proper sense of proportion concerning the relative values of
abstract science and the other dimensions of human life. The following
passage discloses that the problems of Pascal's age were much like our
own:

> I spent a long time in the study of the abstract sciences, but the
> limited opportunity of exchanging ideas with others bred in me a
> distaste for this study. When I began my study of man, I perceived
> that these abstract sciences are not suitable to him and that my
> deeper inquiry into them was leading me farther away from my
> human state than other men were led by their ignorance of these
> matters. I forgave others for knowing so little. But I hoped that at
> least in pursuing the study of man, I might find many companions,
> believing it to be the study truly appropriate to a human being. I
> was disappointed; even fewer people study man than study mathe-
> matics. *The only reason that people aspire to other studies is that
> they do not know how to study man.*
>
> (Italics mine) (Paragraph 144)

In his edition of the *Pensées*, Paepcke sums up Pascal's basic theory
as follows: "Reason and will *(volonté)* are housed and actuated in the
heart; thus the *coeur* constitutes an emotional structure clarified by
Raison and directed by *Volonté*." [68]   In our hearts we intuitively feel
what we must clarify in our thoughts and act upon through our wills. It
was in this sense that Max Ferdinand Scheler (1874-1928) later cited

Pascal's *logique du coeur* as a model for his own "non-formal ethics of value" in his book *Formalism in Ethics and the Non-Formal Ethics of Value.* [82]

Modern as many elements in Pascal's basic concept appear, he remains, in one crucial respect, the child of his age and is unable to escape its conflicts. For Pascal, only one choice was open to the heart, to the faculty of feeling: the choice between self-love and the love of God. Thus love either reduced man to insignificance or changed him into a being of gigantic stature. Either he experienced himself as the child of God, or he performed an act of self-deification. In other words, Pascal, like the other thinkers we have discussed, is under the sway of that narcissistic complex which initially evolved out of the state of dependency, analogous to that of a minor child, which defined man's position in the Middle Ages. In Pascal's view, man could either totally surrender himself to God, or he could give himself over to *hybris* and a grandiose self-love. Thus Pascal's *coeur* never became a genuine source of human solidarity, of relationship between equals. It fails to establish a foundation for the love of one's fellow man, for charity, for sympathy. It does not lead man to other men, but only to the amorous suffusion of the self in God or, once again, to megalomaniacal egotism. Love does not become a standard or guide for man's shared life in a human community. Pascal's evaluation of love between the sexes is even less positive than his judgment of the love of one's fellow man. "Its cause is an indefinable *je ne sais quoi* (Corneille), and its effects horrific. This *je ne sais quoi*, a thing so small that one cannot even perceive it, sets in motion the whole earth, its sovereigns, its armaments, and all its people. Cleopatra's nose: if it had been shorter, the countenance of the whole world would have been altered." [68] (Paragraph 162)

However, Pascal does persistently and energetically attack the principle of self-love *(amour-propre)*:

> It is the nature of self-love and of this human ego to love only itself and to contemplate only itself. But what shall man do? He cannot alter the fact that this object which he loves is full of flaws and base qualities. He would fain be great and perceives that he is small. He would fain be happy and perceives himself to be wretched. He would fain be perfect and discovers in himself countless imperfections. He would fain be the object of the love and esteem of men, and he sees that his faults merit only their antipathy and scorn. This dilemma in which he finds himself engenders in him the most

unjust and criminal passion that can be imagined; for he conceives a
mortal hatred of that truth which reproves him and convicts him of
his faults. He would fain destroy it, but because he cannot destroy
truth in itself, he destroys it, insofar as he can, in his own mind and
in the minds of others. [68]   (Paragraph 100)

Thus self-love is equivalent to self-deception, and people play the
hypocrite when they display love for others. "Human society is founded
solely on this mutual deceit." (Paragraph 100)

For Pascal, affection for other human beings can be justified only in
terms of the bond which God has instituted among men. The love of one's
fellow man is justified only as a variant, indirect form of the love of God.
"There is nothing in other people which intrinsically merits my love, and
I do not deserve that they should love me. For our shortcomings make us
all unworthy of love. We turned into brute beasts when we sought to
withdraw from God's dominion, find happiness, and equate ourselves
with God." (Paragraph 430) In order to be genuinely happy, man must
accept the revelation of "true religion"—that there is a God, that man is
obliged to love him, that his sole beatitude consists in being in him, and
his sole misfortune in being separated from him.

Thus Pascal failed to provide his contemporaries with a concept of
love capable of reconciling the universal urge to individual self-esteem
with a theory of social solidarity. In psychoanalytic terms one might say
that his views remain deeply imprinted by the thought patterns of a small
child, obsessed with questions of impotence and omnipotence. Under
these conditions, a person has no choice but to idealize the giant figure of
the parent, or to identify himself with the parent, thus performing, on this
relatively infantile plane, an act of self-deification. However, the
establishment of a mature relationship—a relationship between equal
partners—requires the move to a different plane or phase of development,
what Freud calls the genital phase. The same hostility to instinctual
drives manifested by man in the Middle Ages is displayed by Pascal
whenever he inveighs against human loathsomeness and depravity.
Pascal anticipates the modern psychoanalytic theory of repression and
denial in his view that self-love is achieved by man's suppression of his
consciousness of his own unworthiness and the unworthiness of others,
which he could not otherwise fail to perceive. If we were honest with
ourselves, Pascal believes, we would necessarily loathe both ourselves and
others. Clearly Pascal is scandalized by that impulse which was
manifesting itself in his contemporaries, to break free of their centuries of
dependency and to soar to the opposite pole of overweening self-esteem.

Feeling that they wished to become too great, he wanted to make them feel small and wicked again and render their egotism repugnant to them. (Cf. Paragraph 420) The lack, in Pascal's *logique du coeur,* of a firm basis for societal relations, as well as its tone of stricture, prevented it from living up to its initial promise. In other words, it failed to supply man with an authentic guideline in his quest to evolve a new, socially-oriented self-image, and a view of life founded on sympathy and charity.

*

Thus it was not the mystic Pascal but the rationalist Descartes who from the seventeenth century onward largely determined the mind-set of Western man in his quest for a new self-image. People simply did not believe that intuitive knowledge, or knowledge acquired through the emotions, represented a reliable source of guidance which could help them to set meaningful goals and plan for their future. Indeed, Descartes and later rationalist philosophers held the view that the emotions merely constituted a "perturbation of spirit" *(perturbatio animi)* which led the mind into error. This is why, in recent centuries, the head has replaced the heart as the "control center" of the human being. In Cartesian philosophy the affective life was devalued, ranked as far less significant than intellectual cognition. The emotions were relegated to a realm of vagueness and imprecision which, as far as possible, was supposed to be illuminated by the light of the intellect. Descartes regarded the emotions, or passions, as bodily acts communicated to the soul in the form of suffering. [15]

In his system of ethics, Spinoza taught how man could—and should—control those emotions (passions) and sensations linked to the body. Employing a mathematical method of demonstration which, with its axioms, theorems and corollaries mimicked a system of geometry, he supplied a kind of therapeutic self-help program for achieving total intellectual control of all affects and of the body: "Theorem 3: An affect which is a passion [Descartes' *passion de l'âme*] ceases to be a passion as soon as we form a clear and distinct idea of it." (*Ethics*, Part II, "On the Power of the Understanding or of Human Freedom.") For an affect in the form of a passion is merely a "confused idea" which can and should be converted into a "clear and distinct idea."

"Theorem 4: There is no bodily affection of which we cannot form a clear and distinct conception." [96]   (*Ethics*, Part V)

In a note following this theorem Spinoza states: "Thus above all we must take pains, as far as possible, to obtain the most clear and distinct knowledge of every affect, so that through the affect the mind is determined to think that which it clearly and distinctly apprehends, and which affords it total composure." "The consequence of this will be that not only love, hate, etc. will be destroyed, but also that desire and craving, which commonly arise from such an affect, cannot become excessive." *"Of such means of combatting our emotions as lie within our power, none can be conceived more excellent than this, which consists in the true knowledge of the same."* (Ibid.)

By exerting the maximum degree of control over his affects (emotions), man at the same time enhances his own perfection. Accordingly, Theorem 40 of Book V of the *Ethics* states: "The more *perfection* each thing possesses, the more *active* it is and the less it *suffers* [i.e., is passive and receptive]. And conversely, the more *active* it is, the more *perfect* it is." [96]

Apart from their more pronounced intellectual character, Spinoza's propositions are not unlike those made by Sigmund Freud two and a half centuries later, when Freud defined the function of psychoanalysis by stating that where there had been Id, there should now be Ego. Freud held that the unconscious portions of the psyche could be controlled if one understood them. Long before Freud, Spinoza defended the principle that the individual could and should take active charge of emotional impulses which initially are only "suffered" by the ego, i.e., by which the passive ego is overwhelmed. Moreover, Spinoza's demand that man clarify the "confused ideas" concealed in the passions can be viewed as the precursor to Freud's central concept, which in its initial stages was more narrowly defined—the concept that psychoanalytic therapy was equivalent to bringing unconscious processes into consciousness. Rendering this material conscious is much like transferring psychic data from a state of obscurity and confusion into one of clarity and distinctness.

When man took the crucial step, or rather leap, out of the Middle Ages, he felt the need to convert his emotional dependency into total autonomy and to eliminate passivity, adopting an exclusively active role. Emotionality involved the experience of passivity or receptivity, which man hoped, in effect, to engulf by the activity of the perceiving ego, the subject of cognition. In the seventeenth and eighteenth centuries, the degree of man's perfection was considered commensurate with his ability to overcome his passivity. Thus in his *Monadology* Leibniz says: "We say of a creature that, to the degree that it possesses perfection, it works upon that which is external to itself; and of another we say that it suffers [passively] to the degree that it is imperfect." [48]   Leibniz also adopted Spinoza's precept that the "confused ideas" which characterized the suffering of the passions must, through activity, be transformed into clear or distinct ideas. Once again we perceive a certain resemblance to a view later held by Freud, who wrote in *The Ego and the Id:* "The Ego represents what might be called reason and presence of mind, as opposed to the Id, which includes the passions." Most people are aware that in this context Freud compares the relationship between the Id and the Ego to that between a horse and its rider. [28]   However, in Freud's model the Id supplies the Ego with the strength to curb the horse, whereas in his time Spinoza could not yet conceive of such a notion. In the seventeenth century it seemed essential to acknowledge the absolute independence of the ego which bridles the passions. This view reflects the will to total activity as a defense against any reversion to the medieval state of passivity.

Naturally the subjugation of the emotions enjoined by Spinoza could not result in man's total renunciation of emotional gratification. What mattered was that man should learn to discipline those feelings which placed the ego in a distressing state of dependency. On the other hand, this gambit also furnished man an opportunity to compensate for the strictures placed on feelings of self-surrender, which weakened the ego, by the expansion of feelings of self-love. Thus, in Freudian vocabulary, what Spinoza and his contemporaries did was to partially convert object libido into narcissistic libido, i.e., object-directed love into self-directed love. However, this behavior appeared to involve a turning away, or emotional withdrawal, from God. Thus the question arose of how man could risk the attentuation of his relationship with God without experiencing unendurable anxiety and guilt. We have already spoken of philosophers' attempts to deny the fact that man was usurping God's power—attempts which took the form of logical demonstrations of God's existence and of the necessity of his role as mediator between spirit and matter. But this mathematical reconstruction of God did not solve the problem of how to master the emotional distress resulting from the altered relationship of the ego to God. How could the ego justify its withdrawal into a magnified self-love?

Once again it was Spinoza who proposed a solution, one which since his day has been used over and over in a great variety of guises. He simply reversed the terms of the argument by equating expanded self-love with the love of God. In the philosophy of pantheism, narcissism does not lead the self away from God, but rather towards him or even *into* him. In his *Ethics* Spinoza states: "Theorem 35: God loves himself with an infinite intellectual love." "Theorem 36: The intellectual love of the mind

of God is that very love with which God loves himself." "Corollary:
Thence it follows that, insofar as he loves himself, God loves men, and
consequently that the love of God for men and the intellectual love of the
mind for God are one and the same." [96]   (*Ethics*, Part V, "On the
Power of the Understanding, or of Human Freedom")

Thus the human ego participates in the self-love of God. Man is
only a mode of God's self-manifestation, and thus in knowing himself he
knows God. Moreover, at the same time it automatically follows that *in
loving himself, he likewise loves God.* In this sense pantheism may be
regarded as a grandiose creation of the narcissistic mind. It facilitates the
total reconciliation of the self-loving ego with God by enabling man's
self-love to dissolve in the narcissism of God, or conversely, by enabling
God to dissolve in the narcissism of man.

This breed of pantheism is based on the *equation between God and
man. Man's self-regard merges with the self-regard of God,* and thereby
man has taken the decisive step towards libidinous self-deification. Love
ceases to block man's path to egocentrism and megalomania, and instead
fuses with them. The alternatives posed by Pascal—the choice between
self-love and the love of God—are apparently suspended, for God and
man become one. The presumption underlying this tactic is well-
concealed. The egocentric exaltation or hypocathexis of the self is
reinterpreted and represented as the unfolding of God's love for himself.

At this point the marked shift towards narcissism has not yet
resulted in any threatening symptoms of antisocial behavior, primarily
because most of man's emotions remain split off from the rest of his
personality. The narcissistic love sanctioned by Spinoza is a highly
ethereal, sublimated love. It has nothing to do with those body-related
affects and passions which are supposed to be totally subject to the
discipline of reason.

*

In Spinoza's time the attainment of intellectual certitude and power
remained the favored means of consolidating one's position. People were
not content to master physical nature by means of the mathematical-
scientific method, but also applied themselves to the objectification and
analysis of their own inner nature, the human body and its associated
impulses. Descartes, who was born some time before Spinoza, had already
developed a comprehensive mechanistic theory of the body. [15]   He
had designated the motion of "animal spirits" as the cause of the
passions—a motion which was communicated to the seat of the soul, the

pineal gland (epiphysis). To be sure, in Descartes' day no one had, as yet, explicitly voiced the expectation that the French rationalist's attempt to interpret the body and its attendant sensations and affective stimuli as a vast mechanical system might one day result in the ability to compute and control every detail of this complex of machine-like functions. However, this notion was undoubtedly bouncing around in the back of people's minds, and played some role in their behavior. In his treatise *On the Passions of the Soul*, Part I, Article 6, Descartes wrote that the body of a living human being differed "from that of a dead person in the same way that a clock or other automaton—in other words a self-acting machine— which has been wound up and thus possesses the physical principle of those motions for which it is designed, and all that is necessary to its functioning, differs from a broken clock or machine in which the principle of its motion is no longer active." In his mechanistic theory of physiology, which elaborated Harvey's discovery of the circulation of the blood, Descartes had in effect paved the way for that faith in medical progress, based on the potentials of technology, which continues to exercise such a vast influence on our lives today. When we see how even emotions which are explained with reference to "animal spirits" are incorporated into this mechanistic theory of man, we perceive that Descartes is the direct ancestor of that modern psychobiology which seeks the causes of psychopathology in the metabolism of the central nervous system. (Attempts to treat manic-depressive psychosis with lithium, to control emotional functioning by drugs such as the powerful phenothiazine group, "megavitamin therapy," research into enkelaphins and into the influence of certain food substances such as chemical preservatives and refined sugar on emotional conditions like hyperactivity in children, exemplify this approach in the contemporary United States.) And if the entire machine functions like a clock, why should it not be possible, and permissible, for a watch repairman—a psychosurgeon, for example—to perform stereotaxic brain surgery in order to regulate the clock in such a way that disruptive passions are eliminated? In other respects as well, Descartes' anatomical views did not differ greatly from those of modern medicine. For he did not, like many later thinkers, regard the cerebrum as the control center responsible for the functioning of the affective processes, but even back in the seventeenth century was turning his attention to the brainstem, the phylogenetically oldest part of the brain which is the seat of the motor and sensory tracts.

The Splitting Off of Feeling,
the Subordination of Woman,
and the Suppression of Humanity.
The Interaction of Psychic
and Social Repression.
Rousseau, the German Romantics,
Schopenhauer, Nietzsche,
Psychoanalysis

The triumph of rationalism was the inevitable consequence of man's urge to overcompensate for feelings of helplessness by achieving total autonomy and overcoming, once and for all, the dependent status, akin to that of a minor child, which he had held in the Middle Ages. To achieve this he had to suppress that side of his psyche which in the past had served as a conduit for his feelings of dependency. In other words he had to repress his emotions, every passive, receptive, suffering aspect of his nature. All passively-experienced feelings were now viewed as undesirable "passions" (from *passio*, meaning "suffering"); as Descartes' *passions de l'âme*, as enemies of the will to power. Even love, in the form of devotion or self-surrender, came to be regarded as trivial because it weakened man's confidence in his own powers, which had to be shored up at all cost. Primacy was assigned to objective, technological thinking because only by employing this mode of thinking could man anticipate a steady growth of his sense of power. His successful efforts to subdue nature through science and technology were accompanied by the attempt to exercise an increasing degree of intellectual control over his emotions. The substantial union of soul and body was dissolved and replaced by an "adversary relationship" between the controlling ego or consciousness and a body which functioned like a machine. However, despite these radical changes in attitude, the basic hierarchical concept of man, which had reigned in the Middle Ages, remained in force, although now the hierarchy had a different structure. The Middle Ages had been dominated by the hierarchical relationship between the divine ruler of the world and man, who was his creature. Now the dominant role was assumed by the rational, authoritarian ego, and the subordinate role by external, physical nature and by the inner nature of man himself, including all his passive emotional states.

But this suppression of the emotions cannot be adequately understood if we picture it merely as a process which took place *inside* the individual human being. The spectacular success of man's efforts to suppress and segregate emotion to make room for an objective, technical, intellectual mode of thinking would have been impossible if these efforts had not been reinforced by a corresponding trend towards schism within society itself.

For it was not the *human being* in general who soared to new heights of grandiose narcissism and who repressed his feelings of passivity and helplessness. Instead what happened was that the *man*, i.e., the *male*, became the champion and embodiment of one aspect of the human personality, whereas *woman* retired to the background, as the repository of the other part of the human personality. Thus one distinctive feature of the psychological evolution of man since the Middle Ages is the intensification of his psychic schism through an increased sexual polarization. One might say that what the human being *wished to become* was assigned to the *man;* whereas what he no longer wished to be, or *wished to suppress*, having ceased to regard it as a desirable part of the personality, was delegated to the *woman*. In any case, the only thing which enabled men to create what we know as modern civilization by the exercise of a megalomaniacal experimentalism and an obsession with power was the fact that women assumed the burden of all their self-doubts, feelings of insignificance, and suffering. For a long time the illusion persisted that this schism in the personality would one day enable men (males) to create a higher form of human civilization which would benefit all the members of society. Today we are compelled to adopt just the opposite conclusion. If women, in that background role to which men had relegated them, had not preserved an understanding, based on emotional data, of our true position in the universe and the principles on which human social relations ought to be based, then the overweening adventurism of men would surely end by destroying the world. Thus today we confront a paradox; those very values which have been disparaged and suppressed for the past three hundred years are now revealing themselves as essential to the salvation and healing of society. The problem is that the principal culture-bearers of these values, namely women, are still living under socially repressive conditions which have improved only moderately in recent years and which, in a multitude of ways, have become firmly entrenched in our basic societal structures. Thus, unless concrete societal changes take place in the relations between the sexes, the reinstatement of humane, emotionally-determined values would be unthinkable.

But before pursuing this problem in the present, we must first return to our analysis of its roots in the past. It is particularly essential that we examine the historical development of the tension between the suppressed emotions on the one hand and, on the other, that technical, objective, intellectual style of thought which was the instrument of the will to power, for this tension profoundly affected our concept of sexual roles. Our look at the past will reveal that the most diverse attempts to rehabilitate the emotions consistently foundered because of man's failure to recognize that the expansion of consciousness, or broadening of psychological horizons, was dependent on his overcoming the gulf between the sexes. To be sure, the attempts of philosophers to reason out solutions to contemporary problems reveal that the rebellious, dammed-up emotions did on occasion break through the defenses of the forces of repression. But we will see that as a rule these breakthroughs were a "flash in the pan" which tended to trigger a new upsurge of masculine narcissism, accompanied by a refusal to accept any responsibility for effecting change and a tendency to take refuge in an ivory-tower aestheticism. Occasionally a brief revolution occurred within the intrapsychic structure of the male, resulting in an enhanced appreciation of that world of feeling which he normally suppressed. However, such changes in male attitudes remained ineffectual in reshaping society as long as men failed to take into account the down-to-earth realities of the relations between the sexes.

Sex roles were clearly defined and underwent little modification until recent decades. The roles of men and women were defined by sexual stereotypes: the man was responsible for reducing natural phenomena to calculable effects and for asserting his dominion over them. His sphere was that of *raison* and *volonté*, or reason and will. The woman was his companion, emotion-bound and submissive. She retained some control in the sphere of the *coeur*, but only in the sense that she always had to be ready at a moment's notice to perform her emotional "service." It was the duty of women to provide emotional nourishment for the men who were "making history" and involved in the serious business of building a new world. Yet at the same time women were expected to strictly segregate this private realm of domestic emotion and to keep it from impinging on the masculine pursuit of world conquest through mathematics and technology. We should, however, not overlook the fact that this kind of sexual stereotyping merely represented a modification or elaboration of role models established long ago by Christianity. In the Christian Byzantine Empire, under Oriental influence, women quickly lost the comparatively high position they had attained in the society of ancient Rome. "Thy desire shall be to thy husband, and he shall rule over thee." This injunction, handed down by Yahweh to woman in Genesis 3:16, became a guiding principle in the organization of the Christian religious community. St. Paul cited Yahweh's injunction in his First Letter to the Corinthians (1 Cor 14:34-35):

"Let your women keep silence in the churches: for it is not permitted unto them to speak; but they are commanded to be under obedience, as also saith the law. And if they will learn any thing, let them ask their husbands at home: for it is a shame for women to speak in the church."

In 1 Timothy 2:11-14, Paul expresses this thought even more clearly, alleging that woman bears the principal guilt for the Fall:

"Let the woman learn in silence with all subjection. But I suffer not a woman to teach, nor to usurp authority over the man, but to be in silence. For Adam was first formed, then Eve. And Adam was not deceived, but the woman being deceived was in the transgression."

During the Middle Ages women were slave laborers belonging to their menfolk and, in economic terms, totally dependent upon them. In addition to their socioeconomic degradation, they were subject to that intellectual dependency on men enjoined by St. Paul. An exception to this rule was the freedom granted women to be educated in the seclusion of certain important convents like Gandersheim and Quedlinburg in Germany. The courtier's cult of service to his lady, as prescribed by the conventions of courtly love, remained essentially confined to the courts of the nobility, and effected no practical change in the inferior status of women, particularly among the common people. However, courtly love was a typical manifestation of a form of behavior often exhibited by men in the course of Western history. Although in the real world women were oppressed, men enjoyed exhibiting devotion—a devotion largely confined to the realm of narcissistic fantasy—to a maternal feminine figure who possessed the idealized attributes of an angel or the Madonna. Probably

Dante never actually saw his Beatrice, or at most caught a fleeting glimpse of her. The canonized virgins of the Church supplied men with images of woman as an inviolable angel. The traits of angelic innocence and chaste maternity celebrated in the cult of the Blessed Virgin Mary—a cult frequently echoed by the poets of courtly love—were the feminine qualities venerated by men, whose one-sided, distorted ideal of woman enabled them, in fantasy, to adopt towards women a role of passive devotion. Men's exaltation and aesthetic glorification of this fantasy-image of a phantom woman, which continues to crop up in later centuries, for example in German Romanticism, was at bottom a clever strategy for denying the reality of woman's social position, which was the direct opposite of that implied by the Romantic cult. In our own day, psychotherapists almost daily encounter in their male patients evidence of this same schizoid attitude, reflecting the contrast between the actual oppression of women on the one hand, and the fantasy of a celestial, radiant mother-figure on the other. This mother image was, and still is, the Western male's model solution to the problem of how to channel and render harmless that portion of his emotional life which he is not capable of repressing altogether. This narcissistic, visionary dream of the angelic female or the divine Virgin Mary, which serves as a depository for those potential needs for tenderness and devotion which the male is unable to suppress, in no way prevents him from exerting an active domination over women. On the contrary, his fantasy makes it easier for him to do so. Many of those artistic works in which male poets have given lyrical expression to their love of a woman—works which we are taught in school to regard as the noblest manifestations of our culture—can also be interpreted as ingenious fantasies, which often stand in sharp contrast to the egocentricity, unreliability and lack of consideration exhibited by their authors in their actual dealings with women. The man expressed or "acted out" his feelings through the art work, the poem, or the song, precisely so that he would not have to act it out in his real-life social relations with women, where it might possibly have become a source of weakness.

In the Middle Ages, despite the fact that men occupied a higher rank in the social hierarchy than women, the disparity in rank between the sexes was still limited by the fact that men and women shared, as brothers and sisters, in their role as the children of God. But subsequently male domination and its counterpart, female subservience, were intensified by males' self-investiture with divine power, effected in the manner already described, through their identification with God. The prerequisite for this successful *coup d'état* was the primacy assigned to the objectivizing, technical style of thought, which in turn automatically deepened the schism between *raison* and *coeur*, thus intensifying the psychological polarization of the sexes. The male, as the personification of reason *(ratio)*, regarded it as his duty to ensure the continuation of what we have tended to call "progress" by reducing women even more thoroughly to a state of intellectual subservience. In short, woman was to be sacrificed on the altar of civilization.

In the seventeenth century the French philosopher Nicolas de Malebranche (1638-1715), who has also been called the first psychologist, devised that pseudo-scientific justification for reducing women to the dependent role of minor children. His argument, which was passed down to modern times via Schopenhauer and Nietzsche, laid the foundations of a prejudice which is still very much current today. In the first volume of the *Investigation of Truth (Recherche de la Vérité)* Malebranche states that because of the constitution of their brains, women possess refined emotions and taste, but by nature have a very limited intellectual capacity:

> On the other hand, truth, which it costs some mental effort to discover, is commonly far beyond their capabilities. Everything abstract is incomprehensible to them. Their imagination is not equal to the task of unravelling complex, intricate problems. It comprehends only the surface of things. It has neither power nor skill enough to plumb their depths and to compare all their parts without wandering in its attention. [51]

The individual ego, around which all philosophical concepts were henceforth to center, was always the *male* ego. It was the man's duty to ensure that the emotional demands of the woman did not sap those energies he needed for carrying out his work as the forger of civilization. Later we will see that even Freud was still dominated by this view of woman. (See discussion of Freud and "penis envy" later in this chapter.)

The proponents of many intellectual trends of the eighteenth and nineteenth centuries, a number of whom were impassioned advocates of the value of emotion and made every effort to raise its status in the eyes of their fellow-citizens, consistently met with failure because they neglected to take into account the need for a fundamental change in the area of sexual relations. A brief examination of representative figures of the period—Rousseau and the German Romantics—will clarify this point.

Jean-Jacques Rousseau emphatically rejected the rationalism of the Enlightenment and instead pled the cause of *feeling*, which he regarded as the more important mode of cognition. Through feeling, he maintained,

man experienced nature and his own uncorrupted essence, which was the
product of nature. Society, not nature, effected man's corruption.
Rousseau recommended that when a child was growing up, he be
sheltered from all forms of societal coercion and be allowed to develop on
his own, in solitude and outside the family circle, with no guidance but
that of a private tutor. The counterpart of Rousseau's glorification of the
emotional bond with nature is his pronounced antipathy towards any
form of social adaptation, towards the idea of the integration of the
individual into groups of corporate bodies, and towards the representation of the individual by another individual or by an aggregate of others.
The human rights championed by Rousseau are exclusively individualistic in character. In every case he is concerned with protecting the
individual against the encroachments of others. His religious views are
consistently anticlerical, and the substratum of his social philosophy, the
theory of the social contract or *contrat social*, is profoundly antisocial.
This philosophy is founded on a radical individualism with anarchistic
components which, as we all know, played a central role in the formation
of intellectual concepts which paved the way to the French Revolution.
[76]

It should be noted that although relationships with women played
an important role in Rousseau's personal life, women are scarcely
mentioned in his social theory.

In Rousseau's writings, the father alone possesses a "natural
authority" over the children. The laws of nature ordain that he must
bring up his children: "The family is . . . , so to speak, the first model of
the political [structure of] society: The sovereign represents the father, his
people the children." [77]   The father is recompensed for his labor by
the love of his children, the sovereign by the pleasure he derives from
power. The essential thing, both in the family and in society, is that the
sovereign or father on the one hand, and his subjects or children on the
other, must revert to the state of autonomy and ultimately abolish all
forms of coercion and all obligation to obedience. [76]   Woman plays
no role whatever in this concept. The ideal is the male who elevates
himself to a condition of limitless autonomy: It is man's "highest law to
watch over his own welfare; his prime concern is that which he owes
himself; and as soon as a human being reaches adulthood he becomes his
own master, in that he is the sole judge of the proper means for ensuring
his welfare." [77]

Thus Rousseau's impassioned apologia of feeling by no means leads
to any new vision of the relations between the sexes or to an elevation in

the status of women. His concern is not with that kind of emotion which facilitates human communication, but rather with the triumph of a self-love which has liberated itself from all shackles.

Like Nietzsche, Rousseau arouses in the psychoanalyst an irresistible urge to reveal the relationship between the philosopher's theoretical views and that repressed psychic material in his personal history which gave rise to these views. In Rousseau's case, the correlative of his intense craving for untrammelled individual autonomy is a profound longing for a mother, which he never succeeded in mastering. He lost his mother shortly after birth, and from that time on conflict-ridden relationships with women played a central role in his life. For years he was devoted to an older woman whom he called "Mama" and who eventually took him as her lover. Rousseau experienced deep feelings of distrust and fears of dependency, which expressed themselves in his philosophy of anarchic individualism and also repeatedly made themselves felt in his personal conduct. Thus, for example—at least according to his own account—he took all five of their children away from his common-law wife, and placed them in a foundling home. Moreover, towards the end of his life he succumbed to a persecution mania, an acute paranoia, and died in a state of emotional isolation. Thus, considerable evidence exists that the difficulties which Rousseau experienced in forming emotional ties—all of which difficulties he rationalized in the ideological tracts—were intimately related to childhood cravings for emotional support, which he was never fully able to integrate with the rest of his psyche and reconcile with his behavior and environment. [40]   Unfortunately, we are unable here to elaborate more fully on this subject.

*

The image of woman did indeed play an important role in German Romanticism. However, if we examine this image closely, we perceive that it is that same old rosy idealization, the creation of male narcissism, which proved in no way capable of effecting change in the actual status of women. We can see this clearly if we examine a representative example, namely a book which is widely regarded as the major work on psychology produced in the German Romantic era. I am referring to the famous book by the philosopher, scientist and physician Carl Gustav Carus (1789-1869), *Psyche: The Historical Evolution of the Soul,* published in 1848. [12]   It was in this work that Carus, long before Freud, designated the *unconscious* as the true, primordial ground of consciousness. He devised a psychology that emphasized feelings, "inwardness." To some extent echoing the Christian mystical tradition, Carus described feeling and intuition as important authoritative sources in the cognition of truth. Carus actually describes the creation of his major work in vocabulary associated with the process of pregnancy and birth, and in his preface assures his readers that he has recorded only that which "came to fruition in his purest hours of contemplation" *(in den reinsten Stunden in seiner Betrachtung)* and which is "untrammelled by the shackles of academic methodology, the true product of intuition subjected to much sober reflection." [12]

In Carus the duality or dichotomy of reason and emotion becomes a duality of the conscious and the unconscious. The unconscious is the realm of feeling, of vision, of an occult sensibility, of sympathy and antipathy, of mystery. Carus claims that by its very nature the unconscious is "divine" and contains greater wisdom than the conscious mind. "Where conscious thought vacillates and perhaps chooses what is false twice as often as it chooses and desires what is true and right, the unconscious idea, when it holds sway, progresses with the greatest resolution and a profound... unconscious wisdom along its measured course, and often manifests a nature of such beauty that it cannot ever, in its full extent, be grasped, much less counterfeited, in conscious life." [12]   The masculine soul is closer to the conscious mind, the feminine to the unconscious. Consequently, by her very nature woman clings "more firmly and directly to that divine thing," whereas man is more egotistical and worldly and thus runs a greater risk of succumbing to intellectual and spiritual rigidity. Hence pedantry, narrow-mindedness, and "getting into an emotional rut" are forms of faulty development from which males typically suffer; whereas women, because of their greater proximity to the unconscious, possess a marked degree of vitality and pliability.

This inversion of the traditional value system, which esteemed reason as superior to emotion, is characteristic of the Romantic movement. The feminine world of feeling is exalted above male intellect, and indeed is even described as the womb which gives birth to male rationality, and to consciousness, in the first place. One might reasonably assume that this attitude would automatically give rise to a movement to redefine the status of women in society and to alter the traditional relationship between the sexes, which was based on dominance and subservience. But nothing of the sort took place. Although the Romantics preached many variations on the theme of devotion to the exalted and divine female principle, ultimately this devotion proved to be, once again, nothing but a male fantasy which did not oblige men to assume any responsibility for effecting social change. In the end the most visible feature of the Romantic ideal is its intellect, for men were more interested in overcoming their *own* psychological incompleteness by appropriating the feminine principle of the unconscious, than they were in aiding the cause of women. The truly complete human being was the *man* who had been enriched by the acquisition of feminine sensibility and emotional depth, and fructified by woman, who opened up to him potentialities which had been barred to him before. On the other hand, the opportunities for women remained as limited as ever. For by its very nature—so Carus claims—the female soul lacks the urge to acquire greater knowledge, and thus of course its psychic growth remains restricted. Carus says of women: "They are seldom capable of emerging from the world to which they are accustomed and resolutely determining their own true path in life. With few exceptions, members of their sex are almost always denied the capacity to genuinely devote their lives to the achievement of a few goals which they have recognized as particularly worthy, and never have their minds devised a great invention which has opened new paths to the genius of mankind."

"For it has been shown...how fundamentally the growth of the soul is dependent upon the increase of knowledge; and when we perceive that the impulse to acquire knowledge comes *less naturally* [italics mine] to the female than the male, this, in conjunction with the fact that the status of women up to now has barred them from opportunities of furthering their knowledge, makes it clear why individuality and strength of character are so seldom encountered in women of mature years."

In other words, Carus has no reason to regard the inferior social status of women as a problem because this status is entirely consonant with the deficiencies of woman's nature.

The goal of human evolution is the *man* "when, in a state of untrammelled, lucid self-awareness, he at the same time perfectly embraces the mystery of the unconscious." Here, once again, we recognize that traditional male mechanism: the narcissistic sanctification of the female which imposes no actual obligations on the male. The man does not elevate the value of women, but rather elevates himself when, in order to perfect his own nature, he decides to appropriate that portion of the psyche which he had previously delegated to the woman. He is concerned with appropriating the feminine, emotional side of the human personality, *not* with giving up his masculine privileges in the educational, legal and economic spheres so that women may have the same rights as himself. However, this very attitude makes it impossible for him to obtain what he wants. In other words, it renders impossible, from the very outset, the integration of the emotions into culture. Such an integration could take place only if *both* men and women supported each other in a process of mutual psychological growth—a process through which women would assimilate as much male rationality as men would of female sensibility. But this essential process of exchange could unfold only if the man, who is actually in control of things, were prepared to give up his dominant role. Instead of advocating that men "open up" emotionally and yield to their tenderer feelings merely as a mode of personal enrichment, confined to the intrapsychic life of the individual, the man would have to confirm his new openness and the renunciation of his defenses against emotion within his actual relationships with women. That is, he would have to transfer to women the power and rights he himself possesses. It is a delusion on men's part to believe that they can liberate their own emotions from oppression if, in their everyday lives, they continue to oppress women. Whenever men fail to make practical changes in the way they treat women, it is clear that their ostensibly revolutionary idealization of feminine traits is in reality merely a strategy by which men can consolidate their own power. The adoration of female sanctity becomes a psycho-economic medium for the discharge of male emotion, the stimulus for a purely narcissistic emotional "high," for relieving the male of any guilt feelings he may have and giving him the feeling that he has done his duty. Ultimately it serves the end of maintaining the relationship between the sexes exactly as it is.

Carus's attitude is typical in that he makes it quite clear that, in the end, *action* is the province of the man, *passivity (suffering)* that of the woman. However, he rationalizes his view by claiming that it reflects a natural difference between the sexes. Then he consoles the woman by telling her that suffering actually becomes her and alone confers on her the fullness of beauty; only rarely, says Carus, does a woman succeed in "performing a spontaneous, self-aware intellectual act." On the other hand, one can justly claim: "The man's character develops primarily through *action*, the woman's through *suffering*, and indeed, as a rule the peculiar strength and beauty of the female character manifests itself with particular power in those cases in which the depth of the woman's emotional life has been tested by manifold trials."

We sense here faint traces of male envy, of the suspicion that men are not capable of enduring suffering like that idealized woman who rouses the man's admiration. But this partial emotional breakthrough or recognition of woman's superior ability to deal with suffering is by no means capable of altering the disastrous course of societal evolution and ending the reign of the rationalistic, technological view of the world. Far from cherishing any such ambitions, the German Romantic ultimately contents himself with the goal of trying to educate the prominent middle class by instilling in its members the ideal of cultivating a greater spiritual and emotional depth. Carus, for example, does not make the slightest effort to relate his ideas concerning the process of psychological self-perfection or self-completion to an ideal of social solidarity. He thinks in terms of an elite group which alone is capable of partaking of that greatness of soul which he describes in such ecstatic terms: "Just as, in a perfect organism, not all the parts may constitute the eyes or the brain, so it is impossible that all human individuals should attain the same level of knowledge; and there will never come a time when the light of reason will be public property, distributed throughout the masses of all nations, but instead [this light] will always form a radiant triumphal wreath about the heads of a [chosen] few."

*

Schopenhauer's theory of ethics is further evidence that adherence to traditional prejudices concerning the psychological difference between the sexes nullifies any progressive initiatives which might lead to the fruitful revision of the self-image of both men and women, and to a restructuring of society. In his prize-winning essay "On the Foundations of Morality" (1840), Schopenhauer took as his premise the idea that the purely rationalistic determination of an abstract principle of duty could never supply an adequate foundation for cooperation and solidarity in human society. He was searching for a suitable motivating force for the regulation of social life, and found it in the *feeling of compassion*. His *ethics of compassion* represented a substantial breakthrough; it was a departure from the purely individualistic orientation of earlier theories of moral philosophy and attempted to create an ethics of human communication. Schopenhauer stated that justice and the love of one's fellow man were the cardinal virtues, and that both were rooted in man's "natural compassion." Compassion was the "wholly unmediated, virtually instinctual participation in the suffering of others." [85]

Schopenhauer attempted to analyze compassion in terms of the concept of identification (commiseration, or "suffering-with"), an idea which the German phenomenologist Max Ferdinand Scheler later took up in the exposition of his philosophy of sympathy. Compassion was the true natural motivation of all moral behavior. Schopenhauer praised Christianity for having preached the value of charity *(caritas)*, the actively expressed love of one's fellow man, as the expression of pure compassion. However, at the same time he pointed out that "in the whole of the New Testament not one single word is spoken against slavery, despite the fact that slavery was universally practiced at that time. Indeed, as recently as 1860, during the debates over the abolition of slavery in North America, the fact that Abraham and Jacob had kept slaves was cited as a justification of the practice."

Here and in many other passages Schopenhauer reveals that he takes seriously the relationship between philosophical theory and political practice. He thinks in far more realistic terms than many of the Romantics, who confine themselves to purely narcissistic speculation. Schopenhauer is skeptical about self-serving theories which under certain circumstances might enable their proponents to practice the opposite of what they preach. And yet in his own way Schopenhauer himself succumbs to that inconsistency between theory and practice which he ostensibly wants to avoid. And once again, the "sticking-point" is his view of the distinction between the sexes.

Schopenhauer conclusively proves that because of their greater instinctual capacity for compassion and their greater proclivity to exhibit the virtue of love for their fellow man, women ought in fact to be the arbiters of human social relations. But then he reverts to the old male prejudice concerning the natural intellectual weakness of woman, thus denying her any possibility of effecting those social changes so desperately needed by all mankind. He becomes enmeshed in logical dilemma, for although on the one hand he represents compassionate feeling as the primordial wellspring of all moral behavior, on the other hand he sets out to prove that woman—the natural representative of compassion—is incapable of behaving rationally and in accordance with moral principles, and thus is incapable of exercising justice. In this way a schism arises in his thought between justice, which he views as a masculine trait, and the love of one's fellow man, which he views as feminine. And yet in his critique of Kantian ethics he had established that in reality it was impossible to realize an abstract formal justice, sundered from its true motivation in the emotions. In terms of this theory, the "feminine" quality of love for one's fellow man logically *had* to play a decisive role in justice. Yet the contribution which only woman could make, she *cannot* make, for in her nature the capacity for love is vitiated by her native stupidity, inconstancy and laxity of conscience.

According to Schopenhauer, lack of self-control is "the reason why women as such, because of the infirmity of their reason, are far less apt than men in the understanding of universal principles and in adherence and obedience to them, and thus as a rule fall short of men in the exercise of the virtues of justice, honesty and conscientiousness. Hence injustice and deceit are their characteristic vices, and their proper element is lies. On the other hand, they excel men in the virtue of love for their fellow man, since as a rule the motivation behind such love is palpable and thus makes a direct appeal to compassion, to which women are unquestionably more susceptible than men."

"The idea of a woman judge is laughable; but the Sisters of Mercy surpass even the Monks-Hospitallers." [88]

Thus indirectly Schopenhauer demonstrates that the element most essential to the creation of social solidarity is rendered inoperative by the fact that it is primarily bonded to the female character, with its irrationality and instability. The product of this dilemma is an ethics which refutes its own efficacy by resurrecting the old dualistic prejudice of the psychological gulf between the sexes. On the one hand Schopenhauer claims that woman is a "culture hero" capable of transforming civilization by rendering it more humane. (In Schopenhauer's usage the word "humanity" is often synonymous with "commiseration," "compassion.") And yet woman cannot render this service as long as the psychological dichotomy of the sexes, which in reality represents an artificial, culturally-induced phenomenon, is treated as a *natural* phenomenon and employed as an ideological weapon. Nowhere does Schopenhauer exhibit less objectivity than in those passages in which he expresses his views about the alleged inferiority of women. He accuses women of allowing their emotions to distort their thinking, and yet he himself displays this same distortion in his grotesque portraiture of women, one example of which can be found in the chapter "On Women":

"Women are ideally suited to care for, raise and educate young children because they themselves are childish, shallow and can see only what is right in front of them. In a word, all their lives they are just big children: a kind of intermediary stage between the child and the man, who is the genuine human being." [88]

Woman "pays her debt to life not through action but through suffering, through the pangs of childbirth, her devoted care of her child, and her submission to her husband, to whom it is her duty to be a patient and cheerful companion." [88]   Schopenhauer could hardly have demonstrated more clearly the extent to which he himself, in his evaluation of sexual differentiation, has allowed his thinking to be clouded by his emotions—a weakness of which he never tires of accusing women.

Moreover, ultimately this biassed gender stereotyping of women compels Schopenhauer to deprive of its central importance that quality of compassion which he has defined as primarily feminine in nature. He takes a different tack in his metaphysical theory that the essential elements in the world—that which binds all living things together—is the Will. The visible world is simply the mirror of the Will. It is a condition of this universal Will to life that, in feeling compassion ("suffering with") for the suffering and death of others, the individual at the same time is feeling compassion for himself, is pitying his own lot. Thus, for example, weeping is a form of compassion for oneself. [86]   Schopenhauer regards as the definitive principle of existence the restless, blind Will which ultimately has no purpose beyond itself. Thus his philosophy does not, in the end, constitute a romantic attempt to reconcile love with the will to power, or *coeur* with *volonté*. He achieves a conclusive break with Christianity and reveals the true nature of that urge to omnipotence whose profile was revealing itself with ever-increasing clarity and intransigence in the unfolding historical process and which characterized the *male-dominated* European civilization. All that remained was the unalloyed, meaningless drive to press forward, the untrammelled urge to master and envelop the whole world. The principle of impotence underlying this narcissistic omnipotence is represented by the individual who is swept along by the universal Will. As pure, blind impulse or craving, life is ultimately condemned as absolutely meaningless and without value. Georg Simmel sees in Schopenhauer's grisly metaphysics the faithful reflection of contemporary attitudes:

"The absolute nature of the Will, which is synonymous with life, does not permit it to rest in anything outside itself, for there *is* nothing outside itself: Thus it expresses the situation in contemporary civilization, which is ridden with longing for some ultimate purpose in life, but at the same time experiences this purpose as an illusion, or as something vanished for ever." [93]

*

Compared to Schopenhauer's views, Nietzsche's theory of the will to power actually appears to radiate a love of mankind. Under Darwin's influence Nietzsche constructed a theory based on the concept of evolution, on the hope that the human race might evolve into a higher form. However, as we have already shown, his challenge to mankind to create the Superman ultimately involves the same self-destructive element we find in Schopenhauer. Nietzsche was profoundly influenced by Schopenhauer, and so his philosophy of will, like his mentor's, necessarily goes hand in hand with a radical contempt for, and negative evaluation of, women. The only love experienced by the male Superman—the dominant figure in Nietzsche's philosophy—is self-love, an unalloyed self-deification. The Superman no longer even needs the nurturing service and devotion of a woman, for he has, as it were, appropriated her emotional powers by incorporating them into himself. Zarathustra celebrates his triumphant achievement of total autarchy and luxuriates in his self-infatuation, his orgiastic delusions of grandeur. In his megalomaniacal omnipotence, he performs the act of self-deification, turning himself into his own intoxicated and intoxicating lover. Woman becomes a dull-witted, tedious appendage. Once it becomes possible for the male Superman to achieve total gratification through the narcissistic resources of his own ego, woman appears completely emptied of psychic content. Full of scorn, Nietzsche speaks of the *marasmus femininus,* the wasting away of woman. [65]   The mysterious treasure of emotional depth, which the Romantic psychologists venerated as a female prerogative, is now appropriated by the male:

"Woman's feeling is all on the surface, a mobile, turbulent scum on shallow waters. But the feeling of man is deep, his flood roars in subterranean caverns. The woman divines his strength but does not comprehend it." [61]

Shallow, silly, lacking strength of will, woman is no longer capable of being—or permitted to be—anything but a mechanical slave: "Woman's happiness is: He wills." "Behold, the world just became perfect! So thinks every woman when she obeys out of total love." [61]   Accordingly Nietzsche flies into a rage at all the "imbecile woman-friends and woman-corruptors among the erudite asses of the male sex" who would no doubt like to "drag women down to the level of the 'general culture,' probably even to the point of reading newspapers and dabbling in politics." [62]   (Paragraph 239 of *Beyond Good and Evil*)

Tempted as one might be to interpret Nietzsche's aggressive cynicism as the expression of a devastating fear of women which he is attempting to control through a venomous defamation of the female character, in reality his views merely reflect, in a particularly radical form, the failure of an entire historical epoch to devise an adequate intellectual formula for solving the problem of sexual relations. Of course no one could take this problem seriously as long as the primary goal of society was to encourage and support the masculine will to power in its uninterrupted pursuit of world conquest. Given the primacy of this goal, it was only logical to shield men from the realm of the emotions which had been assigned to women, and which might have slowed down the male drive towards expansionism.

To be sure, ever since Pascal's day men had been voicing the need to seek guidance in the logic of the heart in order to impose some limit on the narcissistic masculine urge to achieve omnipotence. Nevertheless, this urge always won the day, supported as it was by a science based on the investigation of causality, which by its very nature was not subject to any limit, and by an apparently infinite technological evolution which went hand in hand with this science. The schism between the sexes turned this dilemma into a chronic problem because the males who dominated society felt that they had to repress their emotions, and thus failed to respond to their own fear and suffering—symptoms of the self-destructive effects of blind expansionism—which might have served as signals to warn them of their plight. For fear and suffering had been delegated to women, who had been condemned to silence and thus were prevented from making any effort to alter the dangerous course of events.

*

However, at the end of the nineteenth century women ceased to be docile and tactful and began to resist the idea that they were to serve as the sole custodians and victims of fear and suffering. Their resistance took two forms. On the one hand there was overt resistance, in the form of the initiatives of the *women's movement* which, with periodic intermissions, slowly but steadily expanded its power base. However, there was also a second, covert, unconscious form of mutiny whose character as a resistance movement frequently tends to be overlooked. I am referring to that species of rejection or refusal of conventional modes of social behavior which is commonly classified as neurosis, nervous exhaustion, functional disorder, hysteria, or psychosomatic illness, and the treatment of which is considered the province of the medical profession. Eventually *hysteria* was revealed as the characteristic form of self-expression to which many oppressed women, at the turn of the century, were compelled to resort in order to draw attention to the intolerable circumstances of their lives. Since that time, as neurotic disorders have become increasingly prevalent, hysteria has ceased to be a hallmark of the female sex as it appeared to be when first studied. Nevertheless, representative studies indicate that even today, far more women than men complain of suffering from neurotic and psychosomatic ailments. [7] When, in the nineteenth century, scientists for the first time began to pay attention to the social phenomenon of hysteria (also known as conversion reaction or conversion neurosis), they initially labelled it as an exclusively *female* malady. Actually it was quite logical that, in the wake of the rapid technological advances of the Industrial Revolution, the emotional side of the human personality, which had primarily been turned over to women, should have been subjected to increased stress and driven to rebel. The alienating life styles imposed by our mass industrial society have automatically heightened the incidence of emotional "disorders," which viewed from a slightly different perspective, can also be interpreted as a meaningful protest of human sensibility against dehumanizing social conditions.

In any case, it was under the aegis of women that the disquieting problem of neurosis was ushered into public consciousness. At this point it became necessary to devise a philosophical apparatus which would enable man to understand and bring under control this revolution on the part of the repressed emotions. It was Freud who evolved this apparatus. Yet one might just as well say that his philosophy was—albeit indirectly—handed to him ready-made by his women patients, who revealed to him the world of their ailments, their dreams and their fantasies. To be sure, Freud's task involved more than the mere recapitulation of those promptings fed him by his patients. His most significant achievement lay in deciphering the secret code, the hidden meaning of the signs and indications imparted to him. All the same, it was *women* who, in acting out their conflicts and fantasies, enabled Freud and his pupils and, eventually, broad segments of the public to acquire vital information about their own psychological make-up and the psychological aspects of modern society as a whole.

Thus the first female patients to undergo psychoanalytic examination—Anna O., Emmy von N., Lucie R., Katharina and Elisabeth von R.—were pioneers and pathfinders who, together with Freud, opened the door to a new concept of man.

Psychoanalysis differs from traditional schools of philosophical anthropology in that it does not represent a closed or completed theory, but rather is an "open-ended" system whose theoretical concepts continue to evolve in accordance with empirical data brought to light in the course of actual therapeutic practice. The theoretical assumptions of psychoanalysis are valid only to the degree that they prove valuable in helping us to understand psychological problems arising within a given socio-historical situation. Three facets of psychoanalysis must be taken into account in evaluating its role in helping us to deal with the problem of sexual relations:

1. Psychoanalysis represents a major "breakthrough," an incursion into the hitherto exclusively "masculine" realm of science, in the sense that it turned the "feminine" phenomenon of emotionality into a legitimate object of scientific study. Psychoanalysis compelled medicine—which, being dominated by the technical-objective, masculine mode of thinking, was threatening to degenerate into a form of engineering (i.e., the mechanical manipulation of physical factors)—to confront a different point of view, the "feminine approach," and to acknowledge anxiety, love and suffering as fundamental categories in the study of disease and the practice of therapy.

2. Psychoanalysis has made, and is making, contributions to the theory of the psychology and psychopathology of sexual relations—contributions which must be critically evaluated on their intrinsic merit.

3. Recently psychoanalysis has led to increased cooperation between the sexes, both on the part of clients engaged in couples therapy, family therapy, and group therapy involving members of both sexes, and on the part of cotherapists engaged in "conjoint therapy." In my earlier book, *Engagierte Analysen,* [74]   I have already elaborated on the first of these points. As to the second point, it seems noteworthy that initially Freud's theoretical hypotheses concerning the psychological differentiation of the sexes were by no means particularly progressive. The depth of the gulf which history had dug between the sexes can be measured by the fact that Freud himself was never able to fully grasp the artificial nature of traditional gender stereotypes. On the other hand, one could with equal justice turn the argument around and say that Freud's female patients did almost nothing to show him how little real women corresponded to that artificial, cliché-ridden image of femininity which societal and cultural conditioning had instilled in both sexes. In any case, Freud's analysis of male and female personality development reflects male prejudices to no small degree. As the heir to an ancient patriarchal tradition, Freud to a large extent continued to view the relations between man and woman in terms of the classic hierarchy of the superior and the subordinate, the active and the passive, the strong and the weak.

Before moving on to a closer examination of Freud's false conceptions about women, it might be well to note that these conceptions are not of central importance in his thought, in the sense that his great achievement—unlike the achievements of the philosophers we have looked at—is not reducible to his theoretical views, but consists above all in his creation of the psychoanalytic dialogue, which offered man a fundamentally new and practical technique for effecting a never-ending growth in his understanding and perception of himself. Freud's perceptions were limited by his personal social and cultural background, the structure of his family and his relationship with his parents, and his own individual neurotic traits. Nevertheless, the introspective procedure of psychoanalysis, in the form institutionalized by Freud, held out the hope of a continual modification and deepening of insight into the problems of both men and women, as well as of the relations between them. For psychoanalysis is a *living* science which never ceases to evolve. Each new course of psychoanalytic treatment—whether it is a case of individual therapy, couples therapy, family or group therapy—opens up new avenues of approach, new opportunities to critically review all presently existing general hypotheses concerning man's intrapsychic structure and the nature of his interpersonal conflicts.

As we have noted, Freud himself had great difficulty in appreciating the full extent to which cultural conditioning determined behavior differences between the sexes. His imprisonment within "masculine" scientific thought patterns led him into sexual bias, and an overestimation of the role played by anatomical equipment in psychosexual development. The penis acquired central importance in his theory. To Freud, female psychic development appeared to be determined primarily or exclusively by the female's lack of a penis and her variegated attempts to deal with this deficiency. This "flaw" in her make-up, Freud claimed, engendered in the female a marked disposition to envy. "Penis envy" explained the faulty development of woman's sense of justice. Thus at this juncture Freud has clearly adopted the prejudiced views of Schopenhauer. [32]   He failed to perceive the crucial influence of the patriarchal structure of the family, and of society at large, in the specific formation of penis envy, the castration complex and the Oedipus complex. Thus he ended by resurrecting the old saw about the natural passivity of woman, as opposed to the naturally active nature of man. The woman's Superego always remained subnormal in the sense that it never attained the same degree of strength and autonomy as that of the average male. "We also maintain concerning women that their social interests are weaker than those of men, and that they possess a lesser capacity to sublimate their drives." [32]

On the grounds that women allegedly possessed a diminished capacity to sublimate their instinctual drives, Freud claimed that by nature they bore a negative relation to civilization and impeded men in their attempts to promote its development. Thus in *Civilization and Its Discontents* he writes:

> Furthermore, those same women who originally laid the foundations of civilization by the claims attached to their love soon begin to resist the forward flow of civilization and exert their influence to retard and hold it in check. Women represent the interests of the family and of sexual life. The labor of civilization has increasingly devolved upon men, confronting them with increasingly difficult tasks and compelling them to sublimate instinctual drives, an achievement for which women possess little aptitude. Man does not have unlimited quantities of psychical energy at his disposal, and thus he must achieve tasks through the expedient apportionment of his libido. To a large extent he withdraws from women and from sexual life the energy he consumes in culture-building. His constant association with men, as well as his dependence on his relations with them, alienate him even from his duties as a husband and father. Thus the woman sees herself taking a back seat to the claims of civilization and develops an attitude of hostility towards it. [30]

In this passage Freud clearly identifies with the classic patriarchal attitude towards women. Even if other factors did not make it apparent, his attitude is betrayed by his language, for when he speaks of man's withdrawal of his psychical energy from women so that it can be employed for culture-building, the word he uses for "man" is *der Mensch* (the generic term for a human being) rather than *der Mann* ("man" in the sense of "a male"). By doing this he implies that the male *(Mann)* is the representative or definitive human being *(Mensch)* and the exclusive builder of civilization. The same attitude is reflected in Freud's hypothesis that women who display particularly active, i.e., "masculine" behavior and attitudes, are suffering from a desire to be men, in other words an immature fixation on the fantasy that they possess penises.

Although Freud found it difficult to accept the idea that there were "masculine" aspects to the female personality, he achieved an important advance when he discovered the "feminine" constituents of the male personality and incorporated his findings into his theory. From his friend Wilhelm Fliess he adopted the theory that human beings are essentially bisexual. It was his fateful, conflict-ridden relationship with Fliess—whom, in the beginning, he deeply admired and revered—which enabled him to understand the passive elements in his own nature and to work out his theory of the "feminine" side of the male in terms of negative Oedipal wishes.* But Freud's major contribution to our understanding of sexual relations was *indirect,* and consisted in the fact that he made it possible for other people to develop new views on the subject. He trained a number of important female psychoanalysts who, as women, were now in a position to modify his views in areas in which he had been led astray by "male" prejudices. Karen Horney informed Freud that he had vastly exaggerated the importance of primary penis envy in the development of young girls. [31] He also conceded that Jeanne Lampl-de Groot and Helene Deutsch had grasped, more readily and clearly than he, certain facts concerning female psychological development. Since then countless other female psychoanalysts have helped to eliminate from psychoanalytic theory the stereotypical view of women as passive, envious, undependable and antagonistic to culture. Quite recently, in a large-scale comparative study of the techniques of German psychoanalysts, Adrienne Windhoff-Héritier determined that present-day psychoanalytic practice is governed by principles which, as far as women are concerned, bear little relation to the classic normative principles, based on the notion of female passivity, which had been sanctioned by Freud. Having completed her comparative study of thirty-two detailed case histories of psychoanalytic treatment undergone by both male and female patients, Windhoff-Héritier concludes: "The analytic accounts revealed that therapeutic goals were not determined by the classical view of sex roles, and deviated from those conservative, sex-political concepts of female psychological formation immanent in the Freudian theory of the female nature, which center

---

* Wilhelm Fliess, who became Freud's friend in 1892, was a physician whose hypotheses regarding the psyche, including his belief that sexuality was the basis of behavior, attracted Freud. Freud acted out his love-hate relationship with his father in his relationships with other people, including Fliess, whom he came to venerate as a father-figure and love object, but their relationship broke down—in part, no doubt, because of Freud's instability. This intense relationship with Fliess confirmed the theory of human bisexuality. In addition to the Oedipus complex involving incestuous attraction to the parent of the opposite sex, Freud held that there were negative or inverse Oedipal wishes involving incestuous desires for the parent of the *same* sex, accompanied by murderous inclinations toward the parent of the opposite sex.—Tr.

around the fixed idea of female penis envy, and which interpret all activities of women not traditionally [defined as] sex-specific—including motherhood—as the expression of an attempt to compensate for this feeling [i.e., of penis envy]." [105]

But perhaps the next step on the road to sexual re-education was even more important than the revision of Freud's ideas of female analysts. This development derived from the discovery that neither men nor women, left to their own devices, are capable of developing an adequate understanding of themselves and their roles in society. It has been realized that the two sexes must engage in an intensive interchange of views and feelings, a kind of "role reversal therapy," in order to overcome the series of psychosocial barriers which, in the past, have fragmented their personalities and driven them into mutual isolation. The result of this insight has been the rapid dissemination of various types of group therapy—couples therapy, family therapy, and group therapy in which the membership cuts across sexual lines. These therapeutic settings enable men and women to understand the extent—generally appreciable—to which their emotional conflicts are related to the traditional distortion of the relations between the sexes. In addition to factors specific to each individual, every personal conflict also involves factors deriving from the artificial psychosocial schism of the sexes. Thus each sex needs the other to effect its own cure. For the coercive sexual segregation imposed in the past, which frequently placed an intolerable burden on people, demands that we do more than merely amend psychosocial attitudes on the conceptual, theoretical plane. Above all it is essential that we work on the practical level to achieve a new emotional and sexual equilibrium. Men and women must cooperate with and lend support to each other in their efforts to liberate themselves from a state of distress suffered by members of both sexes, each in his or her own way.

As a rule the emotional damage suffered by one sex is inextricably bound up with that suffered by the other. I once described this mutual involvement of men and women in the following terms: "The visible suffering of the woman mirrors the invisible sickness of the man." In other words, the woman acts out in an overt form the distress which both she and the man experience, but which the man represses or keeps to himself. But the contemporary male is no longer capable of sustaining this repression. In reality his suppressed, inarticulate despair makes him sicker than the woman, even if, in his outward acts, he continues to demonstrate a strength which he no longer feels inside. Thus epidemiological studies reveal, on the average, a higher incidence of observable impairment among men, whose average life expectancy is also clearly shorter than that of women. Hence men would be acting in their own best interests by ceding a portion of their power to women, who in any case are demanding it with or without men's consent. Moreover, men must also permit themselves to experience and express more passivity, tenderness, and even sadness, which in the past they have desperately tried to repress, to their own ruin. But the purpose of this mutual exchange of feelings, roles and powers between the sexes extends beyond its salutory function in enabling both men and women to relieve themselves of an emotional burden. In addition it represents *an indispensable prerequisite for halting the progressive dehumanization of our civilization.* For the distortion of the relations between the sexes is also reflected in the unilaterally "masculine" automation or mechanization of all societal functions, with its tendency to inhibit interpersonal communication, and in the damage inflicted on man's relationship to the natural world—both of which phenomena are now taking their toll on us all. The humanization of our society depends, in effect, on our ability to "feminize" it, i.e., to order it in accordance with more "feminine" values. But our success in doing so in turn depends on whether women, who were made the unilateral custodians of these values, are able to acquire the requisite political influence.

Within the limited sphere of couples therapy, mixed-group therapy and self-help groups of all kinds, all of which are microcosms of the larger society, we clearly perceive the difficulties experienced by both sexes, each in its own way, when they attempt a fundamentally new and unfamiliar form of mutual cooperation. Women, who have long been deprived of their autonomy as adult human beings, are faced with the task of learning how to articulate their feelings and to assert those emotional needs which have for so long been disparaged as trivial and insignificant. On the other hand men, accustomed to assuming a dominant role, must learn to understand that their methods of dealing with problems—through the reification and technological mastery of phenomena—are not the way to open up more meaningful communication. Women are less alienated from their emotions than men are and thus can, so to speak, develop their identities simply by moving forward, or building on what they already have. But men, cut off from their feelings and suffering deeper emotional damage, must go backwards, must retrace their steps until they find the place where they went wrong. They must learn to understand that their deeply-entrenched and internalized ideas of superhuman power, as well as one-sided view of the world as something to be dominated by technology, have proven invalid. However, they have grown used to deriving their feeling of self-worth from the pursuit of power, and thus they undergo a profound emotional crisis when they try to change their attitudes. It is a shattering experience to realize that one has been on the wrong track and that one must now call into question many things which one has hitherto regarded as the source of one's sense of security and identity. Naturally, many older women suffer from much the same kind of problems as men, in the sense that they have identified completely with the female role as it is classically defined and have arranged their lives accordingly. They may find it so disturbing to realize that they might have made much more of themselves and their lives than they have, that they attempt to repress the realization altogether and desperately cling to their previous mode of life, feeling that in any case it is too late for them to change. Many sociological studies which seem to indicate that a vast number of women are completely content to remain in the home, as tradition prescribes, and actually prefer a passive lifestyle, can be explained simply by this fear of new and unsettling ideas and by the fear of failure if they try to change. Once one has chosen certain goals and come to terms with them emotionally, one tends to block out the notion that more meaningful goals may exist and to cling to a lifestyle which may actually be unsuitable. The fear that changing our course will bring on an "identity crisis" and a total breakdown compels us to defend behavior which we may question in our hearts.

Nevertheless, the experiences which psychoanalysts have so far had in working with couples, families and therapy groups composed of both sexes do hold out hope that men and women are in fact making the attempt to restructure their relationship. Countless men—and not all of them young—are demonstrating their ability to see through the classical norms of "masculinity," to recognize their unnatural and emotionally oppressive character, and to allow themselves to manifest more passivity and more openness towards their emotions. They are also learning to abandon their claims to a leadership role, which in any case they could not live up to (or would soon have become unable to live up to), in favor of a relationship of equality and mutuality. Moreover, many women and young girls are asserting their independence in ways which enable men to accept a diminution of their authority without feeling challenged to engage in anxiety-producing competition.

Some representative studies, using the Giessen Test,* a "personality test" designed along psychoanalytic lines, reveal a rising trend among West Germans to value and to take as a rule of life psychical traits hitherto labelled as specifically "feminine." (A full account of these studies may be found in my earlier writings. [7, 75]) The findings arrived at through the Giessen Test conflict with the impression, created in public debates concerning changing sexual roles, that the majority of German women are actually adapting to the "masculine" code of values by entering into competition with men, while all the men are exhibiting an anachronistic chauvinism and doing everything they can to resist any change in the status of women.

To be sure, important as this frequently almost imperceptible change in sexual attitudes or "raising of consciousness" may be, it does not automatically lead to overnight changes in the structure of society. The power of psychical forces is limited by the prevailing social norms and institutions, which in a thousand ways reinforce the ingrained standards of "masculinity" and the dominant role of men who are emotionally fixated on these standards. In the real world of power politics, we see daily examples of the societal intransigence marshalled against every attempt, no matter how modest, to reduce the privileges enjoyed by men. Moreover, whenever efforts are made, in the name of universal emotional needs, to humanize working conditions, living conditions or other social circumstances, these efforts come into conflict with economic and technological interests. In most of these cases, the final decision is still made in favor of the classical "masculine" goals and values. To our male-dominated governing bodies, the desire of human beings to feel happier in their work and home environments and thereby to realize their humanity more fully appears to be a comparatively irrelevant craving for some luxury which we can ill afford. Wherever large-scale political organizations have had the time to establish stable institutional structures, the old hierarchical and patriarchal thought patterns and organizational models have reinstated themselves, regardless of what the self-proclaimed principles of the organizations may be. These

* V. Horst-Eberhard Richter and Dieter Beckmann, *Giessen-Test (GT), ein Test für Individual- und Gruppendiagnostik,* Bern, 1973. Dr. Richter and his colleague describe the test as a diagnostic tool, resembling American personality or psychological-profile tests, with coded questions which enable clinics, counselling centers and group investigators to evaluate how the tested person experiences himself and is experienced by others. The test is depicted as differing from the usual psychological test in that the emphasis is not on individual psychology but on group relationships.—Tr.

patterns and models then become a law unto themselves, often preventing a political body from carrying out what they themselves regard as meaningful reforms. Thus, institutional constraints leave us little latitude for experimentation. For this reason we must make every effort to voice, in a politically effective form, those needs which are emerging more clearly out of the crisis in sexual relations.

PART TWO

THE SICKNESS OF BEING UNABLE TO SUFFER

7

The Projective Conversion of Suffering into Hatred. Medieval and Modern Phenomena Surrounding the Exorcism of Witches, Racial Enemies, "Hereditary Inferiors," Extremists, Parasites and "Dangerous Elements."

Among those key problems of our civilization for which we have found no satisfactory solution are weakness, finitude and human frailty. To be sure, our responses to these phenomena are essentially linked to the relations between the sexes. Yet quite apart from this link, they are a central concern of our culture and relate to many of the polarizations within our society. Besides the polarization of the sexes there is that of healthy and sick, of young and old, of well-adjusted and maladjusted, of the exploiters and the exploited.

The total elimination of suffering became a primary goal of our society, quite automatically, because it is simply the reverse side of the narcissistic urge to achieve omnipotence. Once we decide to rescue ourselves from feelings of despair and abandonment by attaining absolute self-reliance, we find we are condemned to continually fight off the experience of our fragility, vulnerability and mortality. We have to employ various defense mechanisms in our never-ending attempt to keep our emotional balance. In this part of the book we will first take a closer look at these defensive strategies and then try to find more promising solutions to our dilemma than those we have previously employed—the attempts to eliminate suffering, to run away from it, or to despise it.

The following are common techniques for turning off suffering:

1. We decide that suffering is an evil inflicted by someone or something outside ourselves and try to eradicate suffering by fighting its evil source. This is the *elimination of suffering*.

2. We pursue a strategy of avoidance and denial. This is *running away from suffering*.

3. We attempt to rise above suffering, to overcome it by adopting a heroic posture. This is the *contempt for suffering*.

The Elimination of Suffering

The general principle underlying this reaction is the transformation of suffering into hatred. In terms of developmental psychology, Freud traced this reaction back to the early phase in the development of the ego characterized by the search for pleasure and the avoidance of pain. The ego, in a sense, eliminates everything unpleasant, converting its pain into hatred and projecting it onto some external source. [26, 29]   As people grow older they still employ this pattern of behavior as a major defense mechanism. It never disappears completely. Many people use it all their lives to gain relief from their despair, always blaming someone else for their problems and sparing themselves inner suffering by combatting these "guilty" parties. Whenever they feel the danger of depression, they rescue themselves by immediately adopting a hostile attitude. This technique may necessitate having a lifelong supply of external enemies at one's disposal, in order to be able to exorcise the constant threat of depression and collapse. Special tests have been devised to diagnose this particular type of reaction. The specific form of the accusations a person directs against his external enemies is an indication of the degree and nature of the inner affliction which he is trying to ward off. The more a person is crushed by feelings of self-reproach and personal failure, the more diabolical are the traits he will attribute to his external foe.

The strategy of the elimination of suffering plays an extraordinarily significant role in Western culture. In the course of history it has manifested itself in a wide variety of forms. In many cases these manifestations are crude, instinctual and blatant; in other cases they are so well masked by compulsive-neurotic factors and by intellectualizing that at first glance it is almost impossible to recognize them. In general we can say that during the history of Western man the ways of expressing this technique for resisting suffering have tended to become less primitive and archaic. But this does *not* mean that the reaction type itself has diminished in significance.

At the end of the Middle Ages, Europeans faced a dilemma. Their unlimited egocentric self-reliance, with which they sought to compensate for the security they had found in religious faith and then had lost, stood in blatant contrast to the fact that they did not possess any scientific-technological remedy for many of their afflictions; thus in many ways they were really quite helpless. Unpredictable plagues, poor harvests and other disasters repeatedly threatened their illusion that they could quickly eliminate their miseries by exercising their omnipotent dominion over nature. It is easy to understand what tensions resulted from this contradiction between wishful thinking and reality. These tensions provided the social-psychological background for a phenomenon which for centuries has dominated man's effort to rid himself of suffering.

What people did, in effect, was to find a source, an external cause, for every ill they suffered—a cause whose systematic elimination would guarantee them freedom from suffering. The *witch* was a scapegoat onto whom people projected the blame for all the vexations that threatened their confidence in their own powers. In 1484 Pope Innocent VIII signed a bull concerning witches, the *Summis desiderantes affectibus,* which was of crucial political importance. This bull described the crimes of which witches were accused:

> Not without the greatest distress did we recently hear that in certain areas of Upper Germany, as well as in the dioceses and provinces of Mainz, Cologne, Trier, Salzburg and Bremen, a great multitude of persons of both sexes, unmindful of their own salvation, are engaging in fornication with the Devil, and with their magic formulas and conjurations and other abominable arts of witchcraft, that is through criminality and wantonness, slay the children of men and the offspring of beasts, destroy the crops in the fields, the grapes in the vineyards, and the fruits in the trees, torment man and beast with hideous torments both within and without, hinder men and women from having marital relations and prevent conception. [37]

Later elaborations and interpetations of this catalogue of griefs made it possible for people to establish a causal link between witchcraft and every possible form of human affliction. The "successful" witch hunt, by extracting confessions through torture and the the spectacle of public burnings, gave people the illusion that by exterminating witches they could at the same time gradually exterminate all those evils the witches caused. And even though Pope Innocent VIII spoke of witches of both sexes, and despite the fact that sometimes men as well as women fell victim to witch hunts, women were, by the mechanism of projection, made the principal scapegoats for other people's feelings of discontent. The infamous *Witches' Hammer (Malleus maleficarum)*, the standard compendium on witchcraft, written by the Dominicans Heinrich Institoris (H. Krämer) and Jakob Sprenger, also puts the blame for abuses of the black arts squarely on the shoulders of women. The transformation of women into witches was said to take place through sexual intercourse with the Devil. Even a dubious linguistic basis was provided for the predisposition of women to practice witchcraft. The authors of the *Witches' Hammer* analyzed the Latin word *femina* ("woman") as a compound made up of the Spanish *fe* ("faith") and the Latin *minor* ("less"), so that woman was "the one of lesser faith." In any case, most of the one million people burned for witchcraft from the eleventh century onward were women.

It is a persistent misconception that witchhunting in Europe reached its climax in the early Middle Ages, and after that declined steadily. In reality, even before the end of the first millennium of the Christian era, the Church had fought to destroy every form of superstition as "heathen nonsense"—including belief in witchcraft—and at times imposed penance on persons who propagated such superstitious notions. Confessors were encouraged by the Church to do everything in their power to eradicate erroneous beliefs concerning witches or fiends. To be sure, the Inquisition was instituted at the end of the twelfth century to combat heresy, but witch hunts and witch trials did not really become prevalent until the great shift in mental attitudes which marked the transition between the Middle Ages and the modern era. Not until just before 1500 did the wave of witch trials reach staggering proportions, for not until then did the Church definitely decide to join forces with the superstitious belief in witches which in the past she had rigorously denounced and combatted as a vestige of paganism. [37]

However, the Church would not have been able to make use of the witch trials to ensure the preservation of its own authority, were it not for the fact that the masses, of their own accord, displayed a corresponding inclination. The growing readiness to persecute witches must be seen in relation to the onset of the great transformation of consciousness to which we have already referred. Suffering had to be eliminated because man's flight into the narcissistic myth of his omnipotence no longer permitted him to manifest any kind of impotence. The sadism displayed in the torture and burning of witches was fully in keeping with the concept of the harsh and punitive nature of God—that God whom man was preparing to abandon. The mercilessness of this God, as described by the German author Moser in his book *Gottesvergiftung* ("Poisoned by God" [58]),   is reflected in all those horrendous acts through which the postmedieval witch-hunters turned visions of the Last Judgment into a fearful reality.

*

Of course, witch trials came to an end long ago, but the attempt to eliminate suffering by denouncing and destroying external enemies to whom one ascribes diabolical traits persists in countless derivative forms.

The excesses of modern racism have been every bit as barbaric, primitive and nakedly sadistic as the classical witch hunt. The Nazi gas chambers are the funeral pyres where twentieth-century "witches" were burnt at the stake. Modern man has "improved" on the techniques of the past only in the sense that he has introduced certain administrative and bureaucratic improvements into the techniques of manhunting and the automation of murder.

However, it is misleading to think of man's attempt to ward off suffering through projection onto external scapegoats exclusively in terms of such ghastly and extreme behavior as that of the Nazis. For after all, the behavior pattern we observed in the Nazis is one we encounter everywhere. It has become a universal technique for dealing with the problems of everyday life. If we are to make any progress towards overcoming this particular defense mechanism it will not help us to seek examples of it which are so remote that we can easily distance ourselves from them. Thus in a sense I would be merely perpetuating the phenomenon of the witch hunt if I were to cite only such obviously diabolical and repulsive examples that the readers of this book would not see the problem as applying in any way to themselves. Hence, we must look for more banal and contemporary manifestations of the social-psychological phenomenon of the witch hunt.

*

In the political sphere contemporary manifestations of the witch hunt include all emotionally-ingrained, collective prejudices against groups, customs or ideologies, whereby those who succumb to the prejudice feel they can obtain significant relief from their own difficulties by combatting the object of this prejudice. These people make no attempt to engage in any constructive form of self-help. Instead, they typically expect to be released from all their problems once the evil external influences responsible for these problems have been neutralized. The maxims "Do unto others before they do unto you," or "When somebody hits you, hit back," enable people to avoid coming to terms emotionally with the fact that they have indeed been hit and are suffering, or that they are faced with the imminent threat of suffering. The more dependent a person becomes on this projective form of emotional relief, the greater is his susceptibility for engaging in a constant search for enemies and accepting without question theories about these enemies—theories which form the chief propaganda device of many political groups. However, successful attempts by political groups to suppress the enemy are of no help whatsoever to those who fear emotional collapse if they are deprived of their scapegoat. They cannot, in effect, do unto others before others do unto them, for this would be the surest way of bringing about their own ruin. Once their chosen scapegoat has really been eliminated, the only way for them to cope with their problem would be to discover, or to invent, new "witches" to take his place, thus perpetuating the vile game *ad infinitum.*

The recent history of Germany amply demonstrates that the German people have a particular tendency to ward off suffering by means of projection. This tendency is clearly shown by the ease with which political tensions in Germany have again and again degenerated into manifest or veiled "wars of religion." Nowhere else in Western civilization have nationalistic ideas been so strongly colored by fantasies of a special, holy calling to redeem the world from evil. Notions of this kind, sparked by Fichte in the nineteenth century, have repeatedly fueled the flames of martial enthusiasm, or at least inflamed people against minority groups. Mankind—so the theory goes—will finally enjoy the reign of peace and freedom once Siegfried or St. George has slain the wicked dragon. This is the basic stereotypical concept underlying the projective defense mechanism, and although the names may change, the substance always remains the same. After "international Jewry," "international Communism" became the great dragon of the Germans, many of whom see in its destruction the magic formula for instantly eliminating all the woes of the earth. It would no doubt be an instructive exercise to make a systematic social-psychological analysis of the anti-Communist sentiment so widespread in Germany, with the purpose of detecting the role played in it by archaic, magical fantasies. In any case, certain classic symptoms of that projective mechanism we have discussed are clearly operative here. People throughout the so-called "free world" share with West Germans the penchant for viewing the Communist bloc as the current Whore of Babylon.

Among other classic symptoms manifested in this Western anti-Communist sentiment, we must include projective *narrowing* and *distortion of perception*. In other words, people tend to see aggression, imperialism or violations of human rights as occurring only on one side of the world, i.e., only among their enemies.

This anti-Communist projective mechanism also involves a tendency to the *generalized disparagement* of other groups. In other words, citizens of the Western democracies may lump together all the peoples living in the Communist bloc, characterizing them in terms of clichés and regarding them all as uniformly guilty of barbarity, primitivism and aggression.

A similar phenomenon is the *paranoid fear of being infiltrated, seduced, infected and corrupted* by a "fifth column" of the enemy in one's own camp. Whenever a person within one's own group dares to voice any criticism, whenever workers or trade unions make what are felt to be exorbitant demands, or women protest against sexist treatment, students against conditions in institutions of higher learning, pupils against the shortcomings of the educational system, or citizens' action groups against nuclear energy plants, many people immediately jump to the conclusion that these protests are Communist-inspired. At the very least they accuse the protesters of having been "contaminated" by creeping socialism. Typically, people who confer diabolical traits on an enemy attribute to him the ability to employ all sorts of dark and mysterious methods to gain control of the minds and souls of others and to sow universal ruin wherever he goes. This substratum of magical thinking explains the feverish hunt for Communist or terrorist "sympathizers" or "fellow travellers"—after those who are, in a sense, possessed by evil spirits. Citizens of other countries often find incomprehensible the effort which the German authorities put into the surveillance, investigation, registration and professional harassment of leftists, including simple radical democrats. Yet this effort becomes understandable in light of the magical-minded attribution of demonic powers to the enemy. In order to protect the children at school, the students at the universities and the civil servants in their government ministries—i.e., the vital centers of the organism of the state—from any kind of infection, all these people must be systematically kept away from those agents of foreign governments who are lying in wait to infiltrate and undermine all our institutions with their poisonous doctrine. The panicky fear of any contact with these supposed sources of contamination has a strongly pathological character.

A final significant symptom of the archaic mechanism of projection is seen in the fact that, intelligent as they might otherwise be, those who employ this mechanism can no longer be reached by logical proofs which would ordinarily compel people to revise erroneous suppositions and generalizations. Because, for emotional reasons, they no longer *wish* to do so, many people *can* no longer distinguish between Western democratic socialism and Eastern-bloc state capitalism, or even between the liberal Left and outright Marxism. For such people terrorism appears to be merely a logical extension of "left-wing" views.

This type of projection, involving an enemy endowed with diabolical traits, is as visible among certain left-wing groups as it is in the ultra-conservative camp, although of course in this case the devils' horns are on a different set of heads. Among leftists it is the concepts of capitalism, government bureaucracy and police which are "demonized." From their viewpoint, the Western democracies are democratic only on the surface, being in reality controlled by a clique of exploitive conspirators who torture political dissidents and ruthlessly assassinate, in the prisons where they hold them captive, revolutionary freedom fighters and members of radical underground groups like the RAF.* These leftists do not have at their disposal administrative ordinances, constitutional safeguards and other "security agencies" with which to pursue these demons from a position of authority, and thus they are automatically forced to use guerrilla tactics. The use of such tactics arouses McCarthyist attitudes on the part of the opposition, just as the abuses of the hunt for radicals inflame the fanaticism of the leftist underground.

This is not the time or the place to undertake a more thorough social-psychological analysis of the mutual reinforcement of this tendency for opposing parties to depict each other as devils incarnate. However, it should be pointed out that this phenomenon of diabolical projection plays a particularly significant role in contemporary, divided Germany. The spectrum of political sentiment tolerated in German society is narrower than that tolerated in neighboring Western nations. In Germany, political conflicts have a more pronounced tendency to

---

* The RAF (*Rote Armee Fraktion* or the "Red Army Group") is a modern German radical group.—Tr.

degenerate into irreconcilable pseudo-religious warfare with archaic campaigns to stamp out enemies who are treated as heretics. And scarcely anywhere else on this planet have worldwide phenomena such as racism and (more recently) terrorism manifested themselves as virulently as in Germany. [Cf. 67]

*

There is another strategy involved in the warding off of suffering through projection which cannot be viewed in isolation from its political origins and which, once again, has been more clearly manifested in Germany than anywhere else. This is the idea that mankind must be protected from "decadence," from the increasing prevalence of "negative" physical and mental traits, by preventing certain groups—ostensibly the representatives of inferior hereditary traits—from reproducing themselves, or even by exterminating them outright.

Those who practice this strategy have always portrayed themselves as saviors seeking to produce a pure-bred, healthier, stronger and "higher" race—allegedly in accordance with the evolutionary laws described by Darwin. They claim that mankind will be spared infinite misery if people and groups with negative hereditary traits are simply eliminated. In Germany, geneticists, ethnologists, and animal behaviorists were called upon to lend an aura of scientific legitimacy to the work of mass extermination.

In July, 1933, the Nazis passed the "Law for the Prevention of Congenitally Diseased Offspring." As Mitscherlich and Mielke point out, this law "laid the foundation for a development which, on the one hand, led to a compulsory 'coup de grâce' for the incurably mentally ill, and on the other hand, during the war, to plans to exterminate the allegedly inferior races of the Poles, the Russians, the Jews and the Gypsies." [56]

However, many people who were by no means incurably mentally ill were also murdered as a result of the Nazi euthanasia program, [84]and compulsory sterilization was performed on masses of people suffering from diseases or handicaps which were far from being hereditary maladies in the strict sense.

In this case too, as with other phenomena of the Nazi period, one is inclined to feel that one is dealing with some sort of exotic historical anomaly, rather than with a consistent reaction type. Confronted by the outpouring of this horrifying human propensity, we are able, simply by labelling it an exceptional case, to deny that it has any bearing on our own attitudes and behavior. In reality, however, it is essential to take seriously the indications that the ideology which preaches the extermination of "the genetically inferior" is still very much with us.

In 1973, in a chapter on "Genetic Decay," the renowned animal behaviorist Konrad Lorenz expressly drew attention to the danger that society might be flooded with "social parasites," and lamented: "There can be no doubt that the degeneration of genetically-anchored behavior threatens us with apocalypse, and apocalypse in a particularly ghastly form." [49]   In this chapter Lorenz makes it quite clear which allegedly hereditary negative behavior traits he has in mind, for he dwells on the fact that "countless young people have a hostile attitude toward today's society and thus toward their parents as well." He conjures up dire visions of the progressive infantile regression of our society and cites other decadent phenomena such as the increase in juvenile crime and the "attenuation of the capacity for powerful emotions" produced by "coddling" people, especially the young. Just a few sentences removed from his comments on the protests of many young people against their parents and society, Lorenz draws an alarming comparison between this phenomenon and the condition of an organism which is unable to fend off the attack of immature cancer cells: "The pernicious growth of malignant tumors is facilitated by the fact that certain defense mechanisms by which the body normally defends itself against 'asocial' cells, break down or are neutralized by the cancer cells. Only if these cells are treated and nurtured by the surrounding tissue as 'one of our own kind,' can the tumor infiltrate and grow." [49]   Thus are we to conclude that those "immature" young people who engage in any kind of protest are not to be treated and nurtured as "our own kind," but rather rejected or warded off like asocial cancer cells? The author suggests the form our self-defense must inevitably take when he notes that the types of behavior he has observed in young people are based on "phenomena involving genetic decay." How, indeed, could one defend oneself against these asocial cancer cells, if not by taking compulsory measures to prevent them from reproducing? Lorenz does not expressly recommend this course, but what other conclusion can possibly be drawn from his argument?

Lorenz recommends no concrete political policies, just as Nietzsche never suggested practical methods of any kind by which to create a higher race of men or generally "improve the breed." But is it not obvious what practical conclusions are to be drawn from Lorenz's theories about the student-youth protest of the last decades, which is now a thing of the past? Every age has its missionary thinkers who are expected to work out principles which at least point the way to political salvation. The degree to which such prophets meet with an enthusiastic response is an index to the latent proclivities of their contemporaries. Apart from his significance as a behaviorist, Lorenz must be included among those authors of the postwar era who can justly be regarded as preachers of a way of salvation. Thus his warning of an impending "apocalypse" brought on by genetic decay, which he describes as one of the eight deadly sins of civilized man, has highly significant social and political implications. Of course, by now the mood of the times has cooled off, for the youth protest movement has subsided. Thus, at the moment it is no longer fashionable to dismiss outspoken anti-establishment groups as mere clusters of genetic deficients. Not until social tensions in Germany peak again will we be able to determine the extent of the latent tendency among the German people to convert racial or genetic prejudices into a campaign to exorcise the Devil.

Three years after the publication of Lorenz's book *Civilized Mankind's Eight Deadly Sins* (German edition, 1973), one of the states of West Germany appointed as Minister of Justice a man who—according to the *Frankfurter Rundschau*, No. 59, 22 March 1978—had written in his doctoral dissertation in 1936:

> Only a human being of racial value has any right to exist within society. On the other hand, an inferior, good-for-nothing person, or one who exercises a positively deleterious effect, must be eliminated. Details concerning the method of elimination depend on current attitudes of the people. It is not yet clear whether the [German] people are *as yet* capable of understanding the need to eliminate inferior types by killing them outright. However, it is certain that today they at least welcome the extermination of the morals offender and thus sanction the prevention of asocial persons from producing offspring of the same kind. But the law in its entirety must serve the end of improving the race. [Italics mine]

The remarks of Nobel Prize-winner Konrad Lorenz and the case of this West German Minister of Justice (who has since resigned his post) demonstrate that, at least in Germany, a latent inclination still persists to eradicate suffering by projection. Lorenz published his dubious theses long after the Germans had witnessed the ghastly results of the Nazi "Law for the Prevention of Congenitally Diseased Offspring," and yet these theses encountered remarkably little in the way of public opposition. As for the Minister of Justice who had expressed his concern over whether the German people were "as yet" ready to condone the murder of congenital "inferiors," his party and some members of the press dismissed him as the unfortunate victim of a wicked campaign of character assassination. For some time now there has been a growing tendency to invert our moral values and to discredit those opposed to the premature repression of German awareness of the racism and witch-hunting of the Nazi era.

However, during this period of comparative prosperity which Western nations, and especially we in the Federal Republic of Germany, are enjoying at the moment, we should be making a specific, focused effort to examine and deal with the archaic projections which played a depraved role in the era of the Third Reich. Now would appear the ideal time to take a critical look at the thought patterns which wrought such devastation on the world. Yet it may be that the psychological presuppositions for such a critical assessment of our past do not yet exist, because the German people still have such a strong propensity for magical thinking and for trying to exorcise demons they have projected onto people and events. We have noted that opposing political interest groups in Germany have a tendency to blame each other for everything that is going wrong, and to ascribe to each other diabolical characteristics. This trend in contemporary Germany suggests that Germans may in fact not be ready for a constructive reassessment of their past.

Indeed, the frequently dogged effort of Germans to avoid a reflective, self-critical examination of the basic intellectual attitudes of Fascism is a prime example of that elimination of suffering which is the theme of this part of my book. The opprobrium attached to suffering makes it almost impossible for people to assume the emotional burdens of responsibility and guilt. Besides, we feel an overwhelming fear that we will be incapable of bearing the burden of guilt once we have accepted it. As a result, we hide behind the same old repressive clichés: We were really trying to do the right thing, and when our good intentions had evil consequences, it was other people, not ourselves, who were to blame. Anyone who accuses me of anything, we say, is simply trying to divert attention from his own wickedness, and if there is in fact something evil in me, other people have more of it in them than I do.

Nevertheless, we in Germany still need a therapeutic self-help program. We have to face up to our fears and come to terms, patiently and thoroughly, with the monstrous deeds which arose out of the "projective diabolization" of our alleged enemies. It does not help us achieve this task if we spend our time denouncing all the violations of human rights taking place in some faraway corner of the world, while at the same time our own everyday conduct is ruled by considerations of power politics and we shield former Nazis and Nazi sympathizers who used the law to systematically violate human rights, simply because they now share our own political views. Nor, on the other hand, does it serve our purpose to abandon a fellow party member to his punishment merely because he was not clever enough to think up a good excuse for misdeeds he could easily have gotten away with.

The reader will hardly have failed to notice that people become uneasy when a discussion of current events is introduced into the analysis of social-psychological data. The total number of witches burned over the centuries may well equal the number of Jews murdered by the Nazis; yet their memory no longer awakens in us any fear that *we ourselves* may be implicated in the crimes. Most people feel no more uneasy over the crimes of the past than they feel about any crime with whose perpetrators they feel they have nothing in common. In such cases it is easy for them to assume a clearly-defined moral posture. Despite all the theories which have been put forth about hereditary tendencies, we no longer view the witch hunters of past centuries as our own forebears, nor do we view their actions as a part of our personal historical past. But the most recent instances of racist persecution and compulsory sterilization do not permit us to adopt this detached and contemplative pose. Some of that generation of Germans who, directly or indirectly, share the responsibility for the excesses of the Nazi era are still alive and in fact are playing a decisive role in the shaping of contemporary German political policy. Moreover, their children feel that they too are implicated to some extent, for they see the older generation try to repress and hide the effects of memories with which they have not succeeded in coming to terms. Even now we all find it hard to fathom the archaic sadism of which we humans are capable when a particular set of circumstances weakens those control mechanisms which give us the illusion, during times of comparative peace, that we have achieved a degree of ethical maturity. In fact, we bear little resemblance to the ideal image we have of ourselves, and we are afraid to see ourselves as we really are. This fear gives rise to an irrational moralism which, without our being conscious of it, fixates the evil it was intended to dispel. This irrational moralism can drive some individuals to spend their lives compulsively hunting down and denouncing Nazi war criminals, in order to affix to these "scapegoat" figures a guilt in which they themselves by rights must bear a share. Others, driven by the same blind moralism, call down the curse of heaven on the heads of those who *refuse* to give up the hunt for Nazi war criminals. Both these groups are convinced that they are fighting for a good cause and serving the ends of morality; but they only appear to represent a moral standpoint. Actually they are just rationalizing a defense mechanism; both groups are trying, from opposite perspectives, to ward off their fear. Basically, they are practicing the "scapegoat strategy." Yet they do not recognize that they are doing so: instead they attribute this strategy exclusively to those people whose guilt and shortcomings they are trying to denounce.

We Germans are particularly prone to the misapprehension that we are extremely sensitive to moral values, whereas what we mistake for moral conduct is merely the tendency to rashly and radically polarize all situations into black and white, good and evil. These premature value judgments, and tendencies to spy the Devil behind every woodpile, derive primarily from emotional insecurity and from an inability to endure the suffering involved in acknowledging guilt. This inability in turn makes it impossible to face and integrate one's faults and disagreeable traits. There is a perpetual need to conjure up the image of some "devil on the wall," some scapegoat, in order to feel whole and right with the world.* People may become extraordinarily susceptible to the seductions of demagogues who incessantly call upon them to take up arms in some crusade—large-scale or small—against Jews, Communists, radicals, the police, industrial magnates, bearers of "inferior hereditary traits" and so on. Certain politicians, posing as guardians of public morals, go to grotesque lengths to maintain and exploit the public susceptibility to demagoguery and continually widen the rifts in the social fabric by the creation of new scapegoats. To win or hold on to political power, these politicians attempt to activate archaic, deep-lying psychic complexes and emotional dispositions among the public in order to stimulate hatred for their political opponents. There is every reason to believe that political demagogues practice their manipulations with full awareness of their effects, and that they simply accept as part of the game the damage which they may cause by releasing primitive psychological patterns of response.

---

* The Swiss ethno-psychoanalyst P. Parin made an intriguing contribution to the study of this problem in an interview published under the title "Der ängstliche Deutsche: Kleinbürger ohne Selbstbewusstsein" ("The Anxious German: Petit Bourgeois without Self-Esteem") in *Psychologie heute*, No. 10, 1978. Cf. Richter, H.-E., *Flüchten oder Standhalten* ("Stand Fast or Run Away"). [67] —Author.

To be sure, the success of their strategy depends on the emotional immaturity of those persons who are taken in by it. No one can be goaded into joining in a witch hunt unless he is unconsciously seeking a supply of witches or devils to relieve tensions which he does not believe he can deal with in any other way. The fact that pernicious German demagogues, and the gutter press which caters to them, still strike a strong responsive chord among the German people is symptomatic of a widespread psychological instability which even extends deep into German academic circles.

Our susceptibility to demagogues, a trait which we must continually work to hold in check, stems from the mistaken notion that we are behaving morally, when all we are really doing is trying to ward off anxiety. When we concentrate on outside scapegoats we escape nagging self-doubt about our own guilt, which we feel unable to face. Thus there arises a strange paradox: a "moral conscience" derived from our very inability to hold onto our integrity by standing up to self-criticism. No doubt that Minister of Justice we mentioned earlier was at one time sincerely convinced that by advocating the murder of genetic deficients he was actually speaking out for morality. And no doubt the same thing is true of the many people who unhesitatingly supported the mass sterilization of "genetic deficients" or even took an active role in it. Those who militate against heretics, witches, radicals, or "social parasites" invariably regard their actions as a crusade against evil. Moreover, people who advocate closer supervision of political dissidents, harsher punishment for criminal offenders, and the reintroduction of the death penalty are as a rule moved by their desire to save mankind from misery and decadence. They tend to see the breakdown in public morality only among their ideological opponents, who, by their "pseudo-humanitarian" leniency, seem to be opening the doors to crime, decadence, ethical barbarism, and ultimately terrorism. In conclusion, it is certainly important to keep in mind the immoral aspects of demagoguery, which, with its exalted phrases about the "higher" goals of "breeding good stock," "improving the race," and "law and order," demands that our fellow men should no longer be treated as human beings like ourselves, but fought or even destroyed like cancer cells. Yet it is equally important that we view the problem from a different level—a level on which we may be able to relax our rigid defense postures instead of continuing to trade accusations about who is to bear the guilt for the crimes of the past.

I am speaking of the level of the emotions—fear and courage, suffering and compassion. A person who knows of no way to protect himself from suffering but to continually ferret out and neutralize other persons who are supposedly responsible for his pain is, of course, acting primarily out of fear, and not out of any pleasure he takes in the role of witch hunter. At the close of the fifteenth century, when people no longer trusted God to afford them adequate protection, they used the witch hunt in the attempt to exorcise poverty, starvation and pestilence. At the same time they were motivated by their fear of the burden of personal guilt, which they had to confront now that they had lost hope of atoning to God for their sins and obtaining absolution from Him. In principle, the same fears are operative today, and are responsible for that horde of demons we create by projection and then set out to destroy. Moreover, detailed examination of conditions in Germany at the beginning of the Nazi era reveals that the general tendency to react to fear by projection was activated by a combination of factors such as unemployment, hunger, political impotence and moral degradation. (At that time there was a general hostility towards the "ugly German," who was considered responsible for World War I.) This pervasive poverty, oppression and moral degradation stood in such sharp contrast to traditional, nationalistic notions of German greatness, power, and a mission to redeem the world, that it was natural for the German people to try to escape their troubles by blaming them on others. All that was needed was a spark to set them off. Hitler offered them exactly the solution they wanted: a way out of their weakness, a determination to rule the world for a thousand years, and a way to get rid of their feelings of guilt and inferiority by projecting them onto the representatives of universal evil— "international Jewry," "international Bolshevism," "genetic deficients"—whom it was now their task to destroy.

Ultimately it is their own inability to endure suffering which forces people to make others suffer. We continually see large-scale reenactments of that archaic reaction which Freud described as typical of small children: After bumping into some object and getting hurt, the child transforms his suffering into anger at the object in order to regain his sense of emotional well-being. The basic pattern of reaction remains the same, even when the projection expands beyond this level, ceases to involve sheer physical pain or material distress and also, or primarily, involves a feeling of worthlessness. When a person collides not with an inanimate object but with other people or groups of people, the process of shifting blame to others by means of projection can create a never-ending cycle of human misey. An unending quarrel arises to determine just who is to serve as scapegoat for those woes for which no one dares to accept personal responsibility. However, in our culture few people associate "daring" with daring to accept personal responsibility when things go wrong. We almost always equate courage and daring with *action.* A person is courageous if he challenges external foes, sets out to slay the Dragon or struggles against forces of nature more powerful than himself: cold, storms, the waves of the sea or sheer rock cliffs. But in reality there is always more than simple courage involved when a person feels *compelled* to fight in order to maintain his emotional stability. This kind of courage is a flight from a despair which simply cannot be borne. This fear of despair in turn springs from an unendurable clash between the ideal and the real. If, after World War I, the German people had not been obsessed with an inordinate ideal of grandeur, power and moral superiority, it would perhaps have been easier for them to integrate themselves into the community of nations on the level of an equal partner. But they lacked the courage to revise their exaggerated image of themselves. In their narcissism they were not daring enough to live on a more modest scale.

Thus, people must always face the question of how to strengthen those psychic forces which make it easier to endure personal weakness, insignificance and imperfection. The main reason we continue to employ the projective mechanism is our vision of omnipotence and narcissistic perfection, exemplified in its most extreme and graphic form by the Nazis when they set out to take revenge for all the humiliations which the Germans had supposedly suffered; yet this vision of perfection represents, apart from the Nazis, a universal blight on all of Western civilization. All of us are heirs to that historic flight into an inflated sense of our own godlike stature, of which we have already spoken. As we have seen, the men, the young and the strong assume the role of divinity and realize the vision of omnipotence directly, whereas the women, the old and the weak help them to realize and fulfill this vision, and thus indirectly participate in it. Hence we all face a common task: to recognize that it will not destroy us to surrender some of our inflated ideals, but rather will give us an opportunity to develop a new, more meaningful human identity in which we can all share equally. What we need is to reeducate ourselves, to learn a different kind of courage. This includes the courage to retreat or give in, to accept that we are not perfect, to make peace with our own weakness rather than fighting it as "the demon within." Later we will discuss more fully the implications of this reeducation process.

*

It remains for us to consider a special variety of projection, employed as a defense against suffering, which, although in principle is identical to the phenomena just described, differs from them in that we can no longer detect in it any *direct* evidence of that instinctual process which underlies it. At first glance we see no sign in it of fanaticism or aggression. The conflict is no longer that between inquisitors and witches, between the "guardians of law and order" and the "social parasites," between the "higher men" and the "subhuman beasts." The representatives of evil are not human individuals, groups or ideologies. Instead what may happen is that the projection is displaced onto a surrogate enemy which is not immediately recognizable as an enemy at all, at least not in any obvious sense. In fact evil is converted into some sort of material, environmental factor or factors. These factors appear to elude the categories of social psychology and to pertain only to the physical scientist. Witches turn into *bacteria, viruses, food or stimulants such as tobacco, along with various noxious influences, both animate and inanimate, which are believed to exert a toxic effect on the person from without.* This mechanism of displacement is characteristic of the symptomatology of compulsive neurosis, in which the conflict frequently centers around the smallest and most insignificant opponents —dirt, germs and so on.

Science confirms that certain microorganisms do in fact cause disease, that vegetables grown with artificial fertilizer can contain harmful substances, that an unbalanced diet is not good for people and that certain substances consumed by the body, such as tobacco and alcohol, can prove damaging to health. But all of these, and many similar factors, can become the focus of a unilateral and exaggerated battle to the death. Some people turn bacteria, viruses and environmental pollutants into Public Enemy Number One, and all their thoughts revolve around this enemy. At this point we are no longer talking about that essential and highly laudable concern for the environment which manifests itself in rational measures to protect our air, water and foodstuffs from continued irresponsible exploitation and pollution. Instead, what we see here is a full-blown *persecution mania* centering on one or many of a number of phenomena like dirt, bacteria, chemical fertilizers, chemical food additives and other substances harmful to the environment. The elimination of the evil in question, people believe, will not only preserve them from premature death, but will render life itself pure and clean again. A clearly perceptible trait of many hygiene fanatics, vegetarians, consumers of macrobiotic foods, and similar groups is the *moralistic* element in their thinking. There is actually a vegetarian *ideology* which decries the eating of meat as a sort of preliminary form of cannibalism and as one of the principal causes of brutality and violence of all kinds. Many sectarian-minded devotees of macrobiotic foods also take as gospel the relationship between a pure diet and physical, spiritual purification. For a number of years now people who smoke have often been obliged, in the presence of non-smokers, to feel like semi-barbarians or insect pests whose active pollution of the air is practically antisocial.

Ever since the nineteenth century there has been a steady intensification of man's effort to detect harmful agents, external to man, which threaten life, health and often morality as well, and which must be stamped out or at least held in check by civilization.

The discoveries of the great microbiologists Pasteur and Koch introduced a new phase into medicine. Their success in treating infectious diseases awakened an inordinate hope, still widely held, that at last man had discerned the principal cause of disease—the bacterium or virus. There is almost no disease under the sun which someone has not sought to trace to a specific chemical or bacterial source. Moreover, today many people still believe that some day most unexplained diseases will be traced to the effects of a virus or some other type of microorganism. In fact, scarcely a year goes by in which we do not discover new viruses and develop new immunization techniques. On the other hand, in many cases a decades-long search for external agents of disease has produced no results. Furthermore, in the course of the war against germs, man has unintentionally created new sources of disease and caused other kinds of harm, a fact which is frequently overlooked in public discussion. Many bacterial agents develop "resistant" strains, or in other words become immune to the substances designed to combat them. Certain types of virus defy traditional methods of sterilization. This explains how physicians and nurses have inadvertently injected thousands of people with live virus causing liver infection. Thus hospitals and clinics, the principal arenas of the war against infection, have at the same time become one of the prime sources of contagion. Recently, at the Fifth Düsseldorf Conference on Public Health, the public health specialist Franz Daschner spoke of the approximately 500,000 patients in West Germany who every year "contract infections deriving from their hospital stay which put an additional strain on their health." [13]   Moreover, Daschner stated that some *25,000 deaths* result annually from infectious diseases contracted in a hospital setting. The fact that many infectious diseases can no longer be effectively combatted because medical personnel have inadvertently bred a strain of bacteria which no longer responds to antibiotic drugs also plays a significant role in this dilemma. To a large extent the breeding of resistant strains results from the fact that, in order to prevent contagion, vast quantities of antibiotics are put into the fodder of animals destined to be slaughtered for human consumption. This practice is carried on all over the world. As people consume the meat from treated animals, small quantities of antibiotic substances are continually fed into the human organism. Bacteria grow accustomed to these substances and build up a resistance to them, so that, in the most serious cases, a therapy employing the appropriate antibiotic substances will no longer do the patient any good at all. It is a widely-known and disturbing fact that the chemical insecticides sprayed on crops have polluted numerous vegetable foodstuffs. The campaign against the malaria mosquito had to be halted because medical authorities became aware that the DDT which was so effective in combatting the mosquitoes was also harmful to humans. Since that time malaria has once more begun to spread over the world.

Thus, in many respects the massive campaign against substances which have a harmful effect on surrounding organisms is producing no results, or at times dangerous results. The quest for the bacterial agent responsible for many diseases has proved fruitless. Thus, for example, there has for decades existed a wholly unsubstantiated theory that cancer may result from a viral infection, and as a result, untold sums have been expended on research projects which have not resulted in the slightest genuine progress. To be sure, other diseases do involve, in part, the activity of bacteria and viruses, but there is no indication that these bacterial or viral agents are principally responsible for the spread of the diseases in question. The surface of the human body, as well as many of the mucous membranes, normally teem with germs which, in and of themselves, cause no harm whatever, and which become dangerous only if the organism, as a result of exhaustion or unmastered psycho-social conflicts, loses its inherent ability to resist disease. Thus if we wish to remain in good health, we would be wise to give much more attention to preserving or strengthening our innate powers of resistance, rather than to searching for some "external enemy" to combat. Man's efforts to achieve the prophylactic annihilation of all pathogenic insects and microorganisms "threatening" to man, animal and plant appear nothing sort of calamitous. These efforts frequently create fresh sources of damage to organisms, and so the war against disease becomes perverted, giving rise to the very evils it seeks to eliminate.

We cannot free ourselves of the demons we have conjured up to serve us. Once we decide, however unconsciously, to evade responsibility for suffering by devising a persecution theory, we become the slaves of the notion that everything is out to get us. At first we only see one enemy, but new enemies rise up behind them. In the beginning people believed that they could rid themselves of their affliction merely by burning a *few* witches, but eventually they had to burn more and more. No matter how much they stepped up the witch hunts and multiplied the burnings, the persecutors always remained, at the same time, the persecuted, the hunters, the hunted. In much the same way, today we continually discover new and injurious viruses, fungi, carcinogens and other noxious substances. No sooner do we gain control over certain strains of bacteria or virus through immunization or antibiotics or chemotherapy, than new strains pop up which for the time being we can do nothing about. And in our increasingly systematic attempts to liberate human beings, animals and plants from all noxious influences, we are not merely discovering but actively manufacturing (albeit inadvertently) new sources of affliction. We destroy one pernicious substance with the aid of another which in the end proves even more dangerous than the first. We upset the balance of nature because, after making some scientific discovery, we prematurely and overconfidently credit ourselves with the possession of a supernal wisdom which enables us, by artificial means, to direct the course of events more efficiently than nature herself, and indeed to correct nature's errors. Only later do we discover, for the thousandth time, that all we have done is destroy something whose purpose in the natural order we had simply failed to comprehend.

Our deeply-ingrained will to power, and our flight from suffering, are what really—though unconsciously—compel us to carry on a combat as interminable as the labor of Sisyphus. This combat is based on the assumption that some time in the future it will actually be possible for us to conquer death and disease once and for all simply by destroying the last external enemy who exerts a pernicious influence on our lives. We demand that physicians and pathologists explain every single death in terms of some concrete organic cause. We tend to assume that pathogenic substances or environmental pollutants are at least indirectly involved even in degenerative diseases in which external pests appear to play no direct role. Working conditions, diet, alcohol and tobacco are the concrete external agents most frequently blamed for our ills. Moreover, the less we know about certain diseases, the easier it is for us to suppose that in some way they are caused by an *outside source*. We would find it unbearable if a pathologist were to say in his report: Here is a person who died simply because he had to die. He died precisely because everything happened to him just as it was supposed to. He avoided all sources of damage to his health which possibly could be avoided. He received all possible vaccinations in time. He led a healthy life. Now his life has ended in a way consistent with the order of things, just as was proper.

One might remonstrate with the pathologist, pointing out that it never happens that all the organs of the body wear out at exactly the same time. In every dead person one can find organs which, in and of themselves, would have been capable of continuing to live and function, and which only died along with the rest of the body because some other portion of the organism suffered a fatal breakdown. Thus one could, in effect, take this broken-down organ as the starting-point in a quest for the "guilty parties." But after all, who is to say that in a case of death from natural causes, all the organs must cease to function at the same moment? One-hundred-year-old people frequently die of infections, especially pneumonia. This fact nourishes the illusion that they did not really *have* to die any more than persons of any other age. And yet in reality it is only natural that, when the bodily defenses have worn out in old age, disease organisms should propagate at the weakest point in these defenses and bring the person's life to an end. But in the minds of most people this "normal" death represents a rare exception, whereas the average death constitutes a defeat by enemies against whom medical science is obliged to steadily gain ground. The physician finds himself in a very awkward position because he is the focus of most of the magical expectations concerning human omnipotence which still prevail in our culture. Every day he must confront people who have exaggerated notions of his capabilities—notions which to him are an index of the desperation with which people are trying to ward off widespread fears of helplessness and death. He is, in a sense, obliged by profession to become a slayer of dragons; and paradoxically, he can deal most effectively with his difficult task if he does in fact play to the hilt the impossible role imposed upon him, turning himself into other people's ideal of what he should be, and at the same time repressing the fact that he is indeed an actor playing a role.

Most people today take an offensive posture regarding their health and use the weapons provided by science and technology in the attempt to eradicate external enemies which may threaten it. There is a big difference between them and the minority who merely take a defensive posture, hoping to escape external pests by retreating into a "natural" life style. However, frequently even those who develop this defensive posture insist fanatically on the contrast between their ideal of purity on one side and all conventional foods and stimulants on the other. Sectarians and cultists of this sort remain under the spell of the same type of projective mechanism, in that they often feel compelled to keep their attention focussed on external threats and see the avoidance of these threats as their only hope of salvation.

A smaller group of sectarian thinkers, faddists or cultists may turn their backs on science, displaying instead a preference for ancient magical concepts and Oriental mysticism. Religious motifs appear to be playing an increasingly important role in "back-to-nature" movements. On the other hand, the adjusted majority primarily make use of a projective mechanism involving superficial, technologically-oriented concepts of suffering in which health and salvation are not far removed from the flawless state of the well-oiled "organic machine." The unhealthy condition which everyone dreads more than anything else shrivels up until it becomes a mere function of unfavorable blood, urine, weight and blood pressure tests. It appears as the chief task of the medical community and the chief purpose of individual hygiene to keep fit that organic machine which is the body. The progressive narrowing-down of the meaning of the word "hygiene" gives semantic verification of the fact that the mechanism of projection which I describe here is gaining, not losing, ground. Originally the Greek word "hygiene" meant the care of one's health in general. But later, as a technical medical term, it came to refer exclusively to that medical discipline which instructs us concerning the control of injurious substances *external to ourselves*. For example, hospital hygiene does not imply any concern about creating a humane atmosphere, but refers solely to the maintenance of sterile conditions in temperature-control units, procedures for disinfecting surfaces and instruments, the scrupulous attention paid by the medical staff to washing their hands, and so on.

Thus in this variation on the theme of projection as a defense mechanism against suffering, morality is equated with hygiene and hygiene with morality. There will be nothing but goodness in the world, people believe, once bacteria, viruses, dirt, toxic substances and vermin have finally been defeated.

Hysterical Pretense as a Means of Denying Suffering.
The Cocktail Party Culture.
The Compensatory Function of Therapy and Self-Help Groups.

The concept underlying the projective elimination of suffering states that suffering is basically something inflicted on us from outside, something produced by witches, asocial or antisocial elements, extremists, inferior races, social parasites or toxic substances. Once these external causes are eliminated, suffering will disappear.

On the other hand, projection plays no role, or a much less pronounced role, in the phenomenon of "running away from suffering." The following manifestations are involved in this second form of projection:

a) denial through camouflage or "covering up"
b) denial through splitting
c) pacification through substitute gratifications
d) techniques of societal camouflage

Anyone in our society who wishes to be regarded as socially well-adjusted practices the art of concealing suffering. It is considered good form to represent oneself as if one were always feeling in top shape. The technique of artfully covering up signs of deterioration, chronic illness, and even death is prevalent everywhere and is most pronounced in the United States. The etiquette—or perhaps one ought rather to call it the breach of etiquette—surrounding death is the most extreme form of the effort to hide the reality of suffering. In funeral homes the dead are covered with makeup to make them look like young people glowing with health who just happen to be asleep at the moment. We demand that even the dead should attest, in the eyes of their survivors, to man's power to produce eternal fitness.

The root of this practice is the fantasy that one can hold suffering in check or ward it off if one simply ceases to *show* it to oneself and others. Such a fantasy proves effective only in a society characterized by hysteria, in which the most important thing in life is whatever can be seen *from the outside*. People reach some sort of agreement as to what game they are going to play. Then everyone plays along, and in the presence of others react only to the game that the others are playing. The rules stipulate that one must always pretend to be cheerful and confident. One is supposed to show how good one is feeling and to confirm others in the notion that they are fine too. One never wears anything but a smiling face and sees nothing but fellow-players of the game, likewise with smiling faces. People present themselves the way a shopkeeper presents his goods: pleasing, attractive, ready for use. This correspondence between social behavior and the advertising of consumer goods is by no means coincidental. Within the ruthless system of a competitive economy, no one is concerned with what people are like *inside*. The only important thing is their usefulness, their serviceableness. But the only people who really prove useful are those who are physically and mentally "fit." Consequently you must always remain fit, or at least pretend to others to be so. What you are *really* like becomes less and less important. The crucial thing is how successful you are, how you sell yourself, what can be made off you. If a person wants to be successful, either he does not dare to suffer, or he must conceal his suffering so that it does not damage his image, for no one has any use for someone who is broken or damaged. He's out of the game, done for. Thus clearly the hysterical cover-up of suffering is a bitter necessity of life in our society: not a spontaneously invented "style" but a forced adaptation to which people conform in order to survive. The automatic nature of this behavior is a *secondary*, not a primary aspect. In other words, first you are compelled to behave a certain way, and later it becomes natural to do so. Behavior is internalized so that in the end you *want* to be the way you are *supposed* to be. You are voluntarily subsumed into your image, and convince yourself that what is behind the image is not really important. No one has addressed this transformation of man into a mere human commodity as eloquently as Karl Marx.

People reinforce each other in their attempts to deny suffering by giving each other little emotional "boosts" of a socially-prescribed nature which compel those on the receiving end to demonstrate how well they feel. Marriage counsellors and therapists who help train people to communicate better have recently begun to help clients practice exchanging the right "signals," which is automatically supposed to result in harmony in interpersonal relations. If one person deals with another according to regulations, the latter is morally obliged to radiate good cheer. The whole show can easily be staged. In their relationship the husband is supposed to praise his wife's new clothes and her cooking. She is supposed to listen attentively when he talks about his troubles at work and remain patient when he comes home tired and in a bad mood. The game becomes somewhat more complex if she too has a job outside the home. But the rules can be just as clearly defined and drilled into the players in this case as in any other. As Erich Fromm quite correctly notes in *The Art of Loving*, "All this kind of relationship amounts to is the well-oiled relationship between two persons who remain strangers all their lives, who never arrive at a 'central relationship,' but who treat each other with courtesy and who attempt to make each other feel better. In this concept of love and marriage the main emphasis is on finding a refuge from an otherwise unbearable sense of aloneness." [33]   Or perhaps one might more accurately say that this type of relationship does not encourage a genuine mutual sense of well-being, but merely the façade, the superficial display of well-being.

A typical example of the systematic camouflage of suffering is that round of party-going in which certain groups of Americans habitually indulge. They dash about from one party to the next, and no one expects anyone to reply in a negative manner to his perfunctory question, "How are you?" In this situation, the act of taking a friendly, good-humored interest in each other turns into a form of pure theater—but theater of a very important kind. For people are compelled to continually bolster each other up, in a superficial and narcissistic way, so that together they can succeed in glossing over their misery, which might otherwise rise to the surface. Thus it actually makes such people uneasy if a single member of their group does not show up on the cocktail party circuit. Other members of his set resent this behavior because it makes them feel afraid.

Anyone who withdraws from the hubbub of the party scene and becomes more self-absorbed may be hard put to salvage his reputation, for the flight into the social whirl makes one socially acceptable. Of course, in these party-going circles, people regard as the true "flight" any manifestation of introversion or preoccupation with personal problems, and accordingly condemn it. These people feel insecure when they see their system for the denial of suffering being attacked. The refusal to "play along" with the rest is forgiven only if it becomes known that the dropout is seeing a psychiatrist, for in this case everyone anticipates that psychiatric treatment will restore him to normality, so that he can once again go back to playing the game. It is the clear duty of anyone with money to hire a therapist if he feels any discomfort, any disinclination to spend time with people or some more serious form of malaise, in order that the therapist can build him up again and restore him to the flock of happy joiners and party-goers.

In this setting psychiatry and psychotherapy are endowed with a special function: they conspire in maintaining the role that society plays in suppressing suffering. In many cases the sole concern of these professions is to restore the patient so that he is acceptable and functions normally. Of course, as a rule, something else also happens in the course of therapy. In the therapeutic setting, people experience and gratify feelings which are not in demand or even sanctioned outside this setting. Clients engage with their therapists in a form of communication in which they are actually able to reveal their inner lives. Thus, frequently they experience a measure of genuine psychic life, free of the "rules of the game" in the outside world, where one must always remain fit and attractive. Hence, what is labelled a form of medical treatment may actually represent a medium of genuine communion in which a person experiences *more* true psychic health than he does in the bustle of the outside world, whose norm of physical and emotional fitness as a rule reflects no authentic concern with health but is only a symptom of a strategy of emotional repression. Frequently, even the suffering which surfaces in the therapeutic setting constitutes "healthy suffering," even if the patient does not interpret it, or is not allowed to interpret it, as such. Here we see the internal contradiction of this subculture built on the principle of keeping up a façade: everything which is not in demand in the competitive struggle for success, or which is not attractive and easily convertible into cash, is repressed and can emerge only in the therapeutic setting. The crucial conflict which emerges during therapy derives from the fact that many people feel more alive, more meaningful, more fulfilled in their role as patients than they do outside, in the role of the smoothly-functioning cog in the social machine, of the "guy who goes along with the crowd." Thus it is by no means rare that some people, providing they can afford it, turn psychotherapy into a permanent institution in their lives. To do this they frequently engage in a phenomenon which psychoanalysts call "splitting." That part of their lives which ought properly to constitute the authentic reality, they come to regard as an inauthentic mode of existence. Only in their role as patients of a therapist who takes seriously those elements in themselves which they too regard as the most important do they experience themselves as real human beings.

It is true that the feelings experienced by a patient towards a therapist in the course of therapeutic treatment are colored in many ways by the archetypal relationships to the world—and conflicts within those relationships—experienced during childhood. But this reaching back to childhood which takes place in therapy does not involve simply the need to work through problems which were not dealt with and remained unresolved at the time. It also reflects the fact that once the person became integrated into adult society, the world of his emotions was suppressed and deprived of a voice; it became impossible for him to formulate and articulate many of the emotional needs which arose later in his life. As a result, the patient has developed a secondary form of emotional disorientation and has become an emotional illiterate. Thus the regression, in therapy, to the phase of childhood, must in part be interpreted as a revival of earlier emotional structures, and as clues to a new grammar for articulating emotions, necessary to enable the patient to put behind him that speechless chaos which arose out of the repression of his emotional life. Yet, although it is true that patients may attempt to effect an emotional self-regeneration by returning to their childhood, this by no means substantiates the popular view that psychotherapy represents a sort of dumping ground for childish and immature people. The only way to reintegrate important areas of inner life which have been split off is to get back in touch with archetypal images and behavioral prototypes to which the patient was exposed early in his psychological development, and which after childhood were buried under the rubble of time.

As some people are aware, in Germany there has recently been a storm of protest against the rising demand for psychotherapeutic treatment. This demand has been denounced by critics who view it as a symptom of increasing laziness, or a desire to "take the easy way out," and who claim that people should become more self-reliant again and ask for less counselling and care from others. These critics, whose chief spokesman in Germany is H. Schelsky, [83]   take an oversimplified view of the situation, uncritically supporting the norm of "fitness" based on the repression of suffering. They display a marked prejudice against any failure to conform to this norm, viewing such failure as an expression of the desire to comfort.* The increasing demand for help with emotional

---

*   Cf. the author's article "Freiheit oder Socialismus" in *Worte machen keine Politik,* ed. by I. Fetscher and H.-E. Richter, 1976. [73]

problems, which is turning into a regular tidal wave, is in fact alarming, and it makes sense to warn people of the fact that the problem cannot be dealt with simply by a vast expansion of available therapeutic services. On the other hand, there is no justification for disparaging the motives of people seeking help with emotional problems. If psychiatry and psychotherapy are in fact becoming the last place of refuge in our society, a sanctuary where people with a richer or more intense inner life can still articulate their deeper emotional needs, then it is high time that we direct our criticism not at the *patients* but at *society:* for society at large must take some steps to ensure that it is possible for people to function on an emotional level within it, and must see to it that there is some place for the psychic life which has been increasingly channelled off into the domain of counselling, therapy and therapeutically oriented self-help groups. In reality it is our indolent, comfort-loving society, structured around the denial of suffering and the ideal of fitness, which is in need of reeducation in order to perceive its pathological state. But here, once again, we confront the same old dilemma: for years, massive self-created external constraints have caused us to internalize and become fixated on the resolve to deny our personal sickness and suffering. This denial compels us, again and again, to disparage those who fail to "join the party."

The microsociety of social clubs and cocktail parties is the realm in which the various overlapping sociodynamic factors exist in such a concentrated form that they become perceptible to the individual. Many Europeans, after emigrating to the United States, have reported that although they found a super abundance of "nice people" in their new home, they scarcely ever found a real *friend.* By their own account they themselves very rarely succeeded in really "opening up" emotionally, and other people never really opened up to them. For a long time now it has also been a widespread custom in Germany to shroud the fact of one's inner isolation behind a multitude of superficial contacts. This is, in fact, among the most popular modern techniques for denying suffering in that portion of one's life dedicated to leisure-time pursuits. By manifesting a frantic gregariousness, people prove to each other that they are in fact not isolated at all—and yet the very fact that they are trying so hard to prove this shows that in reality they *are* isolated.

Many modern therapeutic training programs based on the principles of game-playing and group dynamics—particularly encounter groups—have a very similar function to the cocktail party. In these group settings, people appear to break through the pervasive shallowness of their experience by organizing into the program the expression of every emotional impulse lying dormant in the participants. Group sessions involve a veritable hailstorm of violent eruptions of fear, sadness and love. Those taking part are absolutely enthralled by this display of unbridled passion. But their emotions function only within the context of these staged theatrical productions. Trickery is used to provoke something natural, and thus what is natural becomes artificial. People are *drilled* into spontaneity—with the result that all spontaneity is lost. The isolation of everyday existence persists unless a more profound form of communication is developed within the context of enduring relationships. In the group itself, this isolation is merely released for a few moments and eventually dammed up again—during planned "sessions" and under conditions clearly laid down in accordance with the group norm.

To be sure, as a general principle it is very useful for people to learn more about the social structures and rules by which they can revitalize buried emotions and introduce them into their social contacts. But it is essential that these rules and social arrangements not be used simply as "techniques" to rechannel outside the society proper that mass of excess emotional energy which is disruptive to "business as usual."

The "self-help groups" [57] which have recently come into vogue likewise fail to avoid this basic dilemma. For the most part these groups enable people to express—generally in a strictly private setting split off from the outside world—aspects of their emotional life which, as *critical* energies, might be more usefully expended within a larger *societal* framework. To be sure, this stricture does not apply to those self-help initiatives explicitly designed to *carry over into the society at large* the therapeutic insights achieved by individual members. It is a matter of some importance to the general public when the representatives of some trait which is normally repressed or stigmatized by society—old people, cancer patients, the handicapped, the socially disadvantaged, vagrants, and so on—get together and try to attract attention to their problems. The key factor is that people who have been taught to be ashamed of their poverty and "inferiority" and to creep away and hide humbly in the background are here taking up the offensive and standing up for their rights. While fighting for public notice and for a practical solution to their problems, they are at the same time exercising a therapeutic influence on many other people, for being forced to devote some sympathy and attention to persons suffering social stigma can enable people to accept their own weaknesses, the awareness of which they have long repressed.*

* The Gray Panthers might be cited as a model of a self-help movement which has exerted an active influence on society at large. This American self-help organization for the elderly not only supplies older people with the chance to engage in stimulating group projects but also supports effective initiatives to influence social and political policies. Moreover, the Gray Panthers attempt to instill in the rest of the population the insight that the neglect of the elderly is not something which occurs by default, but rather represents the inevitable consequence of the misguided ideals of society, and of political strategies which reflect these ideals. [98a] —Author.

The Avoidance of Suffering
by Splitting

Essentially the theory underlying the camouflage of suffering is that this approach enables people to support each other in their denial of personal vulnerability. Consequently that misery, which is supremely important to conceal, is the kind that threatens *all* human beings, or at least a great many. The more remote and exotic an affliction appears, the more readily we can accept it. Naturally what poses the greatest threat to man's urge to deny suffering is the confrontation with death. The tendency of many younger people to reject old and sickly family members and send them off to old people's homes does not, as is frequently stated, stem solely from unresolved intergenerational conflicts. Frequently one factor in the behavior of younger family members is their fear that if they directly observe their elders losing their strength, they will be forced to accept the fact that they themselves are now threatened with imminent destruction. People cannot bear to be reminded of unpleasant things which they themselves will one day have to face. When young parents want to rid themselves of an elderly relative, they may feel ashamed of their fear of aging and death, and employ the pretext that their young children must be spared the painful sight of the destitution which attends old age. In reality, of course, children as a rule experience no problem whatever in dealing with elderly people, even if they are ill. Often children are the only people around capable of talking openly with old people about their infirmities and about death. The openness of our children to their emotions generally makes it both more difficult and less necessary than it is for their elders to repress the fact of death. This observation is borne out by the experience of pediatricians that very often children are also much better at dealing with the problem of an incurable disease in themselves than are adults.

People who are trying to deny suffering and death find it so threatening to be forced to observe the naked, unvarnished suffering of another human being because everyone has an innate disposition to experience directly what someone else is experiencing. Everyone is spontaneously moved, by any expression of pain, to feel the pain himself. The compulsion to feel compassion and sympathy is inescapable because, in psychophysiological terms, it is rooted in human nature. This phenomenon will be discussed in another context in later chapters of this book. However, we must keep in mind that the experience of *fellow-feeling* with another person can, under certain circumstances, turn into a *feeling in opposition to* this person.

Either within or outside the context of sexual perversion, people can develop behavior patterns in which they enjoy participating in someone else's pain. We see this in the phenomenon of *spite* or *malice*, as well as in the many varieties, both conscious and unconscious, of *sadomasochistic relationships*. The traditional relationship between the sexes, which we have already discussed in detail, also contains an element of sado-masochism. In the past the man has unconsciously compelled the woman to take on the role of the sufferer so that he could repress suffering in himself. Despite the fact that a countermovement has sprung up under the leadership of women themselves, this general pattern of the relations between the sexes still continues to play a highly significant role in our lives—a role which extends far beyond sexual relationships themelves. As a general rule we can say that the more fanatically people overcompensate for their fear of suffering by pursuing omnipotence, the more urgently they need the contrasting spectacle of impotence and helplessness to preserve their emotional stability: for their stability is founded on the gratification they feel at the polarity between the weakness of others and their comparative strength. Paradoxical as it sounds, this strategy too is—indirectly—designed to camouflage suffering or make it invisible. A person needs someone else's suffering in order to drown out his own. But one prerequisite for the effective functioning of this particular strategy is that the person in question experiences, to some degree, narcissistic delusions of grandeur. His inflated ego forms a barrier which protects the sadist, making it unnecessary for him to share in, and commiserate with, that suffering which is forced upon the masochist.

We find traces of these kinds of narcissistic and sadistic needs in the behavior of many people who work in the service professions. These people have chosen a line of work in which they are continually surrounded by, or more accurately, in which they look down and survey, the suffering which they repress in themselves. The conspicuous illness and helplessness of others is the foundation of their own sense of security.

They are continually compelled to confirm their exalted view of themselves by organizing personal relationships and structuring groups which fulfill the function of making them feel secure. Just as the morbidly suspicious person is always looking around for potential persecutors in order to reinforce his unconscious attitude of defensive distrust, so the person afflicted with narcissistic delusions of grandeur must continually surround himself with insignificant and wretched people who confirm those feelings of superiority he needs in order to survive. His fundamental narcissism protects him from becoming infected with the suffering of others. Obviously emotional propensities of this kind are a handicap to anyone in the service professions to the extent that they prevent him from maintaining a role of parity, of equal partnership, with other staff members, as well as with his clients. Over and over the visible suffering of others gives him a "lift" so that he can feel as superior as he thinks necessary in order to escape complete destruction. The case of a psychoanalytic patient, which will be recounted in the concluding section of this book, will demonstrate the fact that people with the kind of emotional structure I have just described can suffer almost total emotional disintegration if they suddenly lose the all-important relationship with a person whose suffering has long been their main source of emotional security.

10

Pacification through Substitute Gratification: Scheler's Theory of Surrogate Compensation. From Sexual Taboo to Sex Cult.

In his ethics the German phenomenological philosopher Max Scheler (1874-1928) spoke of a "law of the inclination to surrogates in the event of a negative determination at the 'deeper' emotional level of ego-determination." [82]   Put simply, Scheler is saying that people who are unhappy deep down regularly try to compensate for their unhappiness by providing themselves with as many types of gratification as possible on a more superficial level of existence, the only area of life in which one can obtain gratification as one *chooses*. Whenever someone of this type gets into a situation in which he has it within his personal control to deliberately *manufacture* any pleasure he desires, he compulsively takes advantage of the opportunity to make himself some kind of amends for the fact that, in the core of his being, he is in a state of despair. He flees from his personal suffering, to which he feels he has been abandoned without any hope of defending himself, by frantically procuring some external anesthetic to numb the pain. In reality anesthesia is the essential issue in this whole process.

Warding off unendurable suffering by affording oneself compensatory gratifications which can easily be manufactured on a superficial level undoubtedly represents one of the most popular strategies of pacification ever developed in Western civilization, and one which we have developed to the highest level of virtuosity. The capitalist economic system has institutionalized it, turning it into a fixed norm of society which eternally reproduces itself. Advertisers maintain in us a perpetual sense of deficiency which they promise to appease through the products they sell. People who try to escape from suffering have available to them such a multitude of surrogate gratifications, in the form of the most sophisticated kinds of consumer goods, that they can at any time cover up their inner pain—or in Scheler's terms, a negative determination at the deeper level of ego-determination. "Youthful freshness," "freedom," "unconstrained *joie de vivre*," "self-confidence," "mental harmony," "undreamed-of vigor" are all supplied to consumers through the agency of "dream vacations," "the automobile of your dreams," soap, deodorant sprays, beverages, cigarettes, sugar-coated pills, insurance policies, and even certain brands of underwear. Man's flight to the happy-hunting-ground of modern consumerism has been organized with the utmost efficiency.

Clearly semantic tricks again play a major role in the technique of eliminating suffering. A whole vocabulary relating to suffering and the abolition of suffering is continually being fed to us by advertisers in connection with their products. The emotional confusion these tactics create is not as innocuous as it may appear at first glance. The aim of advertising is to cause us to forget the essential distinction between the different strata of our emotional experience. We are supposed to believe that even a profound inner feeling of constraint and despair is really nothing more than a superficial anxiety or a "bad mood" which can be eliminated through the purchase of consumer goods. We are expected to persuade ourselves that superficial surrogate gratifications, which are designed to distract our minds from the fact that at heart we feel meaningless and unhappy, in fact eliminate this central suffering altogether, instead of merely covering it up. Moreover, the inflationary abuse of certain words appears to be ideally designed to promote this confusion between the *camouflage* and the *elimination* of suffering. For we need language in order to express emotion and differentiate between various gradations of feeling.

Scheler distinguishes between sensible, psychic and spiritual feelings. Sensible feelings are the most superficial and are the easiest to influence at will. Spiritual feelings are the most profound and are directly linked to the ego or essential self. They are inaccessible to direct manipulation. So Scheler takes as his starting-point the fact that "the more closely feelings approximate the level of sensible [or sensory] feeling states, the more completely subject to arbitrary *choice* (and thus to the practical feasibility of achieving certain effects) is the decision of whether or not to have feelings. Even the vital feelings elude, to an appreciably greater degree, practical alteration by the will, and psychic feelings are still less alterable. Spiritual feelings rooted in our person are not in the least alterable by the will.... Those feelings which spontaneously well up from the depths of ourselves as persons, and which for this reason are the least 'reactive' and are altogether free of the dominion of the will, are the states of bliss or despair of the person himself." [82]   By "spiritual feelings" Scheler does not mean feeling states linked to some intellectual content, but rather feelings which "emerging, as it were, from the core of the person, fill up the whole of our existence and our 'world.' It is...in the nature of these feelings that either they are not experienced at all, or they seize possession of the whole of our being." In these feelings we are "our very selves." Scheler describes the world of feeling as it exists on this deepest level in terms of the polarity of *bliss* and *despair*. It is "the being and self-value of the person himself which form the 'foundation' of bliss and despair." In the final analysis, bliss and despair are not really *"feelings" in the sense of being* "transitory emotions." This is what Scheler means when he says that we "can only *be* in a state of bliss or despair, not, in the strict sense, *feel* bliss or despair." [82]

Such subtle distinctions are important because they keep our minds receptive to the fact that below the surface of those emotional impulses which can be manipulated through some intentional act—for example the consumption of goods—there exists a personal state of being which is not embraced by these techniques of gratification. Moreover, we perceive that if we treat language with sensitivity, its powers are in fact adequate to the purpose of drawing these scrupulous distinctions. It would be helpful to us to protect verbal concepts from fashionable jargon which continually shifts their meaning. But good intentions can accomplish little as long as people have a vested interest in the dissemination of linguistic imprecision—an interest which the advertising industry does nothing but exploit.

There is considerable evidence that our society is deeply under the spell of the mechanism which Scheler describes in the law of surrogate formation. This law states: *For the most part we suffer from such an extreme degree of inner despair that we are reduced to fleeing into superficial surrogate gratification.* In this state it does not matter to us that we have lost the capacity to express our deep sense of meaninglessness and unhappiness. We want to cover up the loss with gratifications which can be bought with a "higher standard of living." We no longer want to know what is going on under the surface, if what is underneath is as terrible as we suspect. Thus our advertising oriented economy is actually doing us a favor when it baldly equates suffering with not having certain commodities, when it dilutes the concept of freedom until it means nothing more than ownership of one's own home and the consumption of luxury items, and when it guarantees that a feeling of well-being will automatically result from the use of labor-saving appliances or power substitutes such as a high-performance car. The hidden suggestions made by our economic system accurately reflect our true situation, our dependence on soothing, peripheral surrogate gratifications. Since we cannot satisfy our longing for inner fulfillment, we are only too eager to partake of that mass supply of consumer goods which predominantly caters to the oral, instinctual level of experience. "Man's happiness today," writes Erich Fromm, "consists of having fun. Having fun lies in the satisfaction of consuming and 'taking in' commodities, sights, food, drinks, cigarettes, people, lectures, books, movies—all are consumed, swallowed. The world is one great object for our appetite, a big apple, a big bottle, a big breast." [33]

In a way Scheler's theory of surrogate formation constitutes an inversion of the original psychoanalytic concept of repression. In the Victorian era Freud perceived the *repression of sexuality* as the central factor underlying disorders in the psychological development of the middle class. It appeared to the public at large that the emancipation of the sexual drive represented a revolutionary psychoanalytic prescription for the cure of all man's ills. The fact that in recent years we tend to encounter just the opposite phenomenon—namely the rising tide of the cults of sex and pornography, which are used to repress unendurable despair—suggests an increase in the level of latent suffering in the deepest strata of our emotions. In the past the cause of illness was the sociocultural sexual taboo, but now this taboo has given way to a *cult of sexuality* which constitutes a prominent symptom of societal disorder. The problem of the pathogenic *repression* of the sex drive has given way to the pathological *acting-out* of the sex drive, clearly pointing to the mechanism of surrogate formation described by Scheler. Thus the sexual frenzy of today, which has been exploited and turned into a big-money industry, indicates a vast degree of unconscious suffering: suffering which drives people to look for sedatives or painkillers in the form of surrogate gratifications which can be "manufactured" at will.

The protests of women against the male sex-and-porno cult make it quite clear what sort of problem we are dealing with. These protests give men the opportunity—if they are willing to take advantage of it—to accept the angry responses of women as a potential source of help. After all, women's anger is a clue to the understanding of men's illness, of which the sex cult is in reality a symptom and expression. For only by frantically denying their own inner state of mind can men persuade themselves—although of course the notion is gratifying to their vanity—that the main issue involved in the sex-porn cult is that of the degradation of women. Actually it is above all men who are being degraded—men who, because they are emotional wrecks inside, are incapable of any but the most superficial communication with women, and who can *see* them and *use* them only as instruments for gratifying their most superficial needs and desires. To be sure, the women who are trying to defend themselves against degradation are in fact often powerless to do much about their situation; but in reality they are healthier, and have greater emotional strength, than the men they deal with. These women refuse to confine themselves to the superficial interchange which takes place on the level of purely instinctual function. However, we should keep in mind, in accordance with our earlier discussion of sexual relations in Chapter 6, that at least some initiatives are being made to restructure these relations, and in particular to help men engage in a critical self-appraisal and reorientation.

Scheler's theory of surrogate formation represents a helpful starting-point in our attempt to understand the weaknesses underlying modern hedonism.* This theory makes it easier for us to refute that idea which has constantly been drummed into us, the idea that the feeling of well-being is equal to the total of all the orgasms and instinctual gratifications which one can possibly manage to obtain, and ultimately is equivalent to technological power. The increasing mechanization of life, achieved through technological advances, has the potential to relieve us of some of our burdens, freeing us to direct more attention to those deeper realms of the emotions, concerning which Scheler says that there "we are our very selves." We could, if we chose, begin communicating with and helping each other to achieve a regeneration which springs from the depths of our nature, our essential being, our personhood. But the inability to deal with leisure, to collect our thoughts, to ponder what is deep within, has become endemic. The "negative ego-determination" at the deeper levels of our being continually prompts us to flee into the world of externalities. And yet, as we have already noted, there are some indications that people are gradually becoming more aware of the senselessness of this frantic externalization of reality, and of the fact that it is simply a form of running away.

---

* The doctrine of hedonism teaches that pleasure is the highest ethical goal and presupposes that man strives for the most intense possible pleasure. Aristippus, a pupil of Socractes, is generally regarded as the founder of the "doctrine of pleasure."—Author.

11

Societal Techniques to Veil Suffering. The Defense Mechanism of Objectification in the Social Bureaucracy, in Medicine, and in Psychology. The Strategy of Semantic Camouflage.

Every situation involving suffering has a material element which can be measured, counted, quantified. This element of suffering can be entered into questionnaires, punch cards, diagnostic apparatus and computers, and finds its ultimate expression in numbers, curves on graphs, and verbal formulae which deal with suffering exclusively as a mass of data. The more attention is paid to the material and quantifiable aspects of suffering, the easier it is to blot out the rest.

This is why, for example, social or welfare institutions treat societal afflictions almost exclusively as problems of logistics, rarely as human sorrows requiring human care. The public assistance and relief dispensed to the needy is virtually synonymous with money. Welfare work, as the term is commonly used today, no longer refers to care given human beings by other human beings. In fact it does not refer to any form of *human* work at all, but only to a cash payment whose sum is determined by a computer. It has already become easy to picture a future in which the social service bureaucracy will no longer have any direct contact with the fear, suffering, and hopes of real people, but will gather information and take the necessary measures fully automatically, without any personal communication whatsoever between workers and clients.

In this case the repression of suffering emanates not from those seeking help, but from the members of the social service bureaucracy, who are increasingly dominated by the special laws pertaining to the technological model of achievement. However, many clients of social service agencies are not just looking for someone to organize away or provide economically and technologically for a financial crisis, a physical infirmity or personal isolation. They also want someone to listen to them, to show them that he understands and sympathizes. Moreover, as a rule they are delighted when they are not simply given whatever is due them but are encouraged to active self-help in solving their problems. In addition, they do not want to be treated by social service personnel as anonymous masses of data, but as human beings whose self-respect demands that the official authorities they deal with also behave like human beings. Without some concern on the personal level, the various public assistance programs are merely a form of social technology. People in need of help profit most from contact with social workers who are committed to the ideal of social therapy, who use their whole personalities in treating their clients' social and psychological difficulties as a whole, and have meaningful, probing conversations with them. This is by far the most effective, cooperative way for people to treat each other, and above all the only truly human way. Yet this personalized approach is increasingly being sacrificed to bureaucratic and technically-oriented strategies of problem-solving. Under the unremitting pressure of shifting institutional rituals, the committed social worker who allows himself to get close to people is finding it more and more difficult to hold onto his personal work style.

A parallel development is taking place in hospital treatment. The decor of the hospital, clinic and nursing home, as well as their mode of operation, play down the fact that these institutions administer to the most intense human fears and pain. Life in a hospital is governed by a series of procedures whose principal purpose is to ensure that patients are "prepped" for processing and evaluation by a variety of appliances, and that they are transferred from one of these machines to the next as if they were products moving along an assembly line. Frequently the sick person does not become, in any sense, a whole human being again until, days or weeks after his admission to the hospital, he has been transformed into an aggregation of abstract chemical, electrophysiological and nuclear-medical numerical values. Sociological studies of medical facilities reveal that it is a rare exception for a patient in a hospital, clinic or nursing home to be given as much as five minutes a day to talk with his doctor and nurses. After all, what need is there for talking when automatic data-processing machines give much more precise accounts of exactly where, what and how things are going with the patient, as well as of the origin and recommended treatment of his problem, than could possibly be learned from the patient himself? The sick person, in fact, is not supposed to rack his brains about his medical condition at all, and he is in the care of a new generation of physicans who are also capitulating before the (to some extent) superior intelligence of the machines and leaving all the brain-racking to them.

Naturally people lying in hospital beds do have some kinds of feelings. They brood about what is happening to them, to their jobs, to their families. They suffer from unresolved conflicts which are frequently responsible for the breakdown of their organic functions. They long for some encouragement and reassurance which will fortify their will to get well and to assume personal responsibility for solving their problems. But at first, in the wretchedness of being sick, what is really important to them is simply to be able to feel the nearness and sympathy of other human beings. They would like to be made to feel that even here they are still people, people in whom other people take an interest and to whom they show respect. A patient does not want to have to feel ashamed of the fact that, despite all the care being lavished on him as a physical organism, he is also burdened with a confused, troubled and curious self which has to deal with his illness in emotional terms. It hurts him when he is expected to function smoothly in unison with the rest of the hospital, causing as little trouble as possible. As a rule he is made to feel that in the operation of the hospital he counts only as a physical organism, an "organic machine." Moreover, he is expected to acknowledge the fact that this "organic machine" is being ministered to by ever-increasing numbers of increasingly complex and costly mechanical devices, which light up all his insides, test bodily fluids, and measure the activity of electrical currents, and that these machines represent the primary, the essential form of medical care; for only this type of care is regarded as having a scientific basis and a scientific *raison d'être*. Everything relating to the *emotional* side of an illness can ostensibly be reduced to a private matter which is superfluous in scientific terms and is treated with the assistance of clergymen, relatives and—in really desperate cases—psychotherapists. [72]

This attitude on the part of hospital personnel explains why, in so many cases, psychotherapists are called in as consultants not because the hospital staff believes that emotional problems may be at the root of a patient's illness and are the reason why he is not getting well, but rather because the patient has become a nuisance, forever complaining of pain despite the fact that, according to the findings of all the mechanical apparatus, he has no right to be suffering at all. In other words, rather than devoting special care to the treatment of emotional factors involved in the patient's disease, the hospital staff wants the psychotherapist, as it were, to eliminate the existence of emotional factors altogether. His treatment is supposed to discipline the sick person, to get him to stop letting his psyche exert a disruptive influence on the functioning of that organic machine which the staff believe they have repaired so that it is working perfectly. From the point of view of organic medicine, the psychical aspect of man which comes to the fore in psychosomatic disease is something essentially culpable, a primary irrationality.

Thus at bottom the medical profession functions in terms of a nonsensical or paradoxical principle: To make people healthy, one must not allow the fact that they are suffering to prevent one from concentrating exclusively on what is happening to them physically. Devoting care to the patient's suffering simply interferes with scientific procedures. As far as the scientific practice of medicine is concerned, all that counts are the concrete data, the objective numerical values determined by the machines. Only these numbers supply us with that (in the Cartesian sense) clear and definite knowledge which leads us to the truth. And since every year sees the invention of new and different machines which continually increase the sum of those data which can be extracted from the body, our field of vision is in any case being filled up more and more completely with those abstractions which allegedly are the only legitimate objects of medical science.

*

As I indicated earlier, the true significance of psychoanalysis lies in the fact that it facilitates the articulation of repressed emotion, enabling it to voice a protest which had hitherto remained mute. Psychoanalysts founded a science where, according to the principles of the physical sciences, no science could exist. And every day psychoanalysis demonstrates the absurdity of that unilateral view that man is an organic *machine* whose body functions quite separately from the psychical infuences always at work within it, which in reality affect even the course of the various cancers and help to trigger heart attacks. But inevitably, even while psychoanalysts were struggling to vindicate the importance of the emotional life within the sphere of science, a radically different species of psychology and psychotherapy developed which tried to view the psyche in terms of the same mathematical and technological models that had been successfully used to master the material universe.

This alternative psychology has ceased to concern itself with that highly personal mode of experience in which the self (the subject) cannot be divorced from the object. Thousands of students who have chosen to study psychology because of their interest in their own inner lives and the inner lives of other people have been surprised to discover that psychology—so it is claimed—has nothing whatever to do with an inner life. This brand of psychology, whose proponents regard it as truly scientific, equates the dimension of the psyche with that element in it which can be quantitatively measured. The psychology to which I am referring is, essentially, the *psychology of the learned* (or *conditioned*) *response*, derived from the philosophy of behaviorism, which has already been briefly described. Its adherents no longer ask what emotions cause a particular behavior, and believe that the elimination of this question constitutes great progress. They record only the behavior itself, its evolution and the influences exercised upon it by the surrounding world. Neuroses and psychosomatic ailments are equated with those of their symptoms which are manifested in tangible, external form and can be apprehended by external means. No "inner" cause exists for such disorders. They simply represent inappropriate behavior which must be changed through reeducation, or behavior modification. No attempt is made to investigate inner conflicts.

Of course the inquiry into *when* and *how* inappropriate or mistaken behavior was learned can lead to practical, effective programs for relearning a "healthy" behavior. Behavioral therapy is based on this approach. Communications theory, which describes human relations in terms of model systems consisting of a sender and a receiver, has had a stimulting effect on psychiatry in that it facilitates a better understanding of certain formal defects in communications in the families of the mentally ill. This does inspire the possibility of developing new therapeutic approaches. However, a certain branch of communications-oriented and behavioral therapists who isolate the external data of behavior do so not merely with a view to setting up specific therapeutic problems or goals, but tend to generalize this clinical perspective. They do not allow themselves to enter into the feelings of their clients or patients, and strive to maintain the detached, objective attitude of laboratory technicians. They repress any tendency to identify with the experience of their clients because such identification constitutes a scientific *faux pas*. Clearly there is a direct correlation between this attitude and that technological reification of human problems which I have already described as typical of the climate in many medical institutions and other institutions designed to serve the public. It is equally clear why, as things stand now, psychoanalysts and behavioral therapists find it very difficult to collaborate. As a rule the divisive factor is not the question of which group pursues the more effective mode of therapy. Instead the conflict is a more fundamental one arising from the fact that psychoanalysts search behind external behavior for the interior world of motivating factors, whereas behavioral therapists are actually bent on bracketing out this interior world. Psychoanalysts attempt to enter into and understand the suffering of their patients. To the consistent behaviorist, suffering is merely a suggestive datum peripheral to his real task, the investigation of the phenomena surrounding external behavior. Besides, the behaviorist regards suffering as nothing more than a misleading concept, a mystification. By this view the only accurate knowlege we can glean about suffering is knowledge of that element in suffering which is manifested in behavior that can be observed and measured from the outside. The "inner side" of suffering remains obscure and unreliable. Suffering as such vanishes into the realm of the intangible. This "vanishing act" reflects a hidden purpose, the view that suffering *ought to be* made invisible!

We should not neglect to mention one special variation on the theme of making suffering unrecognizable by technological manipulation. On the surface the phenomenon seems purely *semantic,* but in reality the semantic camouflage is linked to deep-rooted compulsions to social adaptation. The results: Euphemisms are substituted for words which describe misery as misery. Those who are well off invent semantic disguises for the comparative misery of others. By doing so they compel people living under oppressive conditions to feel that they have been granted social validation and, despite the fact that nothing in their real situation has changed, to feel as content as possible with this symbolic satisfaction of their needs. This changing of labels for purely cosmetic purposes is continually taking place all around us. Approximately ten years ago, the whole spectrum of the economically and socially disadvantaged were regarded simply as the "poor," and they accepted this designation. Nor did they demur at the fact that the districts where they lived, which as a rule were segregated from the rest of the community, were called "ghettoes." Recently it has become the custom to describe slums, low-rent districts and areas where facilities are provided for all those in need of public assistance as "community centers," "urban renewal centers," or "centers for social action," although in reality they are centers of social *inaction*. A center for social action is supposed to be the focal point of a community, in which the life of the community is concentrated like the rays of light converging on a burning glass. But in actual fact, as a rule the other citizens of a community have little contact with the denizens of a slum or low-rent housing district. In other words, the life of the community tends to pass these "centers" by. The neologism might suggest the existence of a constructive program to go along with it, if it were not for the fact that, by all indications, the only real change likely to take place is the change of label. In recent years the use of the word "ghetto" has markedly declined in many areas. Other terms which one hears less and less often in the context of sociopolitical debate are "the lower strata," "the economic substratum." Some politicians actually believe that as long as they never use these embarrassing labels, they have made a positive social and political achievement.

These days one is almost tempted to believe that there are hardly any poor, handicapped, or "needy" people left in the world, for such terms are gradually being eliminated from everyday speech. Admittedly it may heighten the self-esteem of many people with problems when they cease to be victims of discriminatory labels. But the elimination of such labels will be of dubious value indeed if it involves nothing more than a make-believe elevation of social status and a make-believe integration into the community. In fact many such changes of nomenclature represent nothing more than cosmetic correctives which are primarily designed to make life easier for those who do not fall into the category of the "needy." The provide a rosy verbal smokescreen which spares us the shock of acknowledging the continued existence of people who are not merely "welfare recipients" but are desperate and poor; of people in need of public assistance, and not merely inhabitants of "centers of social action"; of sick old people, not merely attractive "senior citizens"; of minority groups victimized by discrimination, rather than a society with genuine brotherhood.

Frequently, efforts to modernize and beautify the façades of places which house the suffering in reality reflect the desire to make suffering invisible. Old people's homes and nursing homes are renovated so that they look more attractive from the outside, and new low-rent and public housing facilities are "raised to standard" through the installation of heating systems and showers. Locked psychiatric wards look less bleak after the bars on the windows have been replaced with special glass. On closer inspection we find that in many cases these structural renovations and new furnishings do not actually make places more human, friendlier or more comfortable to live in. The places simply *look* better and can be pointed to with pride. They are less conspicuous and blend better into the surrounding community. Moreover, they participate, so to speak, in technological advances. For a long time now, low-rent districts and public housing facilities have been equipped with paved streets, electric power and street-lights, and telephone booths, just like other areas. Thus they are linked to the technological communications system of the surrounding community. All these innovations serve a useful function. But if nothing more is achieved than the *external* assimilation of a slum to the outside world, and if the only communication with this world takes place on a *technological* plane, unaccompanied by communication with the *people* in the ghettos, institutions, and marginal or minority housing districts "on the wrong side of the tracks," then all this modernization represents nothing more than a new sociotechnological camouflage tactic.

Investigations of the treatment of old people in nursing homes and homes for the elderly continue to reveal shocking instances of abuse. Furthermore, most psychiatric institutions remain desperately under-staffed, and as a result the opportunities offered the mentally ill to engage in therapeutic dialogue and receive aid in the resocialization process are woefully inadequate. Generally, after a temporary improvement, social-therapeutic efforts to better the lot of people in disadvantaged minority communities come to nothing, and everything soon goes back to "business as usual."

However, these cosmetic reforms do achieve one thing: Many of those in distress eagerly repay the efforts to provide them with more pleasant accommodations and, when occasion arises, to describe them by more tactful names, by becoming more submissive and, at times, even willing to violate their own best interests. Thus just before elections were to be held, the citizens of one impoverished community warned each other not to voice any public demands for reforms in marginal or minority communities such as theirs; for if they did so the liberal candidates who were most sympathetic to the cause of the socially disadvantaged might well end up losing many votes. After all, the people said, they were members of that underprivileged minority to whom the majority of society were unwilling to grant further benefits which would be paid for by taxes that came out of their own pockets.

It is essential that we recognize social processes of this kind for what they are. Some social policies are in reality ingenious policies for "wrapping up" misery in a pretty package. And as if this were not enough, these policies actually compel suffering human beings to actively participate in the processes of societal camouflage. The sufferers cease to shriek out their suffering and in the end they themselves are scarcely able to see beneath the make-up and recognize that the suffering even exists.

12

Contempt of Suffering and Contempt of Death. Stoicism, Heroism. The Hidden Pact between the Urge to Live Dangerously and the Fear of Death.

The contempt of suffering takes many forms, ranging all the way from an attitude of imperturbable calm of the type propounded by the Stoics,* to the militant, "heroic" suppression of suffering.

The Eleatics, and later Socrates and Plato, were the first to describe a world of Being reposing within itself in a state of imperturbable calm. In the Hellenistic-Roman era the Epicureans and the Stoics developed this ancient concept into a psychology in which a stark contrast was drawn between a life anchored in self-repose and based on *reason,* and a life in suffering dominated by the passions *(affectus).* The life of reason was regarded as ethically superior to that of suffering. It has become common usage for us to speak of a "stoical attitude" based on man's ability to ward off suffering through active effort. Thereby suffering can be objectified, that is, turned into an external fact. In Seneca we read: "Let nature use our bodies, which belong to her, howsoever she will. We, joyous and courageous, will simply think: What we are losing is something which never really belonged to us in the first place." "Show contempt for pain, for it will either be brought to an end or will end itself." "Even when you yourself suffer misfortune, you must try to yield to the pain no more than reason would have it, rather than custom." [91]   Epictetus taught that even pain could not affect anyone who adopted the proper attitude. "Time frees fools from their pain, but reflection liberates the wise." [18]

* Stoicism was a Greco-Roman school of philosophy which flourished c. 300 B.C.-c. 200 A.D. The Stoic ideal was the Sage who controlled his emotions and was satisfied to possess a single source of beatitude, namely virtue.—Author.

Marcus Aurelius expresses himself in much the same terms: "Pain is either an ill for the body, in which case the body can suffer the distress of it—or for the soul. But to the latter it is granted to assert its serenity and calm—and to refuse to consider pain an affliction." "By remaining collected within itself... the thoughtful soul preserves its serenity, and the governing reason within us suffers no ill effects." [52]

Interpreted in accordance with Scheler's theories, all these notions would mean that in our innermost emotional domain, we can experience a state of being so positive that the effects of potentially depressing sensations can be confined to a relatively superficial plane. When we hear men such as the Stoics speak of serenity, joy and peace of soul, they are clearly referring to something similar to Scheler's "bliss," meaning that inner force which not only makes it possible for people to get along without peripheral surrogate gratifications, but also makes it possible for them to dismiss all troubles and sorrows as essentially trivial.

Obviously, given the dominant attitude towards life in our times, this stoical brand of the conquest of suffering is bound to hold little appeal. As a result, masses of people attempt to find a substitute for the inner serenity and peace they are lacking—often in the form of mood-altering drugs. As most people are aware, in Western nations certain of these mood-altering agents, such as tranquilizers, are purchased in larger quantities than any other kind of drug. For millions of people they have come to be constant companions, helping them to maintain an attitude of permanent detachment towards disquieting, painful and depressing stimuli. What people seek in mood-altering drugs is an inner relaxation and imperturbability distantly related to the Stoic attitude. However, unlike the Stoics they are obliged to procure from an outside source the energy they need to maintain this attitude, for they do not have such energy within themselves.

This technique of passively manufacturing the freedom from suffering by the use of drugs has become a worldwide phenomenon. But despite this widespread dependency on drugs, the ideal of militant self-conquest has continued to survive in our culture. The stereotypical view of masculinity has always involved the avoidance of any expression of grief or pain, and—in Germany perhaps more than elsewhere—this stereotype continues to play a major role in the upbringing of young boys. Don't whine; hold your head high; pull yourself together; bite the bullet. These are among the classic precepts defining so-called "masculine" behavior. It was not so very long ago that clenching one's teeth in order to conceal pain was praised as a supreme virtue. Two

German authors of the Nazi period, Sauerbruch and Wenke, regarded such behavior as the most sublime form of the conquest of pain, which they designated the "heroic." Their hymn of praise to this heroic posture, recorded in 1936 in a book on the nature and significance of suffering *(Wesen und Bedeutung des Schmerzes)*, reveals how closely akin this attitude was to the prevailing spirit of the times. The heroic attitude, they stated, was the hallmark of "the active approach to life of young and unjaded peoples." The individual confronted pain "in order to measure his strength in his own eyes and prove his strength to the world."

Here we have a clear example of the overcompensatory form of defense mechanism against suffering. Suffering is conquered, beaten down like a military adversary. But it remains an *inner* adversary. In this case we do not find the operation of projection, as we did in the strategies for exorcising devils, in which inner conflict is displaced onto an external scapegoat who is made the alleged cause of suffering.

*

Ultimately even the current fashionable preoccupation with a multitude of different physical fitness, diet and exercise programs must be classed among the attempts to suppress suffering through active effort, for they are linked to the ideology that physical activity is the best means of preventing illness and prolonging life. For example, research into heart disease, which people fear more than any other fatal disease besides cancer, has revealed that one contributory factor can be lack of physical exercise. As a result people in many countries have gone in for physical activities of all kinds in the systematic attempt to safeguard their health. The keep-yourself-trim cult is a variation on this same trend, which represents a kind of countermovement to traditional hedonism where one escapes into purely passive forms of surrogate gratification. The dietary cults are also clearly linked to a trend towards asceticism. As we all know, the campaign against overweight goes hand in hand with the current fashion of engaging in countless forms of physical exercise, but the campaign is also directed against toxic substances such as tobacco. The common factor in all these trends lies in the desire to actively discipline oneself into a state of physical fitness which will eliminate, as far as possible, all those factors damaging to health which have thus far been defined by medical science. Many people keep an attentive eye on epidemiological statistics, and whenever possible try to determine, with the aid of diagnostic instruments developed for personal use, how closely they have come to achieving the optimum reduction of risk factors. One might look at this take-charge attitude as a step forward compared to the strategies of pacification and drug sedation, which appear to be characterized by passivity and resignation. However, the excesses in these physical fitness cults strongly suggest that once again we are dealing with an anxiety-ridden attempt to ward off suffering. People try to convince themselves that it is possible for them to exercise or discipline all suffering away, and in this attitude they find themselves, of course, in full agreement with a concept basic to our culture: Man is omnipotent and has the ability to totally arrest the destruction caused by time.

There has been a flood of recent publications, all celebrating running and jogging as the true way of salvation. For a long time a book by James Fixx, called *The Complete Book of Running*, topped American best-seller lists in the non-fiction category. In a review of this book published in the *Frankfurter Rundschau*, H. Tilton states that judging from the promises of the author, jogging was more effective than that magic potion which restored Faust's youth; for it was endowed with the power to prevent heart attacks, retard the aging process, cure depression, improve one's sex life, and make religion meaningful once more. Besides all this, jogging was said to be able to cure the habits of smoking and drinking, to instill better eating habits, and to guarantee a more refreshing sleep. [98]

*

The active effort to prevent or master suffering is linked to inordinate expectations, a form of overcompensation for earlier feelings of helplessness, and leads people to repeatedly seek out exemplars of the *heroic conquest of death*. This explains the enormous fascination exerted over our minds by those "winners" or victors over adversity who—apparently in defiance of the laws of nature—have by some miracle succeeded in resurrecting themselves from the deepest misery. These heroes appear to prove that no suffering is so terrible that it can prevent a person's restoration to greatness, power and physical fitness, provided that he does not allow himself to be beaten. Models of such heroism in the recent past include the perpetually beaming Senator Hubert Humphrey, who for years waged a successful war against bladder cancer, and the apparently indestructible John Wayne, who as an elderly man with only one lung, and then as a man dying of metastisized cancer, could still conjure up the image of the most powerful of Western heroes. The young Englishman Jim Hatfield, a long-time sufferer from heart disease who, after a number of operations on his heart, sailed across the Atlantic, also confirmed the theory of the absolute power of the will when he expressed the hope that other sick people would look at what he had achieved and follow his example (v. *Frankfurter Allgemeine Zeitung*, No. 164, 2 August 1978). A significant number of world-record-holders and Olympic champions have turned to the sport in which they later excelled as a method of overcoming grave illnesses and handicaps. Amputee mountain climbers and blind marathon runners are merely a few among the myriad astounding examples of man's conquest of infirmity and affliction.

These apparently miraculous achievements—miraculous in the sense that they are tantamount to raising oneself from the dead—ultimately belong among that series of everyday trials of strength and courage which enable millions of people to maintain the fantasy of their own indestructibility. The countless little adventures and daring sports feats people perform give them, and those who observe them, a tingling of the nerves which in reality is a secret challenge to death. By proving over and over that we emerge unscathed from hazardous situations we ourselves have staged, we can continue to pretend that we will never be destroyed in any situation. But behind all these little acts of reckless bravado, the fear remains, and to assuage it we must overcompensate by continually performing new feats of daring. Thus the "self-conquest" in which the many little heroes of this world take such pride and which earns them the admiration of others represents anything but the conquest of the thing which threatens them in the innermost core of their being. For it is their failure to overcome their inner fear of their own weakness and finitude, which moves them to plunge into wastelands or take to the seas or the mountains, or expose themselves to any number of *external* objects which inspire fear. *Hence the demonstration of contempt for death is, as a rule, merely a form of overcompensation for just the opposite feeling—namely a particularly acute fear of death.* This is especially true of people who are driven by an inner compulsion to steadily escalate the number or degree of danger of their daredevil performances, and who panic if, for some reason over which they have no control, they are for a time compelled to remain inactive. To be sure, it is a notable achievement of self-help for a person to liberate himself from the threat of depression by means of some perilous adventure. Moreover, it is easy to understand how people could take pride in the fact that their repeated attempts to maintain their emotional balance by this method have generally met with success. Nevertheless we must keep in mind that there exists a clearly-established link between the fear of suffering and the compulsion to seek out danger. In the autobiographies of many people publicly celebrated for their disdain for death, we find—provided that they possess some ability to analyze their own feelings—convincing evidence that the urge to live dangerously is secretly related to a hidden despondency.

Thus, for example, Walter Bonatti, probably the most famous mountain climber in the fifties, describes the period in his life after he had failed in his attempt to scale the southeast wall of the Drus, just following his failure to complete his ascent of K2, the second-highest mountain in the world:

> Before this attack on the Drus, I thought that victory would not mean much to me. In reality defeat plunged me into a state of profound despair. This was really the last drop that made my cup of bitterness overflow; the cup had already been filled to the brim by my failure in the conquest of K2. The crisis has dragged on for too long. A year ago I stopped believing in anything or anyone. I am nervous, excitable, disgusted, unbalanced, aimless and often in despair for no reason. I do not recognize myself.... But one day salvation comes. Depression puts a mad notion into my head. Suddenly a thought occurs to me—the idea of going back to the southwest wall and conquering it alone. It isn't true! I'm not done for yet! One day after another goes by; my extraordinary plan turns into a ray of hope which brings me peace.
>
> (From *The Great Days, I giorni grandi*, Milano, 1971)

The evening before the actual ascent, when he is already beside the rock face, he thinks: "I envy all people who do not, as I do, have to master this kind of task in order to find their way back to themselves.... The following night is terrible. My heart is filled with confusion, like that of a man who has been sentenced to death." [10]

The Grand Prix racecar driver Niki Lauda, who despite having suffered a serious accident has continued racing undeterred, revealed in an interview: "I am afraid of the night. I am afraid that someone is going to jump out at me when it gets dark. Then my heart really begins to pound. But I'm not afraid in my racecar because I'm in control of it." (*Die Zeit*, No. 34, 8 August 1978)

PART THREE

The Task Ahead: Overcoming the Psychical and Social Split within Man

13

The Youth Counterculture and
the Mainstream:
A Challenge to Self-Examination

Thus far we have attempted to show that certain basic social-psychological characteristics of modern Western civilization can be understood as symptoms of a complex which gives this civilization its basic structure. These symptoms represent the traces left by a conflict which took place within the psyche of Western man—a conflict with the medieval image of the one, unique, stern and omnipotent God. These traces permit a hypothetical reconstruction of the following historical process: Man could no longer tolerate his relationship of helpless dependency on his overpowering God. As a result he attempted, as if at a single bound, to acquire divine omnipotence himself by identifying with God, hoping to derive, from his position of absolute personal dominion over his world, a sense of security which he had lost when he ceased to live passively under the sheltering hand of God. He fled from a state of infantile impotence into an illusion of narcissistic omnipotence, and learned to consolidate this illusion by steadily expanding his scientific and technological domination of the world. It now appeared that man was in a position to personally predict the future through the principle of cause and effect and to control it by means of technology, whereas in the past the future had been totally unpredictable and had rested solely in the hands of the Almighty. Every mystery in the universe could, it seemed, be solved by mathematical means. Thus man apparently had at his disposal clear evidence that he was powerful enough to inherit God's function of controlling the world.

But that infantile helplessness and dependency which man supposedly left behind forever when he made his great leap into the myth of his own omnipotence continued to exist deep inside him. Ever since then, impotence has been the repressed, reverse side, the negative identity of our civilization. The persistence of this infantile helplessness is the price we have paid for our abrupt assertion of godlike self-confidence and of that hubristic claim to omnipotence which has dominated Western consciousness in recent centuries. It is the hallmark of the "God Complex," based on the opposition of omnipotence and powerlessness, that the childlike weakness and dependency of medieval man have lived on submerged in the unconscious. Thus, our task in future must be to make these submerged feelings conscious and to reconcile them with that self-image, marked by overcompensatory fantasies of greatness, which has until now determined the very one-sided development of Western civilization.

Unless we are able to effect this reconciliation between the sense of our power and the recognition of our weakness, it is inconceivable that our civilization could ever bridge that gap between the emotional and social polarities we have discussed. Instead we would simply go on being split between activity and passivity, between a power of control without suffering and a suffering over which we have no power of control—and ultimately between infinity and nothingness.

*

Apparently we are passing through a phase in which it is becoming more and more difficult to sustain that fantasy of man's omnipotence which has dominated our culture for three hundred years. Those scientific and technological advances which, for a long time, have lent a solid foundation to this fantasy have, to be sure, continued, and indeed are coming thicker and faster than ever. Man is now able to send satellites into space, breed test-tube babies, perform dazzling feats of genetic manipulation, and implant artificial organs which enable the "organic machine" of the body to go on functioning longer than ever before. But these and many other impressive scientific advances have suddenly begun to appear to us dubious, problematical. An ever-expanding, virtually autonomous supertechnology seems to be getting out of man's control and is increasingly assuming control over human society and thought. [89, 90]   Now that man has mastered the technique of nuclear fission, we are threatened by the spectre of a state dominated by the exigencies of atomic power, a state like that so persuasively predicted by Robert Jungk. [42]   Computer technology is paving the way for the total surveillance of citizens depicted by George Orwell. [101, 46]   Biotechnology is bringing ever closer the day when we will be able to influence human genetic development. We can no longer overlook the interdependence between economic-technological expansion and the growing danger to the ecology. Every year brings further proof that those mechanical devices which were intended to confer on man an ever-expanding power and independence are in fact acquiring a disastrous power over us, increasing our self-alienation, and even directly threatening our survival. Yet we are still caught in a dilemma by our illusion of our own divinity. Our collective neurosis prevents us from imagining any other alternative to the perpetuation of our megalomaniacal expansionism but to plunge back into that state of insignificance, helplessness and terrible loneliness which we experienced in the Middle Ages, and which for over three hundred years has dogged our footsteps in the form of our repressed, negative identity.

If the social-psychological analysis of our society presented here is essentially accurate, then it is easy to understand why the catastrophic predictions of a future based on expansionism and powered by supertechnology should have made people uneasy but failed to induce them to take appropriate action. Our past history allows us to think of only one possible alternative to the eternal progress of ever-increasing power and might: absolute nothingness. After all, our frantic struggle to achieve total technological mastery over the world is not the result of reasoned reflection about the relative usefulness of such a strategy. Instead—in terms of the interpretation presented by this book—this drive derives from a *compulsion* which for the most part is unconscious. Our attempt to scale the visionary heights of divine potency is, in reality, a flight from panic and despair. Ultimately its emotional wellsprings closely parallel those which impelled Bonatti (cf. end of Chapter 12), the famous mountain climber, to launch his record-breaking achievements: in other words, the fear that if he failed to perform these monumental feats, he would lose his identity. From the viewpoint of a detached observer who has not lost his emotional balance, Bonatti apparently chose to voluntarily exchange an inner problem, for which he might easily have found a solution, for an incomparably greater and more dangerous problem. In the same way, the mountain climbing practiced by our entire civilization, taking the form of a compulsion for technological expansion, has carried us directly to the brink of mortal danger—a danger which we have unconsciously chosen for ourselves.

The question is, How to solve our dilemma? Translated into the social-psychological terms elaborated here, this means: How can we overcome that impulse to an eternal flight forward—or rather upward—into the fiction of our godlike omnipotence? How can we curb that fear of nothingness, of total self-annihilation, which has so far prevented us from straying one step from our narcissistic ideal? Or to ask the same question in reverse, how can we fortify the trust in ourselves which we need if we are to look at the repressed side of that inflated self-image with which we overcompensate for our insecurities, and integrating this hidden aspect, see ourselves as a whole? Let us hope that our simply being able to ask these questions is a sign that we are feeling the first subterranean stirrings of a movement towards a collective self-healing—stirrings which at this very moment are seeking a more definitive form.

*

As was previously noted, one supremely important effort towards self-healing is the broad-based trend towards mending the traditional schism between male and female roles. Woman, the socioculturally-elected representative of repressed, negative traits such as insignificance, weakness and suffering, is rebelling against this state of subjugation. Moreover, those representative psychological rebellions on the part of men, cited earlier, reveal that men are taking the first tentative steps towards meeting women halfway. In other words, men—cautiously but, statistics say, in large numbers—are changing their orientation towards traits which have traditionally been labelled "feminine." Thus there are at least hints of a rapprochement between the sexes, even though, on the surface, their overall relations seem to suggest that they are still very much at odds with one another. The tone of many books and other publications by militant feminists, as well as a number of small, belligerent women's groups, could lead one to the mistaken conclusion that what we are seeing today is not a rapprochement between the sexes but rather an aggressive attempt on the part of women to become the rivals of men, and a consequent deepening of the gulf between them. But in reality the current trend towards reconciliation is the dominant one. The social upheavels we are witnessing undoubtedly confirm the existence of a collective trend, on the part of both men and women, to emphasize tenderness and feeling in their lives and to affirm their desire for deeper human contact and for greater emotional openness. Moreover, in all the flurry over the more militant aspects of the women's protest movement, it is easy to overlook that other brand of latent feminism, "male feminism," which we see, for example, in some of the novels of Alberto Moravia, Gunther Grass and Heinrich Böll, as well as in the films of Ingmar Bergman.

In relation to the previously posed questions concerning the problem of how to alter the future, the change in the relations between men and women is exemplary. Here are two groups of people whose relationship has traditionally been based on oppression, and who thus represent the interplay of impotence and omnipotence. Yet they are attempting, however timidly and cautiously, to get closer to each other. This attempt at rapprochement is symptomatic of a growing need to restructure the, traditionally, radically polarized relationship between power and impotence, suffering and the denial of suffering. Moreover, at the same time the rapprochement between the sexes exemplifies perhaps the only efficient and practical approach to the integration of the extremes of power and importance. This approach shows how a greater effort of polarized groups to communicate could result in the discovery of a common position that lies somewhere between the hitherto irreconcilable poles.

*

Women appear to be summoning the strength to work actively to alter their status as a marginal social group and as representatives of the repressed and the inferior, as well as to gradually get men involved in the movement towards liberation too. Yet we must not forget that other new or persisting forms of societal schism, and other processes of disintegration, still prevent us from drawing any overly optimistic conclusions about public attitudes. One schism deserves special mention in the light of our discussion. Although it may not immediately capture our attention, it profoundly affects the microstructures of our society and thus is of the utmost concern to us all. I am referring to the conflict which develops between young people who "drop out" of society and that majority who have adapted to it.

At the same time that women are attempting to move forward into society by achieving emancipation and are urging men to make some appropriate adjustments, their forward movement is intersecting a movement in the opposite direction on the part of many young people who have been dropping out of the establishment and making their homes outside the system, in alternative youth countercultures. For years people were inclined to treat dropping-out as a trivial phenomenon. Thinking in terms of traditional clichés, they decided it was just a fashionable modern variation on the ancient theme of the conflict between the generations—which after all was completely normal. After the boisterous and dramatic student rebellions, people at first ignored the relatively inconspicuous, even clandestine dropout movement taking place among the generation that followed. Often they simply countered the self-absorption and isolation of the disengaged youth by actively shutting them out. However, by now the dropout trend has reached such proportions and taken such disconcerting forms that it has given rise to a widespread disquiet, the same disquiet which already affects the families of dropouts.

The self-isolation of a certain percentage of young people represents, in terms of the views expressed in this book, a displacement of the symptoms involved in the dynamics of social conflict. One might say that, now that collective efforts are being made towards self-healing of the conflict between the sexes, socially-repressed material is manifesting itself in a whole new set of symptoms. Instead of adopting the active role assumed by the liberated woman, young people in many Western nations have adopted an attitude of resignation and have taken over as representatives of the socially repressed. Thus, the battle line between members of the Establishment and the young dropouts has become the central theater where contemporary social conflict is being acted out. At the same time it is also the testing ground which will demonstrate whether the repressed and the repressors can shed their mutual isolation, thresh out their differences, and discover a method for working on their common problems.

In the light of this analysis, the dropout trend within the younger generation ceases to appear an isolated, circumscribed problem, of concern only to those particular individuals or groups who happen to be dropouts. Instead we see it as a problem shared by persons of all age groups, who are trying to live together within our society. The new alternative youth countercultures merely express—by now in a much less obtrusive way than in the past two decades—the fact that our society as a whole is still profoundly disturbed. They articulate the repressed suffering of the well-adjusted. The young dropouts represent everything that most members of society violently shut out in order to preserve their own identity. But those processes being played out among the young show clearly how fragile and threatened is the identity of the majority. In this sense it is helpful and important for us to take a closer look at the ideas and impulses articulated by young dropouts in their esoteric groups. For however confused, eccentric, irrational, pathological and asocial the various manifestations of the youth cultures may appear to the adapted members of society, these manifestations in fact represent the hidden confusion, abnormality, irrationality, sickness and asociability of every one of us. Those people who actually manifest the symptoms of societal malaise are simply unmasking a problem in which everyone shares; their behavior sounds a general alarm and indirectly challenges us all to come to terms with our common conflict.

This "coming to terms" can begin only if those who cut themselves off from suffering are willing to look at suffering in whatever place they have hidden it. First, at least a brief sketch should be given of this phenomenon itself, so that, while treating the theme, we do not indirectly reproduce that same kind of societal repression which we are attempting to clear up.

The dropout movement we are concerned with here takes many forms, all having in common the factor of motivation. Young dropouts feel incapable of going successfully through the socialization process and finding a niche for themselves in a social order which to them appears bizarre and senseless. They feel empty and at sea within the system in which they are supposed to function. Frequently they get caught in a vicious circle in which emotional withdrawal leads to social frustration, and social frustration to further withdrawal. Problems at home, in school, and in learning a trade, as well as unemployment and at times even trouble with the police, contribute to their emotional confusion. Other people label this confusion "instability," "the inability to tolerate frustration," "pathological passivity," "sociopathy." The young fail to pass successfully through the process of inner "toughening-up" which makes it possible for the average young person to achieve that self-discipline which enables him to adapt to the system. But this failure often takes the form of a high degree of sensitivity, emotional openness and genuine human feeling. Incidentally, as everyone is aware, the concept of "being real," of "being up front," plays an exceedingly significant role in the slang or street talk of young people today. One way in which the young manifest their refusal to employ the tactics and strategy of concealment which dominate the customary forms of human intercourse is by their determination to "be real, man."

Where does a dropout end up? That depends, in part, on the amount of anxiety he experiences, on the depth of his urge not to fight back; but it also has to do with the types of alternative life styles available to him, or to which he is exposed. He may take a nosedive straight into alcoholism or drug addiction. Another increasingly important mecca for youthful dropouts is the religious cults which cater to the young. It has been estimated that some two hundred thousand young West Germans are already in contact with these youth cults, and some 150,000 have actually signed over their lives to them. [95]

Another type of subculture is made up of "semi-politicized," i.e., politically aware or engaged young people, frequently university students, who in nations like West Germany may elect to call themselves

"Spontis" (from the German word for "spontaneous"), or "urban redskins" or "mescaleros," or who may not have any particular designation at all.

These politically-oriented groups are the ones with which the public is least familiar, despite the fact that, like the other youth groups, they involve considerable numbers of people. It is estimated that at many German universities, some 10-15% of the students belong to one of these factions, which however are highly heterogeneous in character. They do, to be sure, voice a mood of political protest, but at least for the time being they are displaying no urge toward political activism. W.D. Narr says of the members of the political youth movement: "You no longer commit parricide in order to reform, revolutionize and overthrow the existing society. You merely refrain from attaching yourself to this society at all, you go underground, you lay it all aside, you say goodbye to it all." [60]

A small number of young Germans organize their lives within an alternative subculture of which T. Fichter and S. Lönnendonker have drawn the following sketch taken from a 1978 issue of *Die Zeit:*

> In all the larger cities of West Germany, and in West Berlin, thousands of young people with political goals and concerns live in a voluntary ghetto. The average local 'urban redskin' wakes up in the common dwelling, goes out to buy breakfast rolls at the local bakery around the corner and then gets his muesli [health-food cereal] from Aunt Emma's Store, which specializes in macrobiotic foods, reads *Pflasterstrand, Info-BUG, zitty,* and then—if he is not a devotee of the never-work school of thought—goes to work in a little crafts shop he organized himself, or to an 'alternative project' involving social welfare work; on every fifth day he puts time in at a privately-organized cooperative children's playgroup; he gets his clonker of a car patched up at an auto repair shop run by people with left-wing political convictions; in the evening he goes to see *Casablanca* in a theater that specializes in old films; after that he can be found in a tearoom, in a left-wing hangout, or listening to records in the music joint or disco. The literature he reads in bed at night comes from the co-op bookstore. The ghetto has physicians' co-ops, lawyers' co-ops, women's counselling centers, men's and women's groups. Almost every aspect of life is provided for by some 'alternative' resource... At the same time, the communication between people is intensive compared to that practiced by the average German middle-class citizen. The local urban redskins, Spontis and antiauthoritarian students talk with these 'average citizens' only

when they have to—with policemen, for example, during a police raid. In West Berlin and Frankfurt some people who belong to this 'scene' are proud of the fact that for two and a half years they have not exchanged so much as one word with any outsider. [60]

Only a few of the dropouts in this category move exclusively within a ghetto-like, closed-off alternative system like the one just described, whereas a great many others, at least on the surface, remain halfway integrated with the outside world. Nevertheless, almost all of them undergo a process of inner dissociation which ends in a pronounced degree of detachment. They study or hold down some sort of job without experiencing ambition, without developing "career goals." The way they spend their time in the here and now is more important to them than making provision for their future financial security or position in society. They are repelled by the demonstrative moral pathos with which power politics, whether on a grand or a minor scale, are carried on all around them. Their left-wing orientation gives many of them a jaundiced view of authority, a profound distrust of those Powers That Be who already resent them for their maintenance of a critical aloofness and their refusal to take seriously many middle-class rituals and regulations, and who may well threaten them with some kind of disciplinary action. They want to preserve their freedom to observe things skeptically from the outside, whereas other people expect them to adjust, to "fit in," totally, even on the inside. They refuse to automatically take something seriously just because it is customary, or even obligatory, to do so; yet they pursue with great earnestness any aim of their own group which appears to them to have some substance, even if people "on the outside" happen to consider it frivolous and more or less unimportant. As a rule their relationships with other members of their group are very important to them. In fact, one of their most pronounced traits is their search for contact, for closeness to one another. Another trait, closely related to their guiding principle of authenticity, is the bluntness or straightforwardness with which they act and express themselves. The artifices of concealment, shady dealings, hypocrisy and guile are repellent to them. Those elements in their behavior which other people label as childish, frivolous, tactless and undignified, they themselves experience as sincerity, as a meaningful alternative to the hypocrisies and masquerades of conventional social behavior.

Still other groups are made up of members who get together outside this new species of voluntary ghetto, or who leave the ghettos to live a "natural" life in a commune somewhere out in the country, to do a little farming without the use of artificial fertilizers and to eat food which they themselves have grown. Such groups attract people who feel confined by the restraints of urban life, or who fail to establish themselves as members of some self-contained, sealed-off alternative subculture within the city.

Assuming that the members of the Establishment and the counterculture do in fact portray their common, interdependent social conflicts in terms of a polarity, the question is: *What can the majority of our society learn about their own repressions by looking into the negative mirror image of the counterculture?*

*

Alcoholism and drug abuse are, essentially, merely the most exaggerated forms of that hedonistic behavior, designed to sedate pain, which we have described as one of the standard techniques of our time for running away from suffering. In terms of Scheler's law concerning the reciprocal relationship between the degree of inner suffering and the compulsion to turn to superficial forms of gratification, alcohol- and drug-oriented alternative culture groups signal an extreme of unhappiness which can no longer be muted with widely-used "normal" sedatives such as anti-depressants, valium and sleeping-pills. The young alcoholics and drug addicts regress to the same state of impatience and helplessness which characterizes small children, who are incapable of renouncing immediate oral gratification. But the behavior of addicts is merely an extreme, uninhibited form of the behavior of most orderly, "solid" citizens. In other words, in both cases life centers around the need to anesthetize or sedate oneself in order to cover up a feeling of desolation, vulnerability and general forlornness. Millions of average citizens might do well to note the fact that alcoholics and drug addicts merely exhibit a quantitative intensification of their own problems, and that the only "advantage" they have over an addict is the fact that their use of mood-elevating or sedative drugs is more consistent with social norms than what we habitually term "drug abuse."

On the other hand, the counterculture of the religious cults offers a real qualitative alternative to the values of the society. The religious cults have broken with the old central values of Western civilization. The ideals of the Enlightenment have no place here. The mystical ways of salvation offered by the various new-wave Oriental religions demand absolute faith of their adherents. In this setting the cult of the individual is a thing of the past. The individual dedicates his life to the cult group without reservation. From now on he thinks and does only what the group demands. At their behest he renounces all his worldly goods, all his previous ties, all social norms.

The very fact that it is possible to break radically with the traditional Western way of life—i.e., to follow a way which demands obedience instead of self-determination, blind faith instead of critical rationality, poverty instead of prosperity, uncompromising collectivism instead of the preservation of individual identity—challenges those who have not dropped out by revealing to them the relativity of the world order which they have hitherto accepted without question. Thus they can no longer take for granted the values for which they have slaved, fought and sacrificed all their lives. Moreover, they must now admit that the "reason for it all" simply gets lost when life consists in playing along with the automatically functioning machinery of the social mill. The young religious cultists can immediately tell you the name of their God or the saints revered by their sect. They are emotionally committed. They are absolutely positive that they not only know "the reason for it all," but that their salvation lies in their total submission to their faith. If outsiders remonstrate with them, saying, "But you're losing yourselves!", they reply that it is the others who are losing themselves: "We didn't really find ourselves until we joined the cult. *You're* the ones who lost yourselves long ago, but you don't recognize it, or you simply don't want to notice!" "We're not the ones who live outside ourselves, you are!" "In your eyes we're the outsiders because we are in the minority. You can only think in term of statistics. In reality we are in the very center of the truth. We are more protected in the cult and in God than you have ever been in your whole lives!" And when parents accuse their children of having given up many valuable things—self-cultivation, a discriminating mind, artistic interest, and so on—for the sake of life in the cult group, and tell them that they seem emotionally impoverished since they joined the group, the young people reply that in another sense, which is beyond their parents' understanding, they have become much richer, more clear-sighted, and more knowledgeable than they used to be, and that they pity their parents because they have no access to the truth which has revealed itself to them.

People "on the outside" do indeed find it difficult to recognize their own problems in the youth religion subculture. For at first glance they fail to perceive anything which their lives and the lives of young cult members have in common. The bizarre mysticism of the new religions merely baffles them. The collectivistic life style practiced by many cult groups seems archaic and primitive, and the personality changes which life in the group often effects in people—including a general deterioration and narrowing of mental horizons—frightens rather than attracts others. To outsiders, the world of the cults seems very remote and in no way a disguised articulation of problems common to both groups.

Nevertheless, there is an obvious underlying relationship between the *import* of the two life styles. The flight into total certitude, absolute faith, can be interpreted as an escape from total spiritual rootlessness, from the sense of being cast adrift. And the absolute self-surrender which marks life in the religious cult may simply be a deep-rooted protest against the repellent egocentrism of a competitive society. The narrowing of interests, the apparent intellectual stagnation, could mean the renunciation of the compulsion to always "keep up with what's happening" so that one can participate and get one's share of power. In short, where the young dropouts go depends on where they came from. Their reaction is a response to the situation they grew up in and to the sociocultural atmosphere which surrounds them. This reaction can be summarized approximately as follows: "In your society there are only two possibilities: Either one conforms absolutely, or one makes a new start from the opposite tack. We try to stay far away from you because the pressure you put on us to conform makes it impossible for us to live anywhere near you. We need to live a life style the exact opposite of yours in order not to be swallowed up by you again. Your God was taken over and corrupted long ago by the power politics of the Church and by your own delusions of grandeur. We are unable to free him. Thus we must find ourselves a new God. You have an unalterable conviction that you can and must program your lives and futures through technology and reduce them to mathematical calculations solely on the basis of economic principles. Unlike you, we see our only hope in the possibility of finding sanctuary in a principle of life derived from a completely different culture, a magical, mystical world of the spirit. We need absolute silence in order to meditate and regenerate ourselves from within, whereas your whole approach to life is designed to conceal these spiritual regions by constantly drowning them out with loud noises, by hushing them up on the surface, and by a frenzy of practical activity."

Viewed in these terms, the two positions fit like two interlocking parts of a puzzle. Moreover, as they grow older these same young people form a link between the two polarized cultures. And if the relatives and friends they leave behind later tell them, "We don't recognize you any more, you've become completely different people," they do so not simply because the young dropouts do not want to be recognized, but also because they themselves are often afraid that if they recognize their prodigal children or friends, they will be building a bridge to that alien world which threatens the entire foundation of their lives.

The left-wing politically-oriented alternative culture groups spare other people the ordeal of having to witness religious fanaticism, exotic rituals and a totalitarian collectivism which at times seems almost terrifying. Their behavior patterns are more familiar to people. And yet precisely because they appear less alien, their protest against the established society becomes more tangible and more threatening. Many "Establishment types" experience the attitude of protest adopted by these groups as potentially destructive, as something that could one day explode and turn into a dangerous form of political activism to combat the way of life they themselves support. But quite apart from their sense that their future may be threatened, most members of the Establishment feel provoked by the alternative subculture of the urban redskins, the left-wing Spontis and the other antiauthoritarians because these groups express a certain mood or state of mind which has been influencing people for a long time, but which they themselves never dared to express openly. This state of mind involves a subterranean sense of discontent and discomfort at being exploited and dictated to by established authorities who appear incapable of halting the increasing dehumanization of many areas of life. More and more people are coming to feel that the major political parties and opposing ideological camps are growing increasingly alike, that they are producing slogans but no genuine ideas. Moreover, it seems that the members of every major party feel compelled to overdramatize scandals in the personal lives of their political opponents, or to create media events out of any other halfway interesting and provocative item they can dredge up, in order to establish any contrast at all between themselves and other candidates. To a large extent, political parties, governments and large organizations appear concerned solely with themselves, with the technical functioning of their various bureaucracies, and with maintaining an attractive public image, while at the same time they pay less and less attention to the opinions of their constituents. The latter in turn feel increasingly neglected and let down by a political system in which those in responsible positions often confess—openly and shamelessly—that much of what they do is done purely to gain or to maintain their power. All these phenomena have aroused a dull animosity, manifested in the swelling tide of protest movements, as well as—at least in countries like West Germany and the United States—in a new type of voter behavior. Many people can no longer identify strongly with any of the major political parties. They tend

to experience a general, unfocussed feeling of negativity towards the
established society. But this negativity is spreading. The indeterminate
character of the animosity here is shown by the fact that suddenly people
and groups who have no clearly-defined platforms but are simply *against*
everything and promise that they will represent the interests of the
ordinary citizen, are meeting with a positive response from voters. They
need only say that they want to protect everyone from toxic substances and
noise pollution, badly constructed cities and housing, radioactivity, the
defacing of the natural environment, and excessive government control.
They do not even have to state precisely how they intend to accomplish all
this and what positive projects they have in mind in addition to stopping
everything that is being done wrong. The important thing is that they
portray themselves as exponents of the general unrest, and claim that they
will get rid of whatever is annoying people or making them afraid.

This trend to express negative feelings about the status quo
coincides with the views which the radical Spontis and other alternative
culture groups have been articulating for a long time. Occasionally this
seeming communality of interests leads to encounters between the two
groups—encounters which are confusing to all concerned—during broad-
based grass roots protest actions in which a potpourri of people of all
different stamps and backgrounds get together and find that they are
united, in certain areas, by the same underlying purpose.

Naturally such coalitions are resisted by the Establishment, as well
as by the silent majority whose assumption that they must adjust to the
system became part of them so long ago, and has become so deeply
ingrained, that if any nagging little doubts arise, they have no alternative
but to exert additional pressure to suppress them. The greater the effort it
costs them to suppress their feelings of resentment and their impulses to
protest, the more difficult it is for them not to react with hostility to any
alternative culture movement with slightly radical overtones.

*

Unlike the battle over sexual roles, the conflict between the alternative
youth subcultures and the rest of society has not resulted in anything
which might be regarded as a trend, on the part of the adversaries, to get
together and try to work out their differences. At the moment it is
extremely difficult to predict whether the dropout movement is going to
increase in scope, whether the gulf between the dropouts and those who
"fit in" will deepen further, or whether the situation will result in an
increase in tension, in stagnation, or, at some time in the future, in a

movement towards reintegration. For the time being the whole situation between the dropout and the rest of society is pathological. Apart from their families, who are directly affected by the behavior of dropouts, most of the solidly-entrenched middle class are maintaining a defensive strategy. Many still refuse to look more closely at the phenomenon of the dropout.

Although the number of deaths resulting from heroin abuse has mounted alarmingly, and although young people are becoming heavy drinkers at an earlier and earlier age, counselling facilities for addicts are still totally inadequate in most communities. This fact is symptomatic of our persistent tendency to trivialize the whole problem of addiction. Although the media frequently use the adjective "alarming," this dramatic word anticipates a response which in fact is very seldom forthcoming. The available preventive and therapeutic measures in no way reflect, either quantitatively or qualitatively, the fact that addiction is not a nuisance to be controlled by the police (necessary as such control may sometimes be). On the contrary, in many cases it involves acute emotional illness, to cure which demands the most intensive long-term work with the afflicted person. But this help can be offered only if society as a whole adopts a responsible, positive and sympathetic posture—only if we acknowledge the relationship between our own habit of self-sedation and the behavior of the addict, and see in this relationship a source of solidarity and a reason for commitment to an active role in bringing about change.

But instead the majority of people still feel little more than antipathy and latent desires to punish the addict. Fear aroused by the sense of being personally threatened encourages unconscious needs to simply bracket out the problem, thus enabling oneself to go on repressing the fact that one does in fact feel threatened.* The case history of a psychoanalytic patient, which appears at the end of this book, will provide us with a precise and suggestive illustration of the dynamics of this process. It shows how an addict, to prevent his own breakdown, splits off his addiction from the rest of his personality and inflicts the problem on someone else.

---

*   The unique documentary account, written in German by a fifteen-year-old girl, Christiane F., under the title *Wir Kinder vom Bahnhof-Zoo* ("Us Kids at the Railroad Station Zoo"), edited by Kai Hermann and Horst Rieck, Stern-Buch 1979, reveals that society, in response to its own repressive urges, not only ignores and neglects the affliction of drug addiction, but that some members of this society deliberately promote addiction even in children, in order to provide a plentiful supply of "human commodities" for the child prostitution market, which is tacitly tolerated by our whole society.—Author.

Unquestionably members of the youth-oriented religious cults also frequently exhibit behavior which could be described as addictive. Many sects demand total emotional submission from their members. But if the young people actually grant this submission—and they often do—it reveals that they already had a leaning in that direction and actively participated in their own subjugation. They have been sworn in, but they themselves took part in the oath. But the people they leave behind do not want to admit this fact. They choose to believe that most of the young people who join religious cults would never have cooperated of their own free will, without being worked over, subjected to diabolical tricks, hypnosis and brainwashing, and forced into sexual accommodation. In fact there are reliable indications that many cults do exert a great deal of pressure on their captives to turn them into obedient slaves.* Moreover, clearly some cult leaders have a strong vested interest in the money which they amass through the pious begging of their disciples. But it would be an illusion, a mere attempt to ward off anxiety, to try to dismiss the phenomenon of the religious cults as *exclusively* the fault of wicked seducers with no other than the familiar motives of material greed and hunger for power. To be sure, if we did so, everything would appear to be in order, and at least to some degree the cults would indirectly serve to confirm our traditional norms. Naturally it would be bad enough if the cults were a clandestine profit-making enterprise in the hands of a well-disguised religious Mafia, but at least then it would be easy to tell the difference between oneself and them. Moreover, from this viewpoint it would be easy to simply pity those of our own acquaintances who have innocently fallen prey to cult groups, and whom we could then look on as unsuspecting, passive victims of a criminal syndicate specializing in psychoterrorism. In this case we ourselves could, with an easy conscience, take the side of the confused and innocent victims—despairing, perhaps, if we happen to be members of the cult member's family—but never despairing of ourselves.

This biassed attitude of those outside the religious cult scene does enable them to defend their own identities, but it does not help to eliminate their misapprehensions about cult members. Many efforts to prevent young people from joining cults, or to rehabilitate them afterwards, fail

* Unquestionably, hypnotic techniques are employed to some extent, but the effectiveness of these techniques assumes a certain predisposition on the part of the young people—a predisposition tantamount to a longing—to let someone else run their lives. The recent mass suicide of the followers of the Reverend Jim Jones in Guyana demonstrated in a most tragic manner the ghastly consequences of these destructive suggestions.—Author.

because parents, teachers and clergymen invariably talk to the dropout about the security of belonging to the system, and in general about those positive societal values which he gave up to join the cult in the first place. Frequently young people no longer regard such values as values at all, and experience the security of the system as a societal shackle. Thus counselling and therapy are based on an appeal which tends not to attract but to further repel those to whom it is addressed. For dropouts simply do not experience the system into which they are expected to reintegrate themselves as sheltering and meaningful. Absurd as it may sound, many young runaways and dropouts would be willing to stay at home if only their parents and other central figures in their lives were really as fulfilled and happy as they pretend to be in their own accommodation to social norms. The young apostates have often been exposed to aggression in their pre-cult environment. This reveals to them the tensions to which the people they are leaving behind are exposed because of their own deep-seated lack of fulfillment.

The dynamics just described are most apparent in reactions to left-wing or radical groups. The rage of the solid citizen towards "left-wing deviates" stems not from his feeling that some abstract "order" is being called into question, but from the sense that he is personally endangered by any threat to his system of repression. We have already discussed this reaction in detail with reference to the phenomenon of the projective defense mechanism against suffering. Thus in the present context our primary concern is to find a constructive solution to a societal paradox which at first glance strikes us as absurd: The vast majority of people long for a natural life, for a life of less pressure and constraint, for more spontaneous modes of relating to other people, for deeper interpersonal communication, and for a more responsible voice in personal relationships. Yet after they have spent years being trained to behave in a way quite different from the way they really want to, in the end they crush their own needs, which continually collide with the norms imposed on them from outside. Ultimately, either openly or secretly, they support the persecution of, and discrimination against, precisely those people who represent their own repressed desires. Moreover, among other things this situation also involves a conflict between the generations, for naturally the degree of inner capitulation to the system is proportional to the length of time a person has been exposed to the pressure to conform, and to the extent to which his conformity has become deeply fixated as a result of his having established himself in certain conventional social roles. Thus the fact that, as a general rule, people tend to resist radical alternatives more fiercely as

they themselves grow older is not directly related to the natural aging
process but, for the most part, results from a socially-determined
reinforcement of repressions and the need to relieve oneself of emotional
burdens by the use of projective mechanisms.

*

If we take as our starting point the idea that the youth subcultures which
cut themselves off from society are at the same time cut off by society, that
the conventional majority that feels rejected by the subcultures is at the
same time actively rejecting them, and that at bottom these two groups have
been polarized by an inner problem which they both face, then a
constructive solution must depend upon the possibility of making visible
what binds majority and minority together. Quite apart from any kind of
moral evaluation, this statement makes sense as an elementary *logical*
deduction. Each side of a polarity should always be viewed in conjunction
with the other. Media representatives, scientists, politicians, clergymen and
therapists who treat the theme of subcultures should always present them
in their bipolar aspect. Unfortunately most analyses, descriptions and
political-therapeutic tactics examine only isolated members of an
alternative subculture, or at best the entire subculture *en masse*, and
unintentionally deepen the conflict between subculture and society rather
than helping to treat it. Such an unrepresentative analysis actively
contributes to the process of societal repression which we ought to be trying
to eliminate step by step.

*

Most scientific studies of alternative subcultures, for example, fall straight
into the trap of perpetuating this pernicious strategy of repression. They
analyze the various countercultures as if these represented a single tribe; or
as if the guiding principles shared by the various groups represented a kind
of germ which infects only these particular specimens of humanity and has
spared everyone else. To be sure, recently researchers have begun to
incorporate data concerning family background and childhood history
into their studies of selected alternative groups, and this at least is a step in
the right direction. In scholarly research one can always justify one's
position in terms of methodological arguments—in this case by saying that
if one tries to investigate too much material at the same time, one can no
longer keep the mass of data under control. The questions become too
complex, the field of study too tortuous. Thus, it appears, for the sake of
scientific tidiness one is forced to arbitrarily circumscribe one's material,

for this tidiness is the chief requirement of the morality of science. The researcher eases his conscience by telling himself that one can attack a single problem-complex, with its many ramifications, from many diverse angles and draw on many disciplines, either by studying all these aspects at the same time, or one by one. Thus—so it would seem—in the end it should be possible to piece all the different results together to form a single mosaic; then one would know exactly how everything fits together.

However, in the present case we are not dealing with elements which can be isolated by nature and which are linked together merely by addition. If one does not perceive from the outset that schisms in our society originally evolve out of a reciprocal process of questions-and-answers, or problems-and-responses, and if one fails to pursue this aspect of *dialogue* from the very beginning, then one will never do so later on.

The truth of all this should be immediately apparent to everyone. Moreover, we continually learn that isolated studies of dropout or anti-Establishment groups produce very little in the way of solid results. Someone may record the fact that among the devotees of the new religions, or among the German "urban redskins" and Spontis, there is a higher than average incidence of neurotic symptoms, sexual disorders, introversion, divorced parents, the early death of a parent, or internment in a boarding school or public institution. And yet all these traits, either singly or as a group, can also be detected in many other people who never abandon "straight" society for an alternative, sub- or counterculture. Besides, even if, through the analysis of causative factors, one could draw a profile of "susceptible types," or of combinations of factors which particularly predispose a person to join a religious cult, what practical use could one make of the information? Ought we, in this case, to place the carriers of such traits under special supervision, subject them to certain reeducation procedures, maintain them under a kind of protective quarantine? Thus a unilateral diagnosis of the alternative culture groups, in isolation from the study of the dominant culture, supplies us with no clues about practical solutions to our problems. After we had found out everything there was to know about that one half of the polarity of culture-counterculture, our findings would in no way affect the possibility that our society might decide to pursue a strategy of persecution of deviant behavior which would merely intensify the problem rather than help to eliminate it.

Moreover, studies of the personal histories of cult members frequently reveal that people who have later joined cults or "dropped out," appeared completely "normal" before this aberration: close to their families, scrupulous, gentle, often perhaps even overly well-adjusted. Even the case histories of prominent terrorists sometime reveal these same traits of amiability and tractability. Yet scholars zealously continue their investigations along the same old lines, as if one day they might discover in the individuals themselves, or in their immediate surroundings, some sort of specific religious-cult or terrorist virus.

It is clear that scientists and scholars often serve as the handmaids of societal repression when they approach the problem in accordance with the moral code of scientific neatness. They create a "methodologically sound" approach to their inquiries, thereby bracketing out those complex, intermeshing factors which alone could enable them to arrive at a unified, all-embracing understanding of the problem. But this unified picture also presupposes a desire to understand, which in the present case would mean a determination to include data on the social environment within the context of the explanation. The question we should be asking the dropout is not simply: What is *your* problem, what is driving *you* out of society? At the same time we should be asking: What is *our* problem, what are we doing that makes it hard for you to live among us? What can *we* do to make attractive to you the idea of remaining in our society? To what abuses on *our* part are you drawing attention by your behavior? Do you no longer credit our basic values, or does your disenchantment stem from that fact that we ourselves have betrayed our values and that you are attempting to revive them by being different from us? Does our situation show the same principle as the traditional relationship between the sexes—namely that *one group merely acts out, in a helpless, pathological, confused and aggressive way, what is actually the repressed disease of the other?*

This question is linked to an insight of central importance: Those researchers and journalists who appear to be studying the problem of the dropout in a detached manner are, along with the entire social milieu, themselves implicated in the problem from the outset. They are implicated not merely in the sense that they are to blame, but in the sense that they are suffering from the same problems as the dropout. The recognition of this truth could bring with it an overwhelming snese of relief. When a "well-adjusted" person becomes aware that he is nowhere near as "together," as fit, autonomous, and self-confident as he (and everyone else) pretends to be a hundred times a day in the course of his social activities, he experiences the incredibly liberating effect of openly confessing one's weakness and fragility. Thus we might also interpret the youth protest movements which have been articulating themselves in various forms over the course of the last twenty years or so as an indirect, therapeutically relevant appeal to society to become aware of its own inner anguish, which it has denied on the conscious level, by taking a look at the anguish experienced by these outsiders.*

We can observe this type of self-critical reaction, leading to acknowledgement of one's own implication in an all-embracing societal problem, among the families of young cult members and other dropouts, who sometimes get together to form self-help groups. In recent years we have often met parents who do not adopt a self-righteous attitude and totally disassociate themselves from the children who have walked out on their world, but instead openly confess their own despair and perplexity. They know that they themselves need help, just as they would like to help their young prodigals. But our concern here is not so much the solution of individual problems as it is a question of the dynamics of society at large. Observation suggests that many of the youthful dropouts would be quite content, in the future, to stay within the mainstream of society, if only this society offered them more of those things which they are compelled to seek elsewhere: *communication, sensitivity, a sense of solidarity, and a concern with the essential problems of human life, faith and meaning.* And it would, above all, prove highly beneficial to society itself to take care of some of the human needs which, to its own detriment, it consistently represses. For society has an urgent need to effect its own regeneration— with the aid of sensitive young people whose impulses, up to now, it has foolishly failed to recognize as its own, attributing them to "someone else out there." Indeed, these impulses are themselves a part of society. And if many phenomena of the alternative subcultures appear eccentric, disconcerting, extreme, or even mad, they merely represent the individual aberrations found within any ghetto culture which has been driven into exile by the outside world.

But clearly it is difficult for most people to engage in this kind of self-critical diagnosis and to conceive of a self-help therapy based on the

---

* The recently published findings of R. Grossharth-Maticek, concerning the student radicals, offer intriguing and valuable insights into the interrelationship, the "dialogue," between student radicalism and environmental factors. The author summarizes his findings as follows: "In general one can say that left-wing radicalism is a problem involving multiple factors, and that it occurs as a result of the interaction between the socialization instilled by the family, psychic pathology, sexual disorders, personality traits, and the behavior of academic institutions and governmental representatives. If one link in this chain were to be missing, there would be insufficient motivation for left-wing radicalism to exist." [36]   However, in the public discussion of these findings, comparatively little emphasis has been placed on the contributory social factors. There exists an unmistakable tendency, on the part of both researchers and the public, to concern themselves solely with the more shocking or unusual

recognition of mutual problems, although it appears absolutely necessary to do so. What are the deeper reasons for our persistent defensive posture? Why are we still dominated by an apparently irreconcilable determination to segregate from ourselves those who give up, who withdraw, who drop out, who develop alternative life styles, or who engage in open protest? Why this prevailing urge to downgrade those who differ from ourselves?

Our anxiety and hesitation with regard to "deviant behavior" is a sign of our suspicion that an offbeat life style might represent more than just a slight shift in attitude and behavior—that in fact once one has set out on the path to change, it will inevitably lead to cataclysms on a vast cultural-revolutionary scale. Thus our task should be to completely alter the fundamental relationship between power and suffering, and to abandon the norm, which has held sway over us for three hundred years, of the repression of our awareness of impotence and finitude. However, many facets of our culture are dependent on this norm: not only a complex system of individual behavior patterns, but also the entire hierarchical structure of our social existence both in our jobs and with our families, as well as our economic system and the fundamental concept of man's technological domination of nature. All these phenomena represent the interrelated components of our identity as a society, an identity which we have defined by the formula: Self-preservation through the internalized equation, Man = God. Can we go on living if we give up this support, this over-compensatory, narcissistic way of ensuring our survival? Must we not sink back into a state of helpless nonentity now that we have destroyed the protective God we chose to depose and replace? And is it even possible for us to gradually reform all those social structures which have become so deeply rooted in our culture, and which are based on that principle of omnipotence which has seemed valid to us until now?

---

sexual traits of the radicals. The fear, which the majority of people continue to feel, of accepting any portion of the responsibility for the problem of radical extremism causes them to restrict the scope of, and thus to adulterate, research findings in this area in the very process of analyzing them. Thus in these analyses, we suddenly find political radicalism—how reassuring!—being viewed principally as a product of some orgasmic disorder, of sadistic sexual fantasies, or of homosexual tendencies on the part of those who support radical views.—Author.

14

The Liberation of Corrupted Love

As we have noted, the small child who feels insecure in his relationship with his parents and flees from it into an attitude of narcissistic omnipotence carries with him from that time on, in a repressed form, the same childlike helplessness which—on the surface—he supposedly escaped long ago. Within his intrapsychic structure, the old alternative between defenseless weakness and infinite grandeur lives on in the same proportions it possessed when he was a child. This intrapsychic model, which carried over to the postmedieval relationship between man and God, would explain why our imaginations have preserved not only the archaic, monumental, medieval image of God, but also its antitype: the needy and forlorn little child. It also explains why we cannot quite reconcile with our self-image the idea that partners of equal status can construct a lasting society. The classical constellation underlying our civilization is that of the weak, childlike being burdened with original sin, confronting the towering figure of the Almighty, severe in His judgments, seated on His high throne. By identifying with this omnipotent figure, man created the self-image of an inflated, dominating individual. At the same time he has been carrying around with him the repressed, childlike, obverse side of his personality, like the stunted remains of a Siamese twin: the immature ego of medieval man. This vertically-oriented, asymmetrical relationship between the figure of the superparent and the weak little child is the model which has been psychically internalized by members of our culture, and which per-petuates itself in all our concepts of human relationships. Thus it never became possible for us to develop a model of a society made up of emancipated, adult human beings. Our internalized "God complex" has left a vacuum between the phase of childhood dependency and that of narcissistic inflation. People have either continued to picture themselves as *very small*, an image which they have tried to suppress, or as *very large*, an image which the tactic of repression persuades them is accurate. This alternative does not permit man to develop the kind of self-image which alone can help him, in these difficult days, to find a truly salutary way of living with his fellows: Namely an image of medium-sized human beings, living in a community made up of persons of equal status, who desire to realize their freedom within this community rather than in opposition to it, and who are not compelled to hate or fear their mutual dependency because they experience it as a one-sided form of repression, but rather are able to affirm it as a meaningful and reciprocal way of relating to and relying on each other.

It is the fixation on the antithesis superman-dwarf—a fixation that psychoanalysis calls a complex—that so far has prevented us from creating an image of a society based on the direct, unconstrained, unmediated sense that people are all intimately linked together. Instead of the egalitarian view, we perceive two dominant trends in recent intellectual thought. The first takes as its starting-point the self-deification of the individual ego. This is the Cartesian ego, which posits its own certitude before all else. The same supposition underlies the concept of the individual in the form of the universe-reflecting monad of Leibniz, and the magnificent rational being evoked by the Idealists, as well as the self-seeking human predator of Thomas Hobbes, Nietzsche's raging Superman, and finally the liberated Narcissus in Marcuse's utopia. All these concepts center not, or not primarily, around men in society, but around the isolated individual, man "on his own." In the words of Norbert Elias, man viewed thus is the *homo clausus* or the "boxed-in self." When we take a closer look at Rousseau's notion of the equality of all men—a dream which he bequeathed to the French Revolution—we perceive an anarchistic and utopian equality among extreme individualists. The second trend in recent social thought involves the antitype to the hubristic narcissist, and remains unreconciled with the first trend. This antitype is the small and impotent being, the devout child in the hands of God, whom we find in Pascal; or Nietzsche's slave and herd men, or the immature, stupid, passive child-woman conceived by Schopenhauer.

*

The internally-fixated model of human relationships as hierarchical structures involving an above and below, a superior and an inferior, also totally determines the shape of our *sociocultural patterns of love relationships*. Apart from narcissistic self-love, love is always conceived by us exclusively as love of a person on a lower or on a higher level than ourselves, as a force which travels up or down. Pascal says that we are incapable of loving each other on equal terms. Either one loves oneself or one loves God, or perhaps more precisely, one is loved *by* God. The love between parents and children is a miniature reproduction of that between the all-powerful God and his human children, as is—in our tradition—the love between the male who dominates and protects on the one hand, and the childlike, submissive woman on the other. Even the classical model of the love of the Good Samaritan is in tune with this same principle: The strong man bends down, condescends to help the weak, the poor and injured. We automatically associate the terms "philanthropy" and "charity" with this same motion of bending down in mercy. And it seems to us self-evident that sympathy and compassion involve precisely the same kind of disparity between large and small, between power and suffering. Yet there is no real reason why the "love of one's fellow man" ought not to develop between persons of equal rank, or why people should not sympathize with one another even if no fixed, hierarchical relationship has automatically been established between them.

The association of love with an unequivocally fixed disparity of power is something we take so much for granted that we are almost never surprised at the paradox underlying this notion. Yet it would seem far more reasonable to believe that love, in its purest form, would flourish between people who can communicate with each other unburdened by any kind of hierarchical imbalance between them. Thus, for example, the prevalent modern ideal of the relationship between men and women is that of a bond between emancipated equals, a bond in which the man and the woman love one another as absolutely equal partners. Thus it does not seem at all far-fetched to assume that the love between parents and their growing children would develop with the greatest degree of emotional openness and richness if the children matured into independent and equal companions to their parents, and if the two could achieve a balanced relationship based on mutual giving and receiving. The logical concept behind this idea is that rivalry and conflict are inimical to love, and that the motivation to engage in such rivalry must increase in proportion as one partner in the relationship is more unilaterally dependent on the other.

In this generalized form, the final assumption we have just made is in reality *not* accurate. Many parents find it easy to love their children as long as the children remain small and dependent. But their affection diminishes to precisely the degree that their children start developing into strong and mature people on an equal footing with themselves. Thus feelings of rivalry on the part of parents are intensified by the gradual loss of their initially superior and dominant position.

It is often observed that workers in the service professions feel affectionate towards their clients as long as the clients are in a helpless position, dependent, as it were, on their tender mercies. But they may find the very same clients less and less appealing the moment the latter begin to grow stronger, healthier and more powerful and want more of a voice in their own affairs. This phenomenon is readily observable among physicians, psychologists and nurses. They like their charges as long as they place themselves unconditionally in their hands, assuming the status of anxious, tractable and grateful patients. But as soon as the pathetic patient changes into a convalescent with a critical mind and a sense of self-esteem, he may notice the disappearance of the unclouded feelings of affection which the therapists previously had for him.

In an earlier book I commented on the fact that in many relationships between men and women, the emotional tension between the couple increases at the very moment when they are both trying to be modern and progressive by eliminating the privileges of the male, i.e., by trying to give the woman full equality. [74]   The paradoxical thing about this situation for the couple involved is that the love between them appears to diminish in proportion to the degree in which they succeed in turning into reality a concept which both of them genuinely believe in. The man wants to have a strong and self-confident woman for a wife, and helps her to develop in this direction. She, in turn, wants him to tolerate her resistance to his authority to that she can test her own assertiveness in their relationship. But gradually the man observes anxieties in himself, anxieties which he cannot hold in check. He becomes insecure or even impotent, and is barraged with fantasies of gentler, more passive women who contrast sharply with the partner whom, for reasons of which he is not consciously aware, he has begun to experience as threatening. In other words, just when he is on the road to the renunciation of power, to actually living by the belief that relationships need not and should not be based on rivalry, he is suddenly attacked from behind by these very feelings of rivalry or competitiveness. The resulting tensions can also deeply impair the woman's ability to give herself emotionally and sexually.

Thus many young people with a critical attitude towards themselves and society have had the unhappy experience of making an intensive effort to realize their ideal of a partnership absolutely free of any domination, only to find that they were emotionally incapable of continuing on this path. Many of them experience this discovery as a severe blow to their self-esteem. They feel that they have failed, and are unable to really forgive themselves for their inability to achieve, even within the narrow domain of a one-to-one relationship, any genuine form of that social solidarity between emancipated people to which they attach such importance and which they regard as the principle on which all of society ought to be based.

*

A superficial examination of these examples would seem to indicate that it is automatically easier to love someone when the roles of leader and follower have been clearly defined, than when the question of the power structure is left open. In fact it would appear that equality represents such an intense provocation to feelings of rivalry that it automatically impairs, or even renders impossible, any kind of loving emotional relationship.

It is accurate to conclude that a balance of power creates a decided temptation to develop competitive behavior. But it is not the objective situation which compels people to behave in this manner. Its triggering effect simply makes clear how *emotionally* bound people are to the power principle, and how readily this principle manifests itself in them when they are made to feel insecure by the lack of any clear-cut, unilateral leader-follower relationship. Those parents who are capable of loving their children only as long as the children remain subservient to them are, in their conflicts with their offspring, concerned with domination more than with love. And those physicians who find it difficult to tolerate patients who adopt a role of equality with them have become so afraid of losing their power that they are unable to maintain any affection they might have had for a patient the moment they feel their superiority is threatened. But what happens to couples who agree to establish a relationship of complete balance and equality in which neither will lord it over the other, and yet in the end cease to love each other?

A relatively high percentage of couples in this predicament try to get help through couples therapy. As a rule, there is a marked discrepancy between what they claim is true about their relationship and the reality. Both partners support in theory the principle of absolute parity, and of the renunciation of any kind of domination of one partner by the other. This ideal way in fact represents for them a deeply-rooted norm. They both struggle to remain faithful to their guiding principle. But both may lack the inner strength to confide in each other completely. They try to persuade or compel their emotions to coincide with their principles. They want to discipline or drill themselves into loving each other, building on what they regard as a rational foundation for love. But then, to their dismay, they realize that philosophical convictions are one thing and emotional capabilities quite another. No theoretical principle is powerful enough to overcome a deeply-rooted fear. The inner, emotional dispositions of the partners often run counter to the decisions they have made in their heads. The man proves emotionally incapable of tolerating a woman who is growing stronger and becoming his equal. His mounting fear reveals to him that this concept of equal partnership is simply too much for him. He is seized with panic, and fears that he may fall apart inside and lose his identity if he does not gain eventual control over his partner. He fantasizes that if he fails to curb her progress she will be able to do anything she likes to him. She may make him small and helpless, or abandon him if he opens up to her completely. Thus at the last moment he backs down—a reaction which may to a large extent be beyond his conscious control. Instead of recognizing his reaction as a retreat or flight, he will frequently—all of a sudden—try to discover in the woman traits which justify his withdrawal from her. He will "catch her" engaging in various tricks or maneuvers which ostensibly give him cause to react with a feeling of grievance, and to move into a defensive position. In reality he needs this evidence of the woman's attempts to control him— evidence which he may have totally misinterpreted—in order to rationalize his fear. His self-esteem cannot bear to confront the fact that he has once again yielded to the urge to view things in terms of power and impotence.

But the woman too may play an active part in amplifying the conflict. She too finds it difficult to define her new role, based on the concept of a relationship between absolutely equal partners. For after all, the man is not *giving* her her new liberty, a whole new sphere of life to experiment with, as a sort of free handout. Instead she must *work* to achieve a position of greater power through her own efforts; she must prove that she is a success. Many young women have not yet come to terms with the thousands of intimidating and humiliating experiences they had as girls. Thus their determination to develop themselves further cannot take place without conflicts, without vacillation between fits of hypersensitivity or irritability and fits of depression, between malice and self-reproach. As she attempts to make some progress, the woman finds it intolerable if the man employs towards her the traditional masculine mechanisms of self-defense, and if, when a conflict arises, he turns away from her and shuts off his emotions. She refuses to put up with this sort of behavior and demands that he open up and confront her directly. But she fails to realize that he may be experiencing genuine panic, that it is this which is forcing him to withdraw from her, and that it only terrifies him more when she pursues him in this way. She mistakenly interprets the fact that he has walled himself off from her as an expression of the pure will to dominate, just as he, in turn, misinterprets her probing and hounding of him as the determination to beat him into submission.

In short, for *unconscious* emotional reasons, both man and woman fail to find the solution for which they are *consciously* striving. They themselves provoke a power struggle as a result of their inner tensions, in violation of their progressive concept of marriage. Their love is not destroyed by this concept, nor by the progress which they have made towards cooperation and towards the practical, evenhanded sharing of burdens and responsibilities. Instead it is destroyed by the fact that the emotions of both partners are still, to a large extent, under the sway of those same power drives whose more superficial or external manifestations they oppose so bitterly. It is in fact quite typical that those people who most vehemently promote the principle of equality often have particular difficulty in turning this principle into reality. They fight for the weak against the privileges of the strong, but once they have acquired the authority they desire, they behave in the same domineering way that they have always condemned in others.

But these examples of the behavior of couples who on the conscious level advocate the principle of equality simply go to prove how deeply rooted in our psyches the hierarchical model of relationships really is. People feel an almost compulsive urge to view their life together as a one-sided dependency, either overt or covert. One of the couple is always weak and childlike, the other adult and dominant. Indeed, if this structure is not clearly apparent to both partners, they may unconsciously feel compelled to create it by means of provocative maneuvers. They are moved by feelings of distrust, which can trigger a struggle for power between them despite the fact that they believe that a clearly-defined power structure is just what they are trying to avoid. The problem of the power structure is, in fact, already contained in the distrust which touches off the emotional conflagrations between them, which the couple then mistakenly interpret as a confirmation of some clairvoyant prediction that the relationship couldn't possibly work.

In other words, the generalization that love is the strongest enemy of power appears to be merely a soothing anodyne which contradicts our everyday experience. We encounter the power *of* love far less often than the power *over* love. Though love may sometimes appear to abrogate the power principle, when a real conflict arises, power wins the day against love, which is then shown to be dependent on a relationship of dominance-versus-dependence that continues to operate as it were behind the scenes. If this hidden relationship is challenged, love disappears, or is itself converted into an instrument of oppression in the struggle for power. Love is then demanded from the person in the dependent role, becoming a duty of love or a debt of love. Moreover, the person in the position of dominance reserves the right to employ the tactic of withdrawing his love as a means of emotionally blackmailing his partner. In the face of all these traditional, lopsided and hierarchical prototypes of love relationships between God and creature, parents and children, the dominating man and the dominated woman, the Samaritan who gives and the afflicted man who takes, the countermodel of a love between equals has not yet taken deep root among the guiding principles of our culture.

This is one reason why many groups critical of our present society feel profound doubts as to whether, for example, pronounced emotional needs to form ties with underprivileged groups are in fact a valid motive for members of the middle class to fight for the social emancipation of these groups. For it is feared that these somewhat pathological feelings on the part of a higher social class might contain unconscious elements of that need to dominate by "helping" which was described in Part II of this book, and which in the end would turn out to be at cross purposes with the avowed political aim of the emancipation of a socially disadvantaged group. For the past few years, in countless sociopolitical and sociotherapeutic projects to aid disadvantaged minorities, endless debates have been conducted concerning the possible risks of "charitable endeavors." And when active participants in the projects have stated that their principal reason for working with disadvantaged groups was their intense sympathy for the plight of their clients, they have frequently encountered highly skeptical reactions from fellow workers, if not an outright condemnation of their motives. They have been told that their feelings of loving-kindness could result in nothing but a patronizing attitude. If one really wanted to emancipate these minority groups from their misery one should not condescend to them as if one were the Good Samaritan, but instead ought to strive to achieve a purely objective cooperation with them in accordance with solid professional theory. Charitable inclinations and efforts towards political emancipation were, they were told, mutually exclusive categories, because the emotional inclinations would always block the achievement of the political aims.

To be sure, it seems to make sense for politically engaged activist groups not to allow themselves to be catapulted into a blind emotional pragmatism by a group of naive zealots. But this radical suspicion of "charitable inclinations" in general makes clear how little credence people in some circles give to the idea that love can in fact achieve anything other than to confirm established dependency relationships. Thus the hope that love could serve as a weapon against power has been turned into the very opposite, namely the conviction that love was long ago definitively corrupted by power. Anyone who loves "beneath his class" needs to have a partner whom he can regard as inferior to himself in order to care for them at all. The many people who hold this view have ceased to even consider that there might be another way of interpreting the attitude of a person who wants to help someone else in the spirit of love. Their radical skepticism suggests that they are, in their own emotional lives, so totally obsessed with the principle of power that they are unable to tolerate the idea that other people might be capable of feeling an affection not based on the spirit of oppression. In reality, charitable impulses are not only compatible with the cooperative attempt to achieve liberation, but even provide a particularly solid foundation for this attempt. True as it may be that several people have been so corrupted by the power principle rooted in our societal structures that they are capable of loving only hierarchically—i.e., upward or downward but not "straight across"—nevertheless, it is equally true that other people seek out emotion-based communication as a way to abolish oppression and self-oppression. The materialistic bias that emotion-based inclinations are determined solely by an interest in defending one's economic advantages is, fortunately, not true, or at least not yet, as a blanket rule. The materialist view describes an attitude which appears frequently but not universally. It makes the mistake of explaining the "abondon-ship" attitude, the resigned surrender to the deeply-rooted unconscious complex centering on the power principle, as if it were in fact a faithful, objective response to the truth of our situation. But there also exists a quite different attitude, held by segregated and fragmented groups who seek to establish emotional ties with each other and to abolish the differences which divide them. In these groups the fear of the isolation engendered by an inequality in power outweighs the fear of the elimination of this inequality. But what can we actually achieve by exchanging one fear for another?

15

The Cycle of Life.
The Affirmation of Death:
The Prerequisite for the
Destruction of the Myth of
Man's Omnipotence and for the
Achievement of a Human Mean
between Impotence and
Omnipotence

*"But death is not an event. It is all-embracing order,
and its glimmering reflection rests upon every
transformation, every destruction, every sleep and
every leavetaking. Death, as the law, also determines
the coloration of the living man's experience—it is the
color of suffering."*

VICTOR VON WEIZSÄCKER [103]

The intellectual attitude which has traditionally formed the foundation
of our culture leads us into a paradox, namely the fact that in order to
attain what appears to be greatness and power, we unconsciously give up
the opportunity to affirm our life *as a whole.* When he measures himself
by that ideal of individual grandeur which he has internalized along with
the rest of his culture, the individual is continually compelled to suppress
his feelings of inferiority, not only because his personal significance
within a highly technological and overorganized society is constantly
diminishing, but above all because, as a rule, he can live up to the ideal of
potency and all-round "fitness" only during a very limited span of his
life. As a child and a young man he is still dependent on others and needs
their help. In old age he reverts to much the same state of weakness and
dependency. Between these two periods of dependency lies a middle
phase, the so-called "prime of life." Only during this period—and then

only if he is lucky—can a person attain a position which, to some degree, corresponds to the ideal in which he has been indoctrinated, and which he feels he must realize if he is to have a positive feeling about himself, a feeling of self-respect. He can earn a living by his own efforts—provided that he is not too sick to work, or handicapped or unemployed. He may build himself a little home and feel that he has attained the pinnacle of power as a paterfamilias surrounded by his children and parents, with his wife at his side. Now he has attained the power he always desired as a child, and which he will soon lose again as an old man. At the peak of his career, be it lofty or lowly—when he belongs to the age group of greatest interest to the economy—he will feel particularly respected and sought-after in his role as a consumer. But soon he is past his peak. His strength begins to fail him. His creative impulses and powers of self-renewal grow weaker. He loses his attractiveness. No one needs him any more. There is nothing to fill his retirement years but various types of self-help or occupational therapy. He becomes a member of a "minority group," regardless of how the rest of the society may camouflage or gloss over the fact so that they will not be forced to feel afraid of this coming phase in their own lives.

The more completely the individual has turned over his life to the classical values of the power principle, the more he must suffer when he realizes that for long periods of his life he is not yet, or is no longer a fully worthwhile human being in terms of these values—if indeed he is capable of becoming one at *any* time in his life. Almost as if by his own free will, he forces himself into the position of feeling inferior for long periods of time, simply because he believes during these phases that he is supposed to be something which he is incapable of being.

Of course, what appears to be a voluntary act is really the result of sociocultural compulsion. The child would greatly prefer to regard his childhood as something more than a mere training-ground for the "struggle for survival" which will occupy the middle phase of his existence. He would like to feel happy about himself *as a child*, and to resist attempts by other people to force him into a way of life which, more and more, is degenerating into a mere anticipation and simulation of the adult rat-race. And elderly people would be happy to fill up their final years with activities they find interesting in terms of their own personal needs and talents, instead of playing bit parts in the great Theater of Potency and Fitness, pretending that they acknowledge as the supreme value of life the ideal of growing even bigger, stronger and grander. In reality they must accept their situation and prepare not only to become increasingly smaller and more fragile but finally to die. Even in the middle phase of life, at the peak of his form, a human being would— given the choice—undoubtedly prefer to attach less importance to his transitory surplus of power and potency, in order to avoid having to fear and repress the thought of the catastrophe ahead: increasing weakness and impotence.

As a result of all this, we confront the basic paradox that *people in every phase of life are deprived of the opportunity to achieve fulfillment in the manner appropriate to them.* Whenever life is viewed not as a cycle but as a line which may conceivably go on forever and ultimately lead into infinity, man can never, with any real degree of freedom, come to terms with the paradox that for him this infinite life line curves upward for only a brief span and then sinks downward and comes to an end. Control over the law of causality, which by rights ought to involve the ability to predict and thus to avert death, fails to work its magic here. The chain of cause and effect stretches forward into infinity. But the "organic machine" which, like a watch, was supposed to have been fixed by technological advances so that it would run forever, finds no place in this infinite perspective. Thus the image after which the individual learns to pattern his life does not match what actually happens to him. He finds himself on a course quite different from what he had expected. His vision of a future which he will one day have under complete, final control prevents him from ever fully participating in the here and now, in the present moment of the ascending and descending curve of his life, which—to his own detriment—he interprets either as an ascent towards something which has not yet occurred or as a descent already behind him. If he only understood that at every moment of his life he is in the center of a *circle* or *cycle of life,* he would not have to suffer the perpetual frustrations of the Not-Yet and the No-Longer. Then each point in the circle would be equally meaningful, and death would represent the completion of the circle, included in the plan from the very beginning, and at every moment thereafter. Death in this sense constitutes a true conclusion; and the meaningful preparation for death represents one of the essential tasks of life—whereas the power principle demands that one spend a lifetime avoiding death or at least infinitely delaying it on the premise that it represents a catastrophe, a headlong fall down a precipice which we experience as completely meaningless.

The traditional faith in progress offers us an empty consolation for the pain of our own declining fitness and of death itself. The individual could try to tell himself: "I myself, my generation and the generations which came before me, were not and are not yet capable of infinitely extending their lifespans and indefinitely preserving a grandiose level of potency. But every generation contributes something towards our achievement of that goal, and at some point in the future our grandchildren will have achieved it. In other words, the life curve of the individual continues to decline because we have not yet reached the point of being able to eliminate the causes of arteriosclerosis and of organ deterioration. But, in a sense, by standing on the shoulders of our generation the next generation or the one after that will reap the fruits of the research of all the preceding generations. When this happens, our entire civilization will continue to evolve onward and upward into infinity. As for the individual, who must fall into ruin and be destroyed in complete contradiction to the ideal of omnipotence, he can console himself with the thought that, at least indirectly, he is participating in that eternally rising curve of humanity which transcends his individual life."

But even this faith in progress is no longer valid. The prognostications of the futurologists make it quite clear that mankind must solve certain ecological and economic problems which at the moment appear virtually insoluble, if it is to gain even a temporary respite from annihilation. In any case, no one can any longer think in terms of that continual ascent onward and upward which marked the classical ideology of evolution. Thus, while we can no longer claim that these narcissistic aspirations to omnipotence bear any meaningful relation to the life of the individual, we can nevertheless claim they are justified to the extent that they represent the collectively-constructed, mighty dynamo capable of catapulting all mankind upward into those grandiose heights demanded by our collective ideal. This dream is simply melting away, and with it vanishes the key argument employed by people in our own day, who balance the disappearance of meaning in their present lives against the goal of a glorious, progressive future, for at this very moment this future is proving to be a mirage.

The time is past when we could simply look to the future and exert all our energies to expand our arsenal of technological apparatus for coming generations, so that ultimately our descendants could employ this arsenal as a sort of Philosophers' Stone to safeguard them against disease and old age, manipulate the laws of heredity to positive effect, and guarantee themselves a life of heavenly luxury. Such goals represent the illusory product of our neurotic complex of feelings about impotence and omnipotence. Our contemporaries must find meaning and purpose for their lives themselves, and leave it up to the next generation to make their own choices about what to do with their lives.

To adopt this course, we must give serious attention to the idea of the *circular* or *cyclical nature of our own lives, and of the completion of the circle.* This implies that we must show greater consideration for those who come after us than we have done in the past, when we demanded that they strive to fulfill our own partially-frustrated dreams. Up to now each generation has imposed on the next the crushing burden of trying to realize those hopes which they themselves failed to realize completely. In order to fulfill its obligation to continue manufacturing "progress," each generation has inherited from its predecessor an increasingly huge and complex supertechnology, closely linked to the prevailing social order, which each successive generation must exert great effort to maintain in order to prevent the eruption of total chaos. This kind of preprogramming of the future resembles a relay race in which each generation takes over from the one before. Each generation has saddled the next with an oppressive weight: the narcissistic ideal of omnipotence with which they have covered up their inability to come to terms emotionally with the cyclical structure of their own lives.

The idea of a circle or cycle of life involves the notion that life does not represent a perpetual forward motion, but rather that in the second half of life there is a motion of *return.* This concept frightens people because we have been taught to regard forward-directed motion as the only kind with any value. The term "a step backward" almost invariably implies criticism or self-criticism. Everything good points forward, is "progressive." A person who is courageous, confident and strong looks ahead, not back. But if the line of one's life closes to form a circle, it automatically leads one back to where one started. Thus, going forward ultimately means returning to the beginning. But in this case a return is not a capitulation; on the contrary, it is the active consummation of the cycle of life.

The concept that the motion of life involves a return to the beginning is of ancient origin in the Western philosophical tradition, and made its appearance even in Plato's *Symposium,* where Plato has Aristophanes recount the famous myth stating that sexuality brings back together the two separated halves of the human being, which in a primordial age had once formed part of a single person. [69]   Sigmund Freud incorporated into his theory the concept of a *death instinct,* an inherent tendency of the organism to revert to an earlier stage of being, and associated with this idea his experience of the so-called "compulsion to repeat." In *Beyond the Pleasure Principle* (1920) Freud wrote that all organic drives were "conservative" and aimed towards the "restoration of that which existed earlier" [27]:

> It would be contrary to the conservative nature of drives if life represented a pinnacle which had never been attained before. Instead there must exist an ancient state, an initial starting point which every living thing has abandoned and to which, via all the detours of its evolution, it strives to return. If we may assume that, without exception, every living thing dies of *internal* causes, returning to the inorganic state, then our only conclusion can be to say: The goal of all life is death. And looking farther back still: That which is not living existed before that which is living.

Freud drew a contrast between two forces, Eros and the death instinct [27]:

> On the grounds of theoretical reflection, supported by biological findings, we assumed the existence of a *death instinct* whose task it is to conduct organic life back into an inanimate state, whereas Eros pursues the goal of rendering life increasingly complex by effecting an ever more comprehensive synthesis of that living substance which has been dispersed into particles, and naturally aims at the same time to preserve it. In this process both drives play, in the strictest sense of the term, a conservative role, in that they strive towards the restoration of a state disrupted by the development of life. Thus the development of life is the cause of both the perpetuation of life and the striving for death, life itself constituting a struggle and a compromise between these two urges.

The assumption of the existence of a death instinct leads to the conclusion that there must also exist a natural, psychical correlative to this instinct, a *need to die*. Freud believed that the "dominant tendency of psychical life" towards "reduction, the maintenance of a constant state, the abolition of the internal tension due to stimuli," represented just such a tendency. Borrowing a term from Barbara Low, he designated this tendency the Nirvana principle. [27]   Freud linked his theory of the death instinct to a new analysis of aggression. Sadism and destructiveness now seemed to him to constitute the diversion of the death instinct towards an external object, through the mediation of Eros. Eros wished to halt the self-destruction effected by the death instinct, and therefore diverted its destructive energy outward, away from the self. Hatred became the externalized manifestation of the death instinct.

Since Freud's day the majority of psychoanalysts have agreed to discard, either explicitly or tacitly, Freud's theory of the death instinct. Moreover, in his discussion of the preparation for death, Erik Erikson, who attempted to supplement Freud's developmental psychology, no longer makes any reference to any instinctual drive towards or inherent need for death. He speaks only of a task, forming part of the general task of ego integration during the third phase of "mature adulthood," to accept our one and only life cycle. A person who fails to do this, Erikson states, will fall into a state of despair over the fact that he does not have enough time to try to start a new life or try out alternate roads to integrity. [20]

Indeed, Freud himself deemphasized the importance of his meta-psychological theory of the death instinct by his failure to incorporate it into his therapeutic theory. It remained, so to speak, in the background, assuming the role of a speculative theory segregated from the concepts which apply directly to therapy. The goal of therapy remained the working-through of childhood repressions. It was for this reason that Freud advised that psychoanalytic treatment be recommended only to potential patients who have not yet passed middle age, for he believed that older persons no longer had the psychological flexibility to enable them to bring about any structural changes in their personalities by working through unresolved childhood problems. This fact in itself testifies that he did not intend psychoanalysis to be used as an instrument for dealing with the new and special types of problems which arise in the second half of life.

However, if one proceeds on the basis of Freud's assumption that there is a natural psychological need for a circular conclusion to human life, and if one is capable of resisting the pervasive pressure to turn the traditional ideology of omnipotence into an absolute, then one acquires a whole new perspective on the criteria for giving a more meaningful shape to our lives. The compulsion to continually evaluate oneself in terms of the criteria of narcissistic inflation simply drops away. Given new criteria of value, a child would not always have to dream of a future in which he has finally become big and powerful enough to live up to the ideal instilled in him by his culture, and the elderly person would not be forced to spend all his time feeling envious and depressed, vainly wishing for the good old days when he was strong and powerful. A person could, at every moment of his life, affirm himself as he is and not merely for what he hopes to become or for what he may perhaps once have been. And the purpose of working through childhood repressions would, for an adult, consist not only in directing previously blocked energies towards the strengthening of his powers in the present, but also in reconciling himself with his childhood as childhood, and in the wholehearted affirmation of this childhood now that it is past. But parallel to this reconciliation with the unmastered vestiges of his past would be the task of preparing in a positive way for those *new* developments and opportunities for growth in his life which he will continue to experience until a very advanced age. In other words, one's goal in middle age and beyond would be to become aware of, and to fully gratify, those new and special needs which develop during the second half of life, rather than to adopt a defensive posture and insist that we must radiate eternal youth, fitness, and physical attractiveness, thus risking becoming more and more depressed.

A psychical reorientation of the kind I have just described would also bring with it the possibility of substantially changing the relations between different age groups. Parents would cease to be exclusively, incessantly and impatiently concerned with what their children are or are not supposed to become, for they would no longer need to think of people in their own age group as being in "the prime of life," for which childhood represents a mere preparation. Now they could proceed on the assumption that childhood also represents the "prime of life," and could encourage their children to feel at home in an environment appropriate to children, and to act and communicate according to fantasies and rules suitable to their age and crucial to their sense of well-being. The parents, relieved of the burden of the power principle, would also be less bound by their need to ensure their superiority over their children and to demand that the children make adjustments which serve no other purpose than to confirm the parents in their views and opinions of themselves. They would not, each time their child's way of thinking and behaving deviated slightly from their own norms, immediately see in this a threat to their dominance, for they would not be forced to exercise this dominance in the first place in order to feel adequate self-esteem.

Moreover, under these conditions young people would find it easier to avoid painful and stressful feelings of competition with their parents and other members of the older generation. And aging parents would once again view themselves as being at yet another high point or "prime of life," and would not feel compelled to keep looking back to try to hang tenaciously onto their former position of power. Young people, in turn, would no longer be forced to fear or even hate their aging parents because they saw in their condition the negative aspects of their own future. On the contrary, unconstrained contact with their parents could teach them to look forward to a future which, as their parents have demonstrated to them, is both positive and meaningful.

Anyone who can view his life as a circle and adopt an equally affirmative attitude towards all its phases achieves a whole new orientation vis-à-vis the polarities of large and small, of power and suffering. He becomes capable of accepting himself when he is strong as well as when he is weak, when he is "fit" as well as when he is in need of help. For this reason he is also able to engage in candid communication with individuals and groups who represent those very things which he himself is not. He is not driven, by his own inability to suffer, to ferret out allegedly diabolical agents of suffering, or to delegate his suffering to the weak, deaden his pain through surrogate gratifications, or overcompensate for it by struggling fiercely. Nor does he have any need for the bustle and forced gaiety of the cocktail-party circuit in order to suppress a deep-lying, unconscious depression.

But the individual cannot achieve this psychological reorientation alone. The overcoming of the "God complex," of the myth of man's omnipotence, can be conceived only as a gradual and collective process in which people help each other to break down their fears of helplessness and suffering, and their idealization of omnipotence. The individual must consistently think in terms of a give-and-take relationship: By opening himself up and sympathizing with the weakness of others, he can learn to endure his own suffering. The acceptance of one's own suffering, in turn, is the prerequisite for the ability to minister to the weakness of others. Openness towards one's own emotions goes hand in hand with openness in communication with others.

In the older, traditional schools of psychoanalysis, therapy as a rule was based on the notion that the individual must become freer in dealing with his own emotions. Only then would he be able to open himself up more in his dealings with others. But later it was noted that psychoanalytic therapy itself constitutes a form of social intercourse, of "dealing with others," and that the introspective self-examination within the individual is stimulated by means of a *relationship*, a *dialogue*. Eventually the evolution of various forms of psychosocial therapy and self-help groups confirmed everyone's expectations by establishing that in fact *the individual needs social relationships,* for only through others can he learn to understand aspects of himself which he has hitherto repressed and split off from the rest of his nature, and to integrate them into his personality. Ultimately the individual can comprehend the cycle of his life as a cycle only within the context of a social cycle. He must allow himself to relate frankly and openly to people who represent everything that he himself once was or will one day be, which he would like to become or even believes he could not under any circumstances allow himself to become; for only then will he be able to correctly evaluate his past history, his future and his present situation. People who make him feel anxious or terrified reveal to him those things which frightened him in his own past, and at the same time reveal the things which make him anxious about his future. If he were incapable of coming to terms with this frightening aspect of his past, he would be unable to complete his cyclical path. For the completion of the circle means that one is able to return to one's beginning. But the circle can be closed only if one can gaze at the whole of the road one has already traversed and can affirm it all, accepting it as a meaningful part of one's life, which one is now called on to continue and bring to an end. Unless one does this one will be forced, over and over, to seek new beginnings elsewhere or outside one's own proper sphere and nature; one will wish to eliminate some parts of the life one has lived or wish to relive this part or that part, or the whole thing, all over again. A person in this plight believes that he can halt the inexorable course of life, that he can refuse to accept a fate which, although it is ineluctable, he feels is irreconcilable with that image of himself which he has defiantly asserted in the teeth of fate. And yet he will, again and again, find near him other people who are able to help him to look at the repressed portions of his inner fate, to gaze steadily at the spectral world of his negative self, and in the future, to consciously integrate these negative aspects of himself. But other people are able to offer this help only if he opens himself up to them emotionally, and also is willing to help them in exchange.

16

The Primary Phenomenon of Sympathy as the Disposition to Solidarity and Justice

"The ultimate source of the possibility that human beings may live together in society is not morality but love."

C.F. VON WEIZSÄCKER

The natural precondition for the interaction between self-help initiatives and efforts to help all of society is the disposition to *sympathy*, which binds all human beings together. Sympathy not only involves the capacity to empathize with another person, but also the spontaneous readiness, experienced as an urgent necessity, to spontaneously *feel what another person feels*. If he does not forcibly drive himself into ego-centricity and self-isolation, the individual will find himself inherently and spontaneously bound to the human condition.

The compulsions of the power principle and the tendency to egocentric competition nearly always block our awareness of that sympathy which constitutes an innate and natural emotional bond between all individual human beings. After the magic-oriented natural philosophers, a number of thinkers—first Shaftesbury, then Schopenhauer, von Hartmann and Bergson, and finally Scheler—elaborated the theory that sympathy represents a primary or primordial social phenomenon and the truly authentic method for establishing a social life based on solidarity. It seems essential that we revive the true, original meaning of "sympathy," which nowadays is used only in the most superficial sense, to indicate that we think someone is nice or feels that we are nice.

For the Renaissance thinkers—Paracelsus, for example—who speculated about magic, sympathy signified the spiritual interrelationship between all things in the universe. Four hundred years later, Schopenhauer used the same concept in much the same way, to embrace all phenomena in which it was possible to experience the unified ground of the universe. This root of the universe, the thing-in-itself, which Schopenhauer interpreted as the universal Will, constituted a unity underlying the multiplicity of things. It was sympathy which established this underlying unity, this bond, among them. In Schopenhauer sympathy is a concept which includes three phenomena:

1. Compassion, which, as I have set forth, is the foundation of justice and the love of one's fellow man, or *caritas*.
2. Sexual love with its capricious choice of a love object: *amor*, which maintains the life of the species which takes precedence over the life of individuals;
3. Magic, including animal magnetism and faith healing. In this sense sympathy is to be defined as: the empirical manifestation of the metaphysical identity of the Will [emerging] through the physical multiplicity of its phenomena, by which is revealed an interrelatedness wholly distinct from that mediated through the forms of appearance and which we understand in terms of the principle of sufficient reason. [87]

Thus, sympathy supplies Schopenhauer with proof of the metaphysical cohesion of the universe outside the sphere of intellectual logic, so to speak through the *logique du coeur*. Scheler's thought is closely akin to Schopenhauer's when in 1913, in his monograph on sympathy, he writes:

I do in fact incline to the belief that the feeling of oneness-with-another is both a subjective index of the conviction of the abiding metaphysical unity of all things and (in the case of a *mutual feeling of oneness-with-another*) the apprehension of this unity, representing, ultimately, the ontic presupposition that it is actually possible to experience this phenomenon [of unity]. [81]

The central phenomenon in sympathy is *fellow-feeling*. And this phenomenon—quite independently of any metaphysical theories which may be built on its foundation—constitutes a mystery in that it cannot be deduced from, or explained in terms of, anything else. To be sure, all our studies of "projection," "delegation" (the disowning of our feelings and attributing them to someone else), "transference," "suggestion," and so on, do in fact demonstrate that every conceivable kind of process can play a role in emotional relationships between individuals. We can, as has

often been done in this book, interpret the need to relieve ourselves of
emotional burdens as the driving force behind the splitting off of certain
parts of our own psyche and their projection onto someone else.
Moreover, we can demonstrate that whenever a person experiences
empathy with another, elements from his own psyche invariably enter
into his experience. But the fact remains that there exists a primordial,
unmediated, more or less instinctual feeling-with, rejoicing-with and
suffering-with the other. This instinctual sympathy, in which the barrier
between the self and the non-self is broken down, is technically
designated as "identification," but this term does not explain it.

In the act of fellow-feeling or of feeling-with another, the individual
self reaches beyond itself. On the other hand, we could just as well say the
opposite: The self is seized and carried beyond itself. To be sure, although
it belongs to the nature of this process that it tends to forge ahead and
establish a genuine bond between human beings, it is possible to halt the
bonding process almost at the outset. There is a narcissistic form of
emotional bond which Scheler calls mere reproduced or vicarious feeling,
as opposed to genuine fellow-feeling, or feeling-with. "The vicarious
entry into another's feelings," Scheler says in defining this phenomenon,
"gives us only the *quality* of his state—not its *actuality*. No doubt this is
why we can vicariously experience the joys and sufferings of characters in
novels, of fictional protagonists in a drama, portrayed by an actor." [81]

However, this vicarious experience frequently occurs not only in
relation to fictional characters, but also in relation to real people or
groups of people. Still, the way in which we experience these people, or
the way in which we process our experience, is in no way different from
our identification with the characters in a play. The following example
appears to be an apt illustration of narcissistic, vicarious identification
with the feelings of others.

In my book *Flüchten oder Standhalten* ["Stand Firm or Run
Away"], I described the case of a homeless mother of seven children, the
youngest of whom had frozen to death in an unheatable shed in a mobile
home park, at a temperature of 39°F. Not the authorities but the mother
was put on trial, despite the fact that this illiterate woman had spent a
year battling social service bureaus, trying to get them to install her
housing with some form of heating system. Her plight was described on
television. The magazine *Bild* reported her case to the German public in
giant headlines. Millions of people followed the course of the trial. The
news accounts must have made it clear to everyone that the woman had
been living and was still living in the most acute poverty and distress. It

was only to be expected that at least a certain percentage of the many people who displayed such emotion over the fate of this family would have taken the trouble to write the mother a friendly note or send her or her children a small gift. But only a few people actually contacted the woman or gave her any kind of help. The vast majority reacted as people always react to such tragedies: by enjoying the shudder of horror they felt. Perhaps they may go so far as to get together with family and friends so that all of them can agree to feel the same way about the situation. They convince themselves that what they are feeling is genuine compassion. But genuine fellow-feeling and commiseration would involve communicating with the afflicted persons, dealing with them as real people. In the case of the woman with the seven children, the majority of the public had been concerned with only one thing, namely the *image* of the woman and her children dressed up by the media, just as every day we are emotionally affected by fictional televised tear-jerkers, despite the fact that we know perfectly well that the actors are only playing imaginary people. This reaction, then, represents a purely *vicarious experience* of someone else's feelings. When people vicariously experience an authentic, immediate event, they shut out the fact that it is real. The public, when they identify with people involved in some sensational public event, feel no genuine sympathy for them. In other words, they do not really feel with, i.e., together with these people. No real "togetherness" takes place. The public simply uses the event as an occasion to vent a narcissistic emotionalism which has been lying just beneath the surface. This siphoning off of feeling actually perverts the original impulse of sympathy. People push away an afflicted person, when in reality the principle of sympathy demands that they turn to him with concern. They allow real people to dissolve into unreal phantoms and, if possible, try to portray their purely narcissistic feelings as a sign of social sensitivity.

We must not forget that in our civilization the production and processing of scripts and news stories designed to trigger these feelings of vicarious narcissistic enjoyment long ago became a big-money industry. The television, magazines and sensational press survive primarily by satisfying the demand for the perpetual reproduction of this narcissistic response. The isolation of human beings within our egocentric, competitive society is halfway bearable only because of this staging of a steady stream of emotionally moving, illusory communications with phantoms. This species of "psychohygienic" canalizing of passive feelings, illusory fellow-feeling and illusory pity has inevitably resulted from our fear of allowing ourselves to feel genuine sympathy and thereby to forfeit certain of the privileges of power.

Incidentally, it seems noteworthy that many of the famous literary and media plots designed to trigger strong feelings of identification with their characters involve such a marked degree of narcissism that any socially-oriented feelings they may evoke are absorbed by the egocentric impulses kindled at the same time. There are any number of plots that demonstrate this, notably tales of the Michael Kohlhaas variety.*

By nature the sympathy impulse extends beyond mere feelings of vicarious identification to genuine fellow-feeling. Only in this kind of feeling do we genuinely *sym-pathize* with, share in, the feelings of another. Just as the German word *An—teil* ("sympathy") suggests, the persons involved *share in* (*teilen* = "to share") a single feeling. If the feeling involved is one of suffering, then the person who *feels with* the sufferer takes upon himself the suffering originally experienced by the other. He endures the pain along with the afflicted person and thus relieves him of the burden. The same lesson is found in the wise old saw which states that suffering shared is suffering cut in half. Moreover, in genuine fellow-feeling the hierarchy of a relationship is abolished. A relationship based on superiority and inferiority is replaced by one of equality and solidarity, by a complete sharing. In this way we see fulfilled the primary principle underlying what we might call the sympathy instinct. This is the principle of sympathetic equality between two people. But to carry through the sympathy impulse, we must first make a social decision. The goal of the impulse is the recognition of *sameness in difference*. Moreover, this sameness or equality must be experienced directly, not mediated indirectly through a third term or category such as God. If our emotional identification with another person goes only as far as acknowledging his equality or identity with ourselves as a member of the human species, we will remain under the sway of the power principle. This domination by power leaves the door wide open to hypocrisy, to camouflage of the oppression on which many relationships are based.

A book of marriage counselling, written by O. Funcke in 1908, contains an anecdote pointedly exposing the hypocrisy of an indirect or

---

* Kohlhaas, a cattle dealer who failed to obtain satisfaction through a lawsuit from a German nobleman with whom he had a quarrel, turned to robbery and murder and was executed in 1540. Heinrich von Kleist based his famous novella, *Michael Kohlhaas* (published in 1810), on the chronicle of this real historical figure whose sense of justice led him—like the new "vigilante" heroes of the film industry who take the law into their own hands—to crime and death.—Tr.

mediated pseudo-fellow-feeling. On no account, this book states, ought one to yield to the demands of female domestic servants for more freedom, higher wages, or housing outside the home of the "master and mistress." Nevertheless, a maidservant was deserving of the greatest sympathy and love. "Merely remain ever mindful that even a new maidservant was redeemed by the same Cross on Golgatha, and by the selfsame blood of Jesus Christ, and for the selfsame salvation and glory, as you. If you have a poor memory, write somewhere on the wall in glowing letters, in English or French or any language whatever: 'Our Dora is one of the redeemed, just as we are!' and then act accordingly!" [35]

The primary phenomenon of sympathy is fully realized only when people achieve an identity with each other through the sharing of feelings. Ultimately sympathy is founded on the mystery of a primordial emotional bond by which one links one's own psychical life to that of other people. Anyone who remains emotionally open to his surroundings is spontaneously moved by the emotional experiences taking place around him. He feels what is happening inside other people. He is affected by what they feel. One basic phenomenon involving shared experience is "infectious emotion," which plays a major role in the study of mass psychology. Genuine fellow-feeling is based on infectious emotion, but it is no more identical to it than it is identical to the mere vicarious identification with the feelings of others which we feel with characters in a book. Anyone who succumbs to infectious emotion is automatically carried away by, or caught up in, the emotional impulses of others, but he does not necessarily enter into any kind of genuine relationship with them. On occasion he may not even perceive these other people as people. The "tuning in" of his mood on theirs can take place without his even noticing it, at least for a while. This is because his ego does not consciously participate in the process, which is determined either by suggestion or by uncontrolled autosuggestion.

On the other hand, in the phenomenon of *vicarious entrance into the feelings of others* (like characters in a book), the ego consciously draws a clear distinction between itself and the other person, whose internal state it perceives and, so to speak, uses as a foundation for its own emotions. But as has already been indicated, this contrast drawn between the sufferer and the spectator can become so pronounced that the latter ceases to experience the former as a real person. When this happens, the narcissistic, vicarious identification with the feelings of others bears no relation to the afflicted person except as an image, a phantom. This phantom can be a fictional creation or a person, originally real, who has come to resemble a fictional creation. Frequently the person who engages in vicarious identification is concerned solely with a sort of performance taking place on the theatrical stage of his intrapsychic existence. Only in cases of genuine fellow-feeling does a personal relationship form whose ultimate aim is a total emotional equality or equation between one person and the other. Of course, the barriers of egocentrism instilled in us by our cultural training do in fact make it difficult to achieve this goal. For this reason a decisive effort is required to complete a process which is, however, preordained by an innate impulse that is almost instinctual. Thus, will power is necessary only to bring to fullness or fruition the natural, primordial phenomenon of sympathy.

Human solidarity, in the strict sense, is founded on this authentic, natural fellow-feeling in which one person equates himself with another. Shaftesbury had advocated this same view that there exists among human beings a primordial emotional bond which transmits the highest norm of human existence. He used the term "social feeling," or *sensus communis*, to describe this bond, and insisted that social feelings conferred a "sense of the common rights of mankind" and of the equality of individuals.

Primary fellow-feeling already contains in itself the impulse to help others when they are in trouble. This type of sympathy effects that process which Schopenhauer describes as a mystery: "It occurs every day, right before our eyes, in the small details of life, whenever, in response to a direct impulse and without really pausing to reflect, one human being helps another, springing to his aid or at times actually placing his own life in the most certain jeopardy for the sake of someone he has just seen for the first time, and thinks no more about it. All he has to see is the great distress and danger suffered by the other person." [85]

Scheler is quite correct, in his critique of Schopenhauer, when he says that the latter reduced fellow-feeling to fellow-suffering (compassion, commiseration). In reality fellow-feeling involves more than fellow-suffering; it necessarily involves the exchange of positive as well as negative feelings. One aspect of fellow-feeling is sharing another's pleasure. And as Schopenhauer failed to perceive, even a relationship based on compassion, on fellow-suffering, contains not only the element of suffering but also feelings of gratification. The compassionate person obtains gratification by amplifying his own ego through direct participation in the lives of others. And the person who is the object of compassion receives emotional support from the assistance offered him by others, which helps to relieve him of some of his burden. Moreover, if we examine this process from both sides, we find on occasion that the elimination of "dissociative fragmentation"—i.e., the splitting off of parts of the ego—also plays a role in it.

Through participation in the suffering of others, the compassionate or commiserating being learns to perceive and to integrate into the rest of his personality that suffering of his own which he has repressed. And the suffering person can now share in the strength of the other—a strength which he has hitherto failed to acquire on his own. This kind of mutual help approximates the model of the mutual emancipation of both sexes.

This type of exchange involves cutting one's suffering in half as well as sharing half one's strength. We can, with justice, view the exchange solely from the vantage point of the sufferer, but we are equally justified in approaching it from the standpoint of the stronger person who lends his aid to the sufferer. We adulterate the basic social-psychological phenomenon taking place here, and unduly emphasize the power principle, if we characterize the process exclusively in terms of the fact that the compassionate or commiserating person gives something to another. In the mature, complete exchange of fellow-feeling and in the mutual identification of the partners who share one another's feelings, there is an equal distribution of giving and receiving on both sides. The initial asymmetry, resulting from the splitting off of power from impotence, is transformed, becomes balance and equality. One person gives up a portion of his suffering, and takes from the other a portion of his strength. Just the opposite exchange is effected by his partner.

All overly restrictive descriptions of the phenomena of compassion—i.e., descriptions which concentrate exclusively on the image of the benefactor who, without receiving anything in return, magnanimously lowers himself to help some poor unfortunate and then, as it were, reascends to heaven leaving the wretched being he had consoled down below him trapped in a state of dependency and gratitude—adulterate the basic phenomenon of fellow-feeling by placing it once more within the classical context of power versus weakness and suffering. As a result of this narrow perspective, Schopenhauer's ethics of commiseration are made subordinate to his metaphysics of the Will. The impotence-omnipotence syndrome has been so deeply ingrained in our thinking that it does in fact still continue to make it difficult for us to perceive the central significance of the principle of sympathy as a counterforce to the power principle. Hence we are still ruled by the prejudice that fellow-feeling and fellow-suffering can take place solely within the framework of a fixed, hierarchical relationship. In reality our concern should be to work out processes of exchange aimed at the creation of balanced relationships based on mutual solidarity. Centuries of discrimination against the emotions have radically dimmed our realization that the only primordial human incentive which can motivate people to eliminate inhumane, oppressive relationships lies in the principle of sympathy.

In the past it has proved impossible to adequately understand the potential of sympathy because our habitually individualistic way of looking at the world has prevented us from taking seriously the assumption that there exists a primary state of human mutuality. Fellow-feeling and fellow-suffering have always been automatically reduced to emotional or behavioral traits of the individual. One partner in the relationship has remained in the role of the passive recipient. Only a bipolar or multipolar way of thinking makes it possible for us to view sympathy, in a social sense, as a phenomenon involving relatedness between people—as something which human beings experience together and which compels them to engage in a particular type of behavior towards one another—provided that they are not prevented from doing so by contrary impulses deriving from the "God complex" or man's myth of his own omnipotence.

The primary phenomenon of sympathy is that natural disposition to create a social life based on solidarity and justice, mediated through the logic of the emotions, the *"logique du coeur."* We can make full use of this disposition only if we make further progress in dealing with the impotence-omnipotence complex. The continuing fascination that Nietzsche exerts over our minds shows that deep-rooted fears are still preventing us from eliminating our overcompensatory preoccupation with thoughts of power. This overcompensation is nourished by our old concern that fellow-feeling could easily drag us down once again to that state of impotence and weakness we knew as children and in the Middle Ages, and which, in however rough-and-ready a way, we have for centuries managed to conceal from ourselves by an egocentric concentration on dreams of personal omnipotence. Thus people continually let themselves be convinced that they only need to defeat the enemies of society, keep themselves physically and mentally fit, and perfect a high-powered technology, in order to "rise to the top" and avoid ever tumbling back down into total ruin. This anxiety-based overcompensation causes people to express a purely fragmentary kind of sympathy—a sort of compromise gesture—in the form of an egocentric, vicarious identification with others, or in the form of an oppressive charity presented as "assistance," which firmly establishes children, the sick and the socially disadvantaged in a position of dependency.

Nietzsche can be refuted only by someone who no longer secretly feels afflicted by the helpless, infantile need for security from which narcissistic delusions of grandeur offer a rather ineffectual protection. On the other hand, anyone able to view himself as a *complete human being,* living in a world together with other human beings of equal status, is also capable of feeling genuine sympathy and solidarity with others. This kind of self-esteem erases the fear that one may lose one's emotional balance if one consents to experience fellow-feeling, and that one may be dragged down to a miserable, inferior status. *The sympathetic identification with other people is no longer the least bit threatening to anyone who views himself as a being of "medium stature," one who subsists neither on a level of pathetic inadequacy nor on one of overcompensatory narcissistic self-inflation, but somewhere in between.* He feels no qualms about yielding to his need to form bonds based on sympathy, and by doing so experiences an inner enrichment mediated through other people who share in his feelings and express towards him the same sympathy he expresses towards them. Thus the principle of sympathy increases our opportunities to achieve a general social emancipation.

Identification and fellow-feeling with others is by no means a virtue of the weak, as it has repeatedly been misrepresented. In fact, the only people capable of it are those who are strong enough to undergo personal suffering and therefore are able to help carry the burden of others' suffering. This emotional openness, which is the foundation of *sympathein* or the sympathetic sharing in the feelings of others, is anything but the expression of *ressentiment* or "slave morality." Quite the contrary, *ressentiment* is characteristically the attitude which motivates people to feel that they must disparage anything which, because of their emotional fragility, they believe themselves incapable of feeling or achieving.

Indeed, Nietzsche's interpretation of compassion has something in common with the way in which the Church has traditionally manipulated the teachings of Christ, by simply standing them on their heads. In the Sermon on the Mount Christ says "Blessed are the merciful," and promises that they will obtain in return the mercy which they give others. But the Church has perverted something which confers beatitude into a duty, a debt. *The primary phenomenon of sympathy is*

converted from a natural, innate need into a question of obedience.
Fellow-feeling, fellow-suffering (compassion) and *caritas* are imposed as
commandments, as if what took place through them were not a liberating
self-expansion achieved in conjunction with other people but rather,
primarily, an act of self-conquest which one is compelled to perform.
Moreover, the Church has turned itself into the social authority
responsible for demanding the fulfillment of this commandment and for
seeing that it is carried out. By doing so it has subordinated the sympathy
principle to a power principle created and established by itself, thereby
lending support to our fatal equation: the sense of solidarity based on
fellow-feeling = "slave morality." Sympathetic fellow-feeling and *caritas*
became equivalent to obedience and impotence. And when, at the end of
the Middle Ages, Western man finally engaged in a mass revolt against
his impotent condition, everything which appeared related to this
condition was immediately and automatically deprived of all value.
Social feelings were thrown into the same basket with all the other
passions de l'âme and banned as impulses which dragged people down in
status or which hindered *raison* and *volonté* on their way to the
acquisition of power.

*

History teaches that all efforts to compel people by means of moral or
legal precepts and regulations to live together in a society based on
mutual solidarity ultimately prove fruitless unless at the same time we
succeed in promoting those natural motivations to solidarity which elicit
from people the desired form of social behavior. In other words, as long as
the "God complex," or the myth of man's omnipotence, enforces the
dominance of egocentric claims to power and personal greatness, those
tensions resulting from constant competition can never be truly overcome
by means of legal and ideological norms. At best all that can be achieved
by such attempts to "regularize" behavior is a coercive, rigidly-controlled
society which follows the same pattern as a person suffering from a
compulsive neurosis and which is dominated by a Kantian joyless
scrupulosity. But a society structured in this way will never cease to
provoke revolts by various groups who feel helpless and oppressed
against those authorities who enforce the law. Paradoxically, the more
completely the climate of society as a whole is determined by the power
principle, the more persecutions, sanctions and general suspicion will be
directed against minority groups who try to break away from this
principle. The various "hippie" cultures in Germany and elsewhere, the

German "Spontis" and the "urban redskins," as well as many other alternative subculture groups and grass-roots initiatives, are forced to live outside the mainstream of society, as "outsiders." And yet the themes articulated by these groups could transmit vital regenerative impulses to the rest of society. Without any qualms, the authorities, posing as "defenders of the constitution," manipulate the laws and the constitution, using them as weapons against people who may cherish constitutional values more than they do. A typical perversion—akin to compulsive neurosis—is the sanctification of rules, regulations and rituals, their transformation into absolutes. When this happens, the humanity they were originally intended to protect automatically becomes equated with the pedantic and scrupulous observance of the rules.

Schopenhauer quite rightly emphasized that basic principles and abstract knowledge represent neither the primordial source nor the primary foundation of morality. [85]   The cardinal virtue of justice, he said, was rooted in man's natural compassion. "Ethics," he taught, "is in reality the easiest of all the sciences. Indeed, this is only natural in view of the fact that every person has the obligation to design his own nature, in accordance with the supreme principle rooted in his *heart.*" [85]   But as we already noted in our earlier discussion of Schopenhauer, he failed to consistently maintain this ethical system, which might, in a broad sense, be defined as an ethics of sympathy. He foundered on the paradox involved in affirming that the sense of justice was rooted in the emotions, even while he clung to the prejudice that a thoroughgoing psychological difference existed between the sexes. He adopted the traditional view that emotionality was the natural province of the female sex, which, with the same traditional bias, he regarded as incapable of exhibiting social responsibility. Accordingly women seemed to him unable to act as guardians of social justice, despite the fact that at the same time they possessed the true key to the problems of society, namely that emotional motivation which alone could serve as the foundation of justice.

The only possible solution to Schopenhauer's dilemma is a fundamental change in the relationship between the sexes which would overcome the traditional splitting off of the emotional sphere of the personality and enable the "female" trait of sympathy to serve as a universal human motivation on which to found a society based on human solidarity. As history teaches, every moral order or system which is conceived as purely defensive, i.e., destined to protect society from the encroachments of egocentric impulses to power, always ends up turning into a kind of superguardian which dominates everyone's lives. For every such order or system is limited by its confinement within a "masculine" perspective. And its attempt to protect society, to ward off threats, to avoid problems, and to guarantee security, gives to this social order and to its administration an overwhelming aura of suspicion. Nowadays we are universally skeptical, convinced that if people were given more freedom, they would tend to behave less rather than more humanely, and that they need to be taught more self-discipline rather than more self-liberation. We lack trust in the "feminine" needs for sympathetic identification and for harmony between suffering and power based on human solidarity. Every traditional order of that kind founded on suspicion of human nature, which maintains a belligerent attitude towards antisocial impulses in society, at the same time inadvertently consolidates the weakening of the positive emotional forces of the Opposition, which is likewise concerned with the elimination of antisocial impulses. The primary concern of the traditional social order is to curb or eliminate those elements in society which seem pernicious. Thus, as a rule, when a doubtful case arises the existing order prefers to prohibit, along with antisocial impulses, the expression of needs designed to promote freer communication within the society, rather than miss a chance to strike a blow at its enemies.

It appears essential that any kind of significant movement to break down traditionally dominant, egocentric thought patterns based on the concept of power should be based on *emotion*. After long centuries of repression, the *logique du coeur*, the *ordo amoris* or "order of love," must now assert its right to exist alongside the logic of the head and the will to power. It is easy to condemn any movement to promote the *ordo amoris* on the grounds that it is engaging in antisocial behavior whenever—as is only natural—it opposes turning into absolutes certain illusory values: the pedantic adherence to formalities, conscientious devotion to working or playing along with the system, and the idolatry of rules and regulations. That ideology of formalism and strict attention to duty which is still glorified in the centers of power—and abused by the powerful in order to secure their own position—is an outgrowth of a cultural attitude towards power which we must work to overcome. Moreover, to a great extent we still lack the ability to discriminate between people and groups who oppose formalism because they want to liberate the emotional element of their human nature, and those who oppose it for purely destructive purposes. Often this distinction in motives goes unperceived, and people may foolishly assume that the former attitude invariably leads to the latter, simply in order to implicate it in a wholesale condemnation of any movement towards change and to justify the use of punitive action.

Once again we see how a semantic slip reveals an attitude which pretends to protect what in reality it harms. In West Germany it has become customary to equate people with liberal or left-wing political sympathies with terrorist "sym-pathizers." This practice is a covert disparagement of that fundamental human attitude which this chapter has described as the basic, natural motivation of any positive social behavior. Sympathy, as *sympathein* or "suffering- or experiencing-with," is the name for that mystery of spontaneous fellow-feeling and fellow-suffering which is the emotional substratum of *caritas* and ultimately of justice as well. Thus there is a primordial opposition between *sympathein* and terrorism. The falsification of the meaning of "sympathize" may be a deliberate attempt to strike a blow at that large circle of people who express their sympathy bond with underprivileged, minority social groups who are discriminated against by the rest of the population. The principle of sympathy aims at the social reintegration of people who represent the suffering repressed by society, whereas those who believe, however unconsciously, that they *must* continue this repression create witches and devils to be the victims of their perpetual need for Inquisitions and persecutions.

17

Sympathy and Trust

Erik Erikson designates the first component of the healthy personality as the feeling of basic trust. The first achievement in a child's development is the choice between an attitude of basic trust and one of basic mistrust. In his essay on basic trust, from the chapter on the "Eight Ages of Man" in his book on *Childhood and Society*, Erikson says: "The general state of trust, furthermore, implies not only that one has learned to rely on the sameness and continuity of the outer providers, but also that one may trust oneself and the capacity of one's own organs to cope with urges; and that one is able to consider oneself trustworthy enough so that the providers will not need to be on guard lest they be nipped [while the child is teething and often bites the nipple]." [20]

But before this basic trust can develop as a result of a dependable relationship between the child and his providers, based on the gratification of the child's oral needs, there is another element in his relationship to the world around him which must come first: the primary phenomenon of sympathy. Of course the mother begins to feel an emotional bond with the child as soon as she feels him move inside her body during pregnancy. This kind of immediate fellow-feeling or rapport with her child becomes complete only after his birth. The mother rejoices and suffers with the infant when he kicks about happily or when he is feeling fretful. She herself feels well when she sees that her child is happy. And of course nothing gives her greater satisfaction than to entice him into a smile or a gesture which she can interpret as a sign of contentment, or even as a positive mark of affection. The infant awakens to life with a sense of being "tucked in" and surrounded by this positive closeness, this shared feeling, which is by no means merely a secondary effect of a well-functioning bond based on oral gratification. Nursing or feeding an infant is only one aspect of maternal devotion, which is also manifested in picking up the child, singing and smiling at him, and tending lovingly to his physical needs. The infant in turn makes his mother feel accepted when, through his movements and later through smiling as well, he shows her how happy it makes him when she treats him with affection. Thus the direct emotional bond, involving "tuning in" to each other's feelings, represents the earliest characteristic of the mother-child relationship. The mother is open to the feelings in her child, and her feelings move in unison with his, just as the child in turn engages in a continual emotional exchange with the mother in the course of which he only gradually comes to acquire his own individual identity.

The sympathy bond forms the foundation on which the child's relationship with his mother, as well as with his environment, develops until it reaches the phase characterized by Erikson's pair-of-opposites, trust and mistrust. Thus sympathy is present from the very beginning. The mother experiences its presence on a primary level, without having to make any special effort. It is not something which she has to manufacture and which the child must, in the strict sense, learn from her. On the contrary, the existence of sympathy presupposes an *experiential process*, an ongoing relationship firmly built on trust, or on mistrust. The crucial thing in this process is the treatment of the child by the people responsible for his care—in other words whether those people display the traits which Erikson calls sameness and continuity. Whereas sympathy, being a primary phenomenon, is a given of human nature from the outset, trust must be *earned*. The mother, or rather both parents, must actually *do* something in order to win the child's definitive trust. And the child learns that he must respond to his parents in a certain way in order to earn their trust. Thus in this sense it is somewhat doubtful whether one can speak of a *basic* trust and a *basic* mistrust, for this attitudinal category is clearly a secondary phase of development, one mediated by previous experiences, which does not represent a "primary" or "basic" phase.

If the bond of trust does eventually develop, it simply signifies the continuity, in the course of childhood maturation, of a relational structure which was, so to speak, prefabricated by the natural sympathy bond. Fellow-feeling includes the impulse to help. Thus if the mother allows herself to be continually guided by sympathy, she automatically comes to care for the child in a responsible and dependable way. The child, in turn, will continue to respond postively to his mother. He automatically suffers along with his mother when he perceives that he is causing her distress, and thus will make a spontaneous effort to avoid such undesirable disruptions of their relationship. For on the primary level, it hurts the child as well as the mother when he sees her in a negative frame of mind. Thus his impulse to change the situation is not a strategic ploy, the result of his calculation that he must propitiate his mother if he is to continue to be fed and protected by her and to have confidence in her care. This kind of calculation would already reflect the existence of a foundation of mistrust, mirrored in the child's sense that he must reward his mother because she is not sufficiently motivated to be good to him of her own accord. Of course this kind of calculation of personal advantage might also conceivably create a smoothly-functioning relationship between the two. But the basis for this relationship would be similar to that between two very judicious men doing business together: For the sake of his own advantage, each of them tries to make the other feel good and to live up to his end of the bargain. At the same time each of them is aware that he would cease to get anything out of the other the moment he neglected or offended him in some way. In this sense Erikson's account of the category of trust is not convincing, for he describes as an essential characteristic of "trust-worthiness" the concern that those who provide for us should not come to feel that they are in danger of "being nipped."

If, like Erikson, we define so-called basic trust as a two-sided emotional relationship, then this relationship cannot be founded on the fact that each person fails to desert the other only because the other does not let him down. Instead, genuine trust involves the conviction that other people's actions as well as one's own are, in the deeper sense, determined by sympathy. Thus, one does not seriously believe the other person capable of simply "skipping out" if one ceases to continually "pay him back" for his help. Therefore, the phenomenon Erikson defines is not "basic" trust either in the temporal or the causal sense. It represents the product of a preexistent mistrust. People affirm each other's worth in an egalitarian, mutually helpful display of care and devotion—a sort of "mutual admiration society"—so that none of their partners will run out on them. They demonstrate their reliability so that they will not be deserted. Precisely because one distrusts others, one protects oneself from being "left in the lurch" by constantly showing that one can be counted on. One pursues a preventive tactic. But in the back of one's mind one continues to think about the danger which one is holding in check by these tactics.

Our Western "complex," centering around feelings of impotence and omnipotence, plays a very small role in the life of a young child. If he maintains a sympathetic relationship with those around him and—under optimum conditions—this relationship turns into one of authentic, stable trust, then the distinction between large and small has, for a long time, surprisingly little effect on the child's attitudes. A trusting child of this sort fearlessly runs over to adults who are complete strangers to him. He approaches, with complete trust, large animals like dogs or horses. He speaks to strangers without any signs of constraint. In other words, he behaves as if he were as big as adults, or as if they were as little as he. In his attitude of "beatific trust," he proceeds on the assumption that a difference in physical size does not prevent equality in an emotional bond. In accordance with the principle of solidarity based on sympathy he is guided by the feeling that his needs are as important as those of others, no matter how old, distinguished or wealthy these others may be. And he takes it for granted that his questions are just as important and just as worthy of being answered as those questions which older and bigger people address to him. When children like this, who are not broken in spirit, look upward at other people from down below, being down below does not yet involve the ideas of being impotent, oppressed, threatened or inferior, and "up above" does not involve notions of power, domination and superior worth. Within the context of the sympathetic mutual sharing of feeling in which a child of this kind is still deeply rooted, it seems perfectly natural that, as a human being, he feels that he is on an equal footing with all other people. The child feels like an authentic and valuable person because, on the level of sympathy, he can make others happy or sad just as they can him. And the child expects other people to listen to him just as he listens to them. He is grateful because they can tell him many things which he himself does not know. But it does not occur to him to feel inferior or helpless because of the disparity between their knowledge and his. For he sees that the adults around him are seriously interested in the feelings of a small child, in what he thinks and imagines. The significant feature here is mutual concern and mutual respect, which make for a balanced or egalitarian relationship. When a child of this kind is suffering and experiences care and devotion from his parents, he does not feel that his parents are being condescending, generously lowering themselves to his level, but rather has a sense of his own importance because of the great concern they show over his condition. Moreover, a small child in turn often sees "grownups" suffering from a pitiable state of despondency or depression. Children only two years old are often perfectly well aware that under certain circumstances they can exercise an important therapeutic function in helping their parents or grandparents out of an emotional "low." They can tell that a stroke of the hand, an affectionate glance or an encouraging suggestion that they play some game together can have a cheering effect on a mother when she is depressed. And every therapist who works with children knows families in which one or both of the parents need a child as desperately for his (or their) emotional stability, as the child needs his relationship with them. How many conflict-ridden marriages are dependent on the mediating function of small children, who tend to subdue tension!

In short, in a relationship based on sympathy special proportions apply, proportions which do not correspond directly to the physical and economic relationship between two people, and indeed may even be at variance with them. The child-parent relationship demonstrates in a particularly graphic way that the *logique du coeur,* the *ordo amoris,* establishes a common foundation or source of orientation—not a hierarchical relationship, but one which by nature is based on equality of value, and is independent of age, sex, wealth, and so on. From the very outset the principle of sympathy which is founded through this emotional logic involves nothing but a *sharing,* a *mutuality of feeling,* in which the distinctions between individuals are not abolished, but possess only a relative significance. For if one person can do something better than another, he does not exploit this fact to enchance his personal power, but rather allows the other person to participate in his achievements. Individual differences make for complementary relationships in a society in which each person feels complete only in conjunction with others. In terms of the self-image of parents, this means that the important thing is not the ways in which they surpass their children, but rather the fact that *without* their children they would be much less than they are with them. The children are part of themselves, yet the parents view themselves, on the contrary, as a complement to their children.

The attitude of appraisal and comparison does not become really significant until the question of power is posed. This happens when primal sympathy and the trust derived from it are destroyed by mistrust. The power principle isolates the members of a community from one another. Each begins to be invaded by the fear that his life with the others is not based on sympathetic solidarity, but that everywhere he finds an above or a below, a never-ending struggle to rise to the top, or a sense that he must fight to defend his "room at the top." This fear teaches a person to view himself and other people in a completely new way. He draws a sharp dividing line between himself and others, and at every encounter he evaluates who is in a position superior or inferior to himself and which personal characteristics offer advantages or disadvantages to anybody in the use of power.

Every child learns about the excessive importance of the power principle—learns it not naturally but unnaturally. For in the beginning the only thing which seems natural to the child is that open, carefree closeness which transmits to him a sense of freedom and at the same time of being protected and sheltered. But soon, within his own family as well as in other contexts, the child learns that this reality of sympathy and solidarity gets buried beneath a reality of a completely different order, which denies communal life within a horizontal social cycle and selects a vertical, hierarchical structure. The greater the effort parents must expend to establish themselves socially, the more readily the child will feel drawn into this same struggle. And the parents will see it as their duty to prepare the child, as soon as possible, for the merciless competition he will meet in the labor market, by hardening him emotionally. Moreover, parents frequently do not make any particular effort to keep from taking out on their child those unmastered conflicts and hurt feelings stirred up in them by their own social failures. Thus the child immediately learns the rules prescribed for those who must play a subservient role, a role with which he must soon come to terms in the world outside his family.

But perhaps the child may grow up in a family who try to eliminate from their private family life all trace of destructive competitiveness. A modern trend does exist for families to try to establish a private little domestic universe which sets up a contrast to the reality outside it—a universe supposedly founded on sympathy, trust and a sense of belonging. An individual family, however, is hardly ever in a position to maintain a private world order which conflicts with the structure of the society as a whole. One fact has been clearly established by the social-psychological research of recent decades: Even the most "liberal" of middle-class families, who try to create a climate of sensitivity to others, tolerance, mutual care and solicitude, and who maintain ideals of emancipation and progress, are unconsciously affected by the dehumanizing forces at work in the societal macrocosm. We have already discussed the problem of veiled rivalry between two married people who pretend, on the surface, that their relationship is based on equality. Children perceive the discrepancy between their parents' theoretical claims and their actual feelings and behavior. But usually the children too have split off one part of their emotions from their consciousness. Parents who believe that children should be raised free of repressions often remain blind, nevertheless, to their own secret attempts to use their children as a personal emotional anchor. Liberal-minded parents may try to draw a contrast between their domestic life style and the conventional,

conservative norms and behavior patterns of the outside world. The more
blatant this attempt, the more pressure the parents may unwittingly be
exerting on their children to adopt the role of allies against society at
large. The children are compelled to play along at the game of belonging
to a loosely-structured, liberated family, and thereby end up in a curious
dilemma. In the usual, relatively authoritarian family structure, the
parents' avowed concept of child-rearing is in total accord with the actual
style in which they raise their children. The parents do just what they say
they will do. But many parents with markedly "liberal" or "progressive"
notions about child-rearing exercise, unconsciously and in a roundabout
way, much the same kind of pressure on their children as more
authoritarian parents, because the strain and tension of their relationship
with society as a whole filters through into their relationship with their
children. As a result, the children may feel confused, for in this case the
parents are saying something different from what they are doing.
Indirectly they are demanding that their children either not perceive or, at
the very least, not *express* what is happening to them. The children are
forced to endure the repressed authoritarian aspect of their parents, but
dare not identify this authoritarian aspect as such or call it by name. They
do not even know why they are suffering, for the things which are
disrupting the family are, officially, not supposed to exist. The radical
extremist protests of many young people who grew up in families of this
kind represent nothing more than a delayed explosion, and expression of
opposition which the young people could neither formulate nor express
during childhood.

Unnatural as this may be, in the course of their development the
average child and young person are led away from the sense of the
sympathy bond between people to an attitude of egocentric vigilance,
from trust to distrust, from candor to tactics. When his world, which was
structured along a horizontal plane and was based on the sympathy
principle, cracks in two, the child is forced to fit his feelings into the
hierarchical types of relationships prefabricated for him by society. He is
forced to acknowledge that the emotion-based logic, which initially urges
people to share in the feelings of others on an equal basis, has been
annulled by the power principle. Intimacy and closeness no longer seem
to be universal, shared human needs, in the experience of which people
confront each other as equals. Instead, closeness and intimacy can be
dictated only to subordinates by those high in the hierarchy. The same
craving for closeness, if it is expressed by persons lower in the hierarchy
towards those higher up, will be denounced as "importunity,"

"insolence" or "pushiness." The need to communicate inner feelings becomes the exclusive prerogative of those in decision-making positions. The powerful, those in command, the parents, have a right to freely express their sense of inner oppression. Those who are weak, small, subordinate, or children—no matter how overwhelmed they may be by ideas and impulses—have no choice but to release these tensions in their contacts with persons even weaker, smaller and lower down in the hierarchy than themselves, or wait until they are invited to do so by those above them. Devoted love is something which the superior demands of the inferior, as in the traditional relationship between the sexes. The love which the superior gives the inferior is a form of condescension and generosity, an act of grace, a big-hearted display of magnanimity.

Those emotional elements integral to the primal and natural *ordo amoris* encourage relationships between people of equal status, all of whom feel that they exist on the same human level and who engage in a more or less equal exchange. These elements lose their meaning once a person comes under the rule of the power principle. Some people internalize the new and perverted meaning and finally arrive at a monumental error: They begin to believe that sympathy, *caritas* and compassion are the foes of any movement towards political reformation which tries to abolish the domination of man over man. Those who believe this fail to understand that by disparaging profound and basic human needs they are actually rehabilitating that power principle which they have tried to oppose. Without realizing it, they carry on the traditional repression of the sympathy principle, although this principle supplies the most powerful motivation we have for moving towards a society founded on solidarity and justice. This fatal error stems from the fact that sympathy has been corrupted and exploited by a system built on disparities of power, so that people achieve it solely as a form of "collaboration with the enemy" and totally overlook its cultural-revolutionary potential.

Genuine fellow-feeling and compassion are the basis of *caritas*, not in the sense that they represent alms or comfort disposed from the higher to the lower echelons of a hierarchy, but rather in the sense that they are an attempt to abolish injustice and discrimination. The sympathy principle demands the recognition of equality, the genuine sharing of strengths and weaknesses, a balance between giving and taking. It demands the political emancipation of the oppressed, but *not* the mere inversion of the relationship between oppressor and oppressed which occurs when the former victims of discrimination achieve a position in which they in turn can discriminate against others. The sympathy principle compels us to experience solidarity with those who have been cut off from, or have dropped out of, society, socially-disadvantaged minorities, the groups of outsiders and advocates of alternative life styles who have deserted the mainstream of society. This solidarity is based on the recognition, by those who have cut certain groups out of the social body, of their own kinship with these groups, and on their ability to learn from the disadvantaged and the dropouts how they ought to go about changing society so that everyone may live a wholesome life together. Moreover, the principle of sympathy teaches those in the service professions, whose job it is to help others, to accept their own weakness and affliction as they go about dealing with the weakness and affliction of others. Viewing life as a circle or cycle which always turns back upon itself implies that in confronting other people who appear quite different from oneself, one is also invariably encountering oneself in a past or future phase of one's existence. The person who for the moment is playing the role of the "strong helper" discovers in the child who is weaker than he, in a frail elderly man, or in a person sick and in pain, that which he himself was or, in one sense or another, will soon become. Whereas at the moment he happens to be in the position of giving more help than he receives, soon the shoe will be on the other foot and he will need more help than he can give. And in the open, sympathetic participation in one another's joys and sorrows, each person shares with the other that which at this particular moment he does not happen to be himself, but which nevertheless belongs to the cycle of his life. This sympathetic sharing expands the momentary, present-day self, turning it into the whole Self of his entire life cycle. And at the same time he helps other people to achieve this same self-completion. The classical alternatives—egocentrism versus altruism, individual freedom versus collectivism, the active versus the passive life—lose their immediacy as central categories for orienting behavior as soon as the principle of sympathy is given precedence over the power principle, which is the basis of all these polarizations.

18

Power and Manipulation

The principle of sympathy is opposed to the principle of power, but their conflict has become virtually indetectible. For our society—organized as it is around the concept of power—has perversely made it impossible to gratify our needs for sympathy outside its own hierarchical structures. As we have already shown, for the most part fellow-feeling, *caritas* and love connive with, or fail to oppose, the "corridors of power." Rather than abolishing hierarchical relationships, they often indirectly help to consolidate them. Moreover, whenever people actually join collectives or communes, suspend artificial societal polarities, and establish equitable relationships, their behavior continues to reflect the covert or overt domination of our society by the power principle. This domination is expressed in two ways:

1. The collective combats an external enemy, or at least adopts a defensive posture and closes itself off from a world expressly defined as evil.

2. The mutual solidarity of the group is enforced from above, in the form of constraints exerted by a strong authoritarian power.

In both these cases the primary human need for solidarity based on the sympathy bond is exploited by the leaders to manipulate others. Thus solidarity perversely becomes a tool of anti-solidarity. The most blatant example is war. Erich Fromm sums up the situation very astutely in *The Anatomy of Human Destructiveness:*

> War, to some extent, reverses all values. War encourages deep-seated impulses, such as altruism and solidarity, to be expressed—impulses that are stunted by the principles of egotism and competition that peacetime life engenders in modern man: Class differences, if not absent, disappear to a considerable extent. In war, man is man again, and has a chance to distinguish himself, regardless of privileges that his social status confers upon him, as a citizen. To put it in a very accentuated form: War is an indirect rebellion against the injustice, inequality and boredom governing social life

in peacetime, and the fact must not be underestimated that, while a soldier fights the enemy for his life, he does not have to fight the members of his own group for food, medical care, shelter, clothing; these are all provided in a kind of perversely socialized system. The fact that war has these positive features is a sad comment on our civilisation. If civilian life provided the elements of adventurousness, solidarity and idealism that can be found in war, it may be very difficult, we may conclude, to get people to fight a war. The problem for governments in war is to make use of this rebellion by harnessing it for the purpose of war; simultaneously it must be prevented from becoming a threat to the government by enforcing strict discipline and the spirit of obedience to the leaders who are depicted as the unselfish, wise, courageous men protecting their people from destruction. [34]

Many people recall the time they spent in fighting units, in bombed-out cities, or in prisoner-of-war and refugee camps as the high point of their lives because of the sympathy and solidarity with others which they experienced in these situations. Looking back, people often feel that they have never in their lives felt as truly human as they did during a war. Later they go into raptures over those days of unconditional intimacy with their comrades-in-arms, the spontaneous way they all stood up and sacrificed themselves for each other in times of emergency and danger. They are confused by the fact that this feeling of fellowship and solidarity, which they experienced as emotionally liberating, was linked to the vicissitudes of war and all its terrors. Why, they wonder, can't they feel this sense of community in peacetime. If they think about it they are bound to conclude that the destructiveness, which in wartime is directed exclusively against an external enemy, has in peacetime been incorporated into all aspects of our "normal" social order. Everywhere we encounter boundaries between people; inequities and domination; the privileges of wealth and property. Boundaries and inequities, whose ostensible purpose is to protect individuals or groups from one another, ultimately perpetuate the concept of egocentric and imperialistic power. The very form of our social structure—structures which we ourselves freely chose—reveals that we are still the victims of our centuries-old, blindly-pursued obsession with power. Now we must confront the truth that our social order does more to protect power than to protect people. Ironically, people who are suspicious of others' efforts to enslave them ultimately lose their souls to the tyranny in themselves, a tyranny which can never be effectively legislated out of existence precisely because it is within them. Likewise, the "justice" of our society is not the genuine justice of sympathy and *caritas* but merely an ostensible justice resulting from our entrenchment in traditional relationships based on superiority and inferiority.

Our longing to overcome the constraints of the power principle is now driving increasing numbers of young people into the new alternative subcultures. But tragically, many alternative groups and sects fail to realize their ideal of an intimate, intercommunicative and communal life style. Instead they produce a replica of the old order, once again sanctioning the power principle. Communities and cults often adopt a fanatically defensive posture towards the environment they left behind them. Authoritarian demagogues establish themselves as "father figures" in the cults and turn the group bond into something rigid and stringent, fixating group norms and the penalties for violating them. Group members hermetically seal themselves off from the outside world and develop an underground code as a protection against those "traitors" who may be tempted to "sell out." The shared paranoid determination to screen themselves from society and the outside world—which of course has been depicted as heresy or sin incarnate—automatically arouses in the inner sanctum of the group an intense urge to stick together and rely on each other completely. The devotees feel that for better or worse, they are indissolubly chained together, and so they are driven to break down all the barriers created by the egocentric attitudes which have been drilled into them. Group members undergo regression, attempting to merge into a mass entity like a herd of livestock. But to the horror of people outside the group, its members experience this merging not as a loss of personal identity, but as the cure for an individualism which they feel was both onerous and senseless. Many young people who were formerly timid, modest and distrustful, are able to integrate themselves into the group totally and without inhibition, and experience this ability as exclusively pleasurable and positive. So intoxicated are they by what they take for an experience of liberation, that young cult members overlook the fact that they have actually lost their autonomy and turned into dependent children. They are like addicts who need to belong more than anything else, and any attempt at critical self-evaluation is annulled by the gratification of this need. The fact that the gurus or cult leaders themselves demand group cohesion and try to break down all individuality in order to fit everyone into the same mold helps to reinforce those sociodynamic factors which tend to eliminate individualism in the communes and cults.

*

People have a primary need to form social ties. Yet our social structures are dominated by the concern with power. As a result it has been easiest to gratify the need to form social ties in catastrophic or emergency situations, such as war, and in social structures modelled on the religious sect, which claim to be in opposition to society and form a counterculture. Paradoxical as this may seem, it is extremely difficult to establish relationships based on a natural sympathy bond within society itself. For our society has organized down to the nth detail the hierarchical, superior-subordinate patterns of relationships which separates individuals, sexes, generations, social classes and races. And fraudulent labelling long ago legitimized this hierarchical structure as the optimum model of social existence. A person who wishes to live out his life within a close-knit social circle often finds himself confronted by two unhappy alternatives: Either he may lose himself in some kind of fanatical counterculture group, or if he chooses to remain *within* the dominant culture, he may gradually become one of a nation of sheep. It is not easy to navigate between Scylla and Charybdis.

But despite the difficulties, increasing numbers of people are trying to develop more meaningful relationships, at least in marriage and the family. In sexual partnerships they are trying to prove sensitive, dependable, and capable of enduring stress. In increasing numbers they are cultivating, within those areas still characterized by a measure of freedom, a feeling of solidarity based on emotional closeness, empathy, and forthright and intensive communication. Moreover, one reason why we are seeing so many groups of all kinds springing up spontaneously all over the Western world must surely be that people are searching to form relationships that are not based on the conventional patterns, seeking committed and responsible ways of communicating and making contact with each other. To be sure, movements to effect societal change are no longer characterized by the enthusiasm and soaring hopes which only a few years ago lent wings to many social initiatives. Today people are quieter about their efforts to bring about change, and are proceeding with greater caution. Most fear that they may end up reproducing those same disillusioning results which they observed over the past two decades whenever people tried to be *too* close, set up overly ambitious norms of social solidarity, and generally demanded more of life and themselves than they could fulfill.

Meanwhile experiments with new models of social interaction continue almost unnoticed by the general public. Despite, or perhaps because of their relative inconspicuousness and unobtrusiveness, they may achieve important work. But of course experimental groups— women's groups, men's groups, single-parent and consciousness-raising groups, groups of the parents of handicapped children, self-help couples therapy and group therapy groups, groups of non-professionals working together on social projects, grass-roots political movements, religious discussion and study groups, and so on—do not provide solutions *in and of themselves.* They can provide a helpful framework within which people are at least able to develop their social sensibilities, and perhaps even to fortify their courage enough to engage in unified action. But such groups can have unfortunate results. Exposed to adverse pressures from devotees of the power perspective both inside and outside the group, members can easily become entangled once again in just the opposite kind of movement from what they really wanted. Self-help groups readily degenerate into narcissistic, closed-in minisects; political activist groups into groups of irrational zealots and genuine "combat units"; and alternative-culture communes into way-stations on the path to alcohol and drug abuse. Yet despite their many difficulties, a number of recently-developed model societies are still "holding out" without deviating markedly from their principles.

Here and there, even in the world of work, attempts are being made to develop new types of relationships, new cooperative initiatives. Despite the increased threat of unemployment and the many fears aroused by it, the number of people who numbly consent to be just a cog in the social machine appears to be slowly but steadily decreasing. People want to work together more, to gain more experience, to have more of a voice in what is going on, and to have more notice taken of their needs. The threat of continuing automation, ecological problems, the findings of modern research on working conditions, is increasing not only grass-roots awareness of the need for solidarity, but also people's determination to take a more active role in planning for the future so that they will not be surprised by unfavorable changes.

Here, once again, we must ask what we can actually *do*—what strategies we can employ within what social and ideological framework— in order to make progress in the right directions, and to forestall any negative results which might arise from the pursuit of social models such as I have just described. As a rule we tend to regard only the practical aspects of our problems as of any real import. Yet if we attempt to propose practical solutions, we often find ourselves—quite mistakenly— being confused with those who believe that the new human being we are seeking can be manufactured under the right conditions. It is always the proposed solutions to problems that stick in people's minds. Of course constructive social theory always involves active effort to turn theory into reality. But the opposite is also true, that one cannot manipulate reality except on the basis of some critical social theory. Moreover, for far too long our misguided view of the omnipotence of Man the Maker has led us to disregard the realm of inner motivations, which alone can give us energy to elaborate new sociocultural ideals.

All the foregoing reflections are directed towards making a single point: By our exclusive concentration on sheer manipulation, pro- duction, action, we have consistently evaded asking questions about the meaning, the purpose of our action. Traditionally we have thought of human society as an object about which we can make calculations and predictions, and which we can manipulate. But now we must confess that this claim already implies a unilateral urge to control everything—an urge which represses and undermines those feelings which provide us with standards of what a human being ought to be and to do within the circumscribed area of personal relationships as well as within the broad realm of social planning. Every day we continue to allow ourselves to be talked into believing that it is a good thing for us to view "objectively" and unemotionally those problems which we all share as a society. But in reality what we need to do is to find out what it really means to be a human being. And to do this we must learn to place more trust in our emotions and less trust in our one-sided urge to turn everything into an object of technological control, concentrating only on its technical aspects. It is one of the principal tasks of this book to show that the urge to objectify the world, far from being totally emotionless, itself stems from an unconscious, emotion-based motive: namely that "complex" which has been discussed here as the "God complex" or the myth of All Mighty Man.

PART FOUR

CASE HISTORY:
AN OBJECT LESSON IN
OVERCOMING THE MYTH
OF OMNIPOTENCE

Preface

The following psychoanalytic case history graphically illustrates that that ideal of grandeur and power which has traditionally dominated our culture leads to ineluctable destruction. Human existence is by nature compounded of a mixture of greatness and smallness, strength and weakness. The complete human being is the one who can integrate these two sides of his nature. A person who wants to be stronger than he really is inevitably burdens himself with a perpetual dread that he will be attacked from behind by that weakness which he does not want to acknowledge as a part of himself. Once he has chosen to segregate greatness from smallness, regarding one as good and the other as evil, the chances are that he may never again be able to reconcile them within himself. One who wishes to rise in the world, no matter what the cost, perceives any forces which may tend to pull him downward as a deadly threat. The repression of the weaker side of the self drives it into an archaic, chaotic state. The tension between the two aspects of the self becomes a vicious circle which tends to escalate and—in accordance with established sociocultural norms—compels the person to flee into an increasingly excessive and hubristic overcompensation. He finds himself forced to fantasize that at some point he will finally have overcome for good that dangerous aspect of his nature—that vulnerability, insignificance and misery—which undermine his overweening pride.

Conflict within the self is always reflected in the sphere of social relations. Those capable of viewing themselves as they realy are—figures of medium stature, a meeting-ground of childish weakness, youthful strength, and the fragility of old age—are also capable of living with other people on equal terms. By cooperative participation in one another's lives people find that the differences between them act as a positive, mutually complementary force, and they become aware that they are simply meeting at different stages of the same life cycle. Each person sees in all others what he himself once was or is going to become. Moreover, the primary disposition to sympathy enables each person to arrive at a state of sameness-in-otherness with every other person. For the mystery of sympathy does in fact make it possible for us to achieve,

. through feelings, an identification with beings other than ourselves, and
to experience their lives as if they were our own. But anyone who
disparages and suppresses all that is small in himself in order to realize an
ideal of grandiose splendor, automatically alters his posture vis-à-vis
society or other people at the same time. He can no longer live on an
equal footing with others. Once he has erected a hierarchy in his inner
world, this hierarchy necessarily becomes the guiding principle of his
social behavior as well. The way he relates to the outside world depends
on how he deals with his own psyche. A person cannot strive to establish
equity between the powerful and the impotent members of society if,
within himself, he idolizes all manifestations of power and execrates and
subjugates manifestations of weakness. If, in order to maintain his
emotional balance, a person feels compelled to overcompensate for any
weakness, he will automatically behave towards other like an autocratic
sovereign ruling over his subjects. Moreover, this autocratic person will
feel compelled to demand that other people, who in his eyes are weak,
love what they themselves are not and hate what they are. For only
through an act of masochistic self-condemnation can the weak confirm
those who wish to appear strong in their belief that they are in fact both
morally and materially superior, regardless of how shaky their claim.
This self-loathing demanded of the weak and oppressed drives them to
the abyss of emotional suicide. In the end rebellion and murder seem to
them the only alternatives to masochistic self-destruction. For this fatal
escalation to destructive forces seems to be the inevitable, logical
conclusion of the rebellion against Pascal's dictum that man can find
meaning only living as a Something between Nothing and Infinity. A
person who cannot tolerate his own vulnerability and tries to escape
death by identifying with the infinite will be overtaken by death all the
same—a death he experiences as a ghastly nothingness.

   More than twenty years ago the true character of the inner and outer
power struggle was graphically revealed to me through my contact with a
patient whose psychoanalytic case history is recorded in the following
pages. It was in the course of treating this patient that, for the first time, I
fully understood the relationship between inner, personal conflict and
the problem of relating to others. Consequently this course of
psychoanalysis became for me an object lesson, and represented the final
incentive for devoting my psychoanalytic knowledge and methodological
skills primarily to family, group and social therapy.

   But this case did more than simply teach me a great deal about the
need for getting involved in socially-oriented forms of psychotherapy. It

also taught me important things about my own psychological development, and at the same time supplied to me, in the graphic, concrete form of a psychological family drama, the basic ideas expounded in the first three parts of this book.

In my description of the course of Martin's treatment, I place the greatest emphasis on my attempts, as a therapist, to work out the personal psychological history of the patient in terms of his relationship with his father, and pay far less attention to certain other aspects of his case, such as how the two of us dealt with the transference-countertransference relationship between us. The aim of my presentation is to document what has been treated in the theoretical groundwork of this book: *the full destructive potential of the relationship between a power cut off from suffering, and a suffering cut off from power.* Inevitably it has been necessary to neglect many other aspects of Martin's case which would have proved of particular interest to professional therapists. Obviously certain facts have had to be presented in fictitious form to protect the privacy of those involved.

Martin Tells His Story

At a social gathering a pale young man came over to me and said that he would like to speak with me for a moment alone. When we had a chance to slip away, he told me, his manner hesitant and embarrassed, that he would like to consult me as soon as possible about going into therapy. He was not certain, he said, whether he actually wanted psychoanalytic treatment, but he did know that he *needed* it, and that without a doubt it was his last hope. If he did not force himself to get into therapy, things would be all over with him soon. But he would very much like to tell me about all this in greater detail as soon as I had time to see him.

A few days later we met in my little apartment, where I had begun to see a few patients for analytic treatment in addition to carrying out my duties at the clinic. I found myself seated opposite a tall, heavy young man of athletic build. He gazed at me with intense but depressed-looking eyes set in a face which still appeared somewhat childlike. Again he spoke with hesitation, sometimes even stammering. Once again he tried to make me understand that, although he was in fact in a really disastrous state, he was not certain that he was capable of really working hard at therapy. Besides, he had already completed four months of analysis with a female therapist, and finally broke off the therapy of his own accord. He hemmed and hawed a bit when I asked him why he broke off this analysis. Probably he had told his father too much about what was going on in these sessions, he said. Then somehow his father had gained too much influence over the situation. (Later I was to learn that in this first analysis Martin had in reality experienced, in a dramatic form, impulses to kill his father. He had had to struggle with an intense urge to parricide. Then he had fled his analysis.)

Actually he saw no way to help himself. Moreover, he felt a powerful inertia, an urge to just let things slide, to leave them as they were. On the other hand, he believed that he had to do something about himself soon. If he could not stand therapy now, things would be all over for him. He was simply incapable of going on living.

In explaining his present situation he told me that he had been trained as a professional actor, but that he had actually played only a couple of bit parts and sometimes worked as a dubber for foreign films. He lived alone in a furnished room. Most of the time, except when he was working, he lay around in bed. He spent a lot of time sleeping. He could not manage to get up the energy to do anything but eat his meals or go out to an occasional movie. He was interested in filmmaking, and had already thought of someday becoming a cameraman. Otherwise he felt completely listless and uninterested in anything. Sexually he had always been impotent. Three years before, his marriage had been annulled on the grounds of his impotence, and he had suffered a great deal because of the way his mother-in-law had abused him for his sexual failure.

He could not manage money at all and had substantial debts. As soon as he was paid his wages, he usually drank up all the money by making the rounds of various bars. Each time before he was paid, he made up his mind that he was going to get through payday without making a tour of the bars and getting drunk, but once he had the money in his pocket, he would feel a great deal of anxiety. Then he could not help "making the rounds." It was easiest for him to resist temptation if, the day before payday, people were particularly pleasant to him. But as soon as anyone frowned at him or looked at him in a funny way, he was done for. Then he was overcome by a kind of compulsion. Unless he managed to pay off a couple of his debts right after he got his money, before he had set foot in the first bar, he would be unable to pay them at all. He was uneasy as long as he had any money in his pocket: he felt like he had to blow it all. "The money always runs out much sooner than I do. If there were any money left, I'd go on boozing till I keeled over."

He habitually invited other people in the bars to have a drink with him. He used to gamble and play at dice at the same time, but never really enjoyed it. Alcohol never made him cheerful and expansive, only morose. Often he used to sit glumly in a corner. In the end he got into the habit of always picking up some prostitute. He invariably felt compelled to pay the prostitutes beforehand, despite the fact that they themselves usually did not want him to. Whenever he attempted to perform a normal sex act with a prostitute—which happened only rarely—his penis usually went limp again very quickly. He never arrived at the point of ejaculation, so he preferred to be satisfied manually. But it was best when he could get the prostitutes to hit him. Being beaten was the only form of pleasure he really longed for.

His period of "making the rounds" of the bars often lasted for two days after payday. Twice now he had lost an acting role because he had not turned up at the theater when he was supposed to. But he was, quite simply, incapable of behaving normally as long as he still had money in his pocket and was making the rounds of the bars. He could not rest until his pockets were empty.

In addition he had problems with his voice. He worried that suddenly he would no longer be able to speak properly. He also had chronic asthma. At times he felt short of breath and was afraid that he was not going to be able to breathe. He took a steady stream of asthma pills. "I'm simply a lump of flesh incapable of living."

*

Gradually, as the analysis progressed, the information Martin had supplied me during our first interview was supplemented by further disclosures, until I finally acquired a more complete picture of his family and his personal history. The dominant figure was Martin's father, the scion of a family of teachers from Silesia. At the age of ten the father had been sent to a boarding school where he was apparently an outstanding pupil. Then he had attended a technical school to be trained as an engineer, and had rapidly risen to the top of his field, becoming a department head and finally the director of a famous institute of technology. There he performed administrative work and did research, both with great success. In addition he held honorary offices of considerable importance in various organizations. He had divorced his first wife, whom my patient knew little about, and married a Finnish woman twelve years his junior. This marriage produced my patient and a sister two and a half years younger. Martin had a half-brother from his father's first marriage, but had seen him only a few times in his life. The half-brother had completely divorced himself from the family. Martin knew nothing about him except that he had supposedly become a fanatical Marxist and had had a falling-out with his father.

His father had completely dominated his mother. She had not even learned enough German to get along in Germany on her own. But his father had obviously been very pleased that she was unable to stand on her own two feet. Martin always felt that his mother treated him coolly, but he did not know whether this might not have been simply a reflection of her own inhibitions. In any case he could scarcely recall her ever having shown him any affection. But then, he said, this probably had something to do with the fact that even at a very young age, he had already begun imitating his father. Thus she presumably displayed towards him some of the aversion she felt, but did not dare to express, towards his oppressive father. His mother had always shown more affection for his sister Ellen, and she had taken great care to ensure that Martin never harrassed his sister or took advantage of her in any way. He had several very painful memories of his mother unjustly accusing him of having mistreated Ellen. Actually, his mother had always been very lonely and had clung to Ellen as the only person who could give her emotional support. Martin's father had lorded it over her so much, and made so little effort to involve her in his many and varied interests outside the home that—at least in Martin's eyes—there had never been anything approaching an emotional bond, a true marital communion, between his parents. His father had, in effect, virtually remained a bachelor whom his dependent mother had had to serve in various domestic capacities. But none of these matters became clear to Martin until later in his analysis. And it would take a year and half of therapy before his image of his mother, initially shadowy and rather negative, acquired more precise outlines, and Martin began to exhibit more amiable feelings towards her.

Psychoanalysts frequently observe that the central figures in a patient's childhood initially exist in his mind in a shadowy form, and that the patient gradually begins to perceive them as more complete, rounded-out individuals only when he has made some progress in working on his repressions. Only at the end of his therapy, when Martin became, to some extent, capable of breaking free from the father who had taken him over body and soul, was he able to feel close to his mother, as he now pictured her, in a way he had never found possible before. At first he could picture only the careworn and rather rejecting mother who gradually grew sicklier and finally died of cancer when Martin was sixteen years old.

Martin had the impression that his sister had never succeeded in growing up and becoming a real adult, any more than he had. Although she was their mother's favorite, their all-dominating father had kept her from growing up. Her father had prevented her from completing her education, and she had left school early. He had never allowed her to learn anything but how to play the violin, which she could play well, but only when her father was not at home. In his presence she became inhibited and played badly, often hitting wrong notes. After her mother's death she became, in effect, her father's maidservant.

Most of Martin's earliest memories were of the time when he was between three and four years old. He recalled that his father had wanted to buy him some shoes. For some reason Martin had resisted. In response, his father had beaten him right there on the street, so severely that Martin had fallen to the pavement. This sight aroused the anger of a number of passers-by, who rebuked Martin's father. Another time, when a domineering boy had ordered him to do something, Martin had hit him on the head with a child's spade. As punishment Martin was once again soundly thrashed by his father at home, and reviled in the harshest terms. He also recalled that one day he had tried to light a cigarette for his father, but had struck the match the wrong way so that the heads of the other matches in the box burst into flame. The incident had made his father violently angry.

He had been around five years old when, as a joke, he had sneaked a washcloth away from his father while the latter was in the bathroom. But he had done it in open view of his father, so that he was certain that his father had seen the whole thing. Moreover, he had even held the washcloth in such a way that his father could not have avoided seeing it. Later his father had questioned him about the cloth, and Martin had said he did not know. His father completely misinterpreted Martin's reply and took it to mean that the boy was seriously denying having committed this petty theft. Then the father gave Martin a terrible beating.

Around this time his father had occasionally shown to various acquaintances a photograph of my patient as a small child, probably no more than two years old, ostensibly swiping a cookie from the table.

The theme of theft was to play a highly significant role in Martin's psychoanalysis. Ever since around the age of fourteen, Martin had frequently stolen money from his father, and his father had never once spoken to him about it.

In contrast to his attitude during the final phase of treatment, in which Martin attributed some positive features to his memories of his mother, at the beginning of therapy the only experiences with her which he could recall left him with feelings of deep disappointment. Actually the only time she paid him any special attention was when he had harassed his sister and thus made his mother angry at him. When his parents were out, Martin did in fact harass his sister. He used to tell her ghost stories. Once, when he was playing croquet in the garden, his sister picked up a wooden croquet ball and threw it at his head. He started to run after her, and she fled to her mother for safety. His mother grabbed Martin and beat him furiously. So he butted his head into his mother's midriff and acted as if he were raving mad. He could not get his mother to understand that his sister had started the whole thing by throwing the ball at him.

For as long as he could remember he had been totally fascinated by his father. He automatically adopted all his father's opinions as his own.

His father had always been like a god to him—but he was certain that this was exactly the impression his father wanted to create. His father believed that he was better than other people. Martin had never heard a single remark from his father suggesting that the father had ever regarded another person even as his equal, much less his superior. Letters, and a critical essay written by the father, confirmed Martin's estimate of his father on this score. During Martin's psychoanalysis, the father wrote a treatise on Goethe's *Faust*. In his introduction to the manuscript he referred to himself, as the author, in the third person, saying among other things: "One cannot infer that the author was proud of or delighted by the solitude to which his so-called 'know-it-all attitude' has, with few exceptions, condemned him throughout his life." Later in the manuscript the father, speaking directly about himself, says: "By this time I have encountered and known quite a number of our dear German countrymen, and have arrived at the bitter but unassailable conclusion that the direct influence of persons such as myself can do nothing to change things.... People do not hear or see. They do not even want to do so, so what is a poor wretch like me to do?"

In a letter to Martin, his father reflects on the image of himself which he presents to his son: "Your father exercises a remarkable fascination over you, an effect which is in part attraction, in part repulsion. At times you see him as the man who has a profound influence on others; the fate of his colleagues, to a degree, depends on him, and he has department heads, assistants, expert advisers serving under him; he has power; he is in control; at home he is the one who says how things will be; he earns the money we all live on; everything comes from him and through him; he can do everything; he thunders away on the piano; he iceskates and skis; he has bathed in the oceans of the world; he can use a woodplane and a file; he is an accomplished archer; he dons his dress-coat and goes to big banquets; he knows everything; he loves and knows all about mathematics; he knows machines, knows how they work; he himself can make tools and things which look 'store-bought'...etc., etc."

"With a father like that looming over me, I could never become potent!" Martin would exclaim later in his analysis. And "My father puts himself in the position of God, so that I can't possibly climb up there!" However, his father was not only overwhelmingly magnificent, but was also on the point of suffocating from his own loneliness. In the aforementioned manuscript the father remarks about himself: "I must confess that I am on the point of *suffocating* at least seven times a week. Often I feel as if something were eating me up from inside." The analysis would reveal that Martin was clearly aware of this side of his father's nature, and that he was certain that his father needed *him* in order not to suffocate in his own solitude. But it would also reveal a dilemma: The father needed a broken-spirited, totally helpless and vulnerable son in order to preserve his own emotional balance. Martin believed that essentially his father had always loved him more than his mother had, but in some way his father had smothered him. His father had, he said, injected him with some drug so that he could not move. In reality he was not living his own life. For example, when he visited prostitutes and let himself be beaten by them, he felt ashamed not for his own sake but at the thought that the son of a father like his should behave in this fashion. Whenever, as a boy, he had made something with his hands, his father would look at it and say, "Well, that's very nice, but now leave me alone!" And then his father always made the same thing so perfectly that Martin himself could never live up to his example. Actually he had always felt a great longing to get close to his father, and wanted to cling to him, but his father never allowed him to get close to him and had always been absolutely pitiless. Martin never dared to contradict him. From earliest childhood he had always adored his father and uncritically adopted all his views; but by doing so he had never managed to find himself. Instead, like an actor, he had imitated and repeated by rote everything which he saw his father say and do. Perhaps even his choice of profession was related to this need to play the actor and mime the role of his father.

Concerning his sexual development Martin reported that around the age of eight or nine he often used to lie in bed with his sister, and they had engaged in sex play together where he had touched his sister's genitals. Several times their mother had caught them at these games. On occasion the brother and sister had even removed their pants. Then he had had his sister strike him, and he had struck her in return. This experience aroused him sexually, and later he repeated the same game with a young male friend. The only person with whom he had ever had a really good relationship had been his school friend Klaus, to whom he had been very close between the ages of eight and thirteen. He had been deeply devoted to Klaus, who had been his superior intellectually and was therefore more successful in school. Yet he had always had the feeling that he needed Klaus more than Klaus needed him. When Klaus moved to America with his family, Martin had hardly been able to survive the separation. He had cried for a long time and felt completely forsaken. Soon after that he stole money from his father for the first time. Around the same time he had had two experiences with homosexual men. They had tried to seduce him but he had been repelled by the whole thing. His aversion to homosexual activity persisted. However, emotionally he had repeatedly felt attracted by assertively homosexual males, and these men in turn had often shown an interest in him. Later, when he became fully aware of his impotence with women, he deliberately forced himself to get involved in a friendship with an active homosexual. He thought that if he could not "get it on" with women, perhaps he might have homosexual inclinations. But he had not been able to bring himself to engage in actual homosexual acts.

When he was fourteen, a nineteen-year-old girl had tried to seduce him on the beach. He had experienced only a brief erection. The girl had gotten angry, insulted him, and treated him with contempt. It had been a terrible experience for him when his penis, after going limp, had touched the sand. He felt absolutely wretched.

At around this time he had one day seen some paper money lying on the table next to this father. He had grabbed the bills, run out of the house, and picked up a prostitute in the center of town. The prostitute took him to her room. Then he gave the girl fifty marks and ran straight home. The girl had cried when he gave her the money.

During this period, characterized by the loss of a friend, the sexual failure with the girl on the beach, and the beginning of his thefts, his schoolwork had deteriorated radically. At that time he had a very strict teacher who grew annoyed at his laziness and lack of interest in his work, and even beat him with a cane. Yet despite his poor performance in school he was not held back and was finally dismissed with a so-called "emergency wartime certificate" signifying that he had passed his final examination. For a short time he served as a soldier in the war.

Again and again, his relationships with girls broke up as soon as the girls discovered his impotence. He had begun to masturbate with great frequency and intense feelings of guilt when he was twelve. Often he had to masturbate several times in succession until he was really worn out and finally felt a sense of comparative relief. Four years before he had met the woman who had become his wife, although their marriage was subsequently annulled. Like his sister, she had been three years younger than he. Other people had always found the girl quite cool and unappealing, but she had had a youthful sweetness which he had found entrancing. But perhaps his relationship with his mother-in-law had been even more important to him. She had still been a youthful and charming woman who basically was more sexually appealing to him than her daughter. However, it had been the mother who had insisted that the marriage be annulled at once because of his impotence. During the annullment proceedings he was accused of having homosexual tendencies. After the dissolution of his marriage he had had many brief relationships with girls, but his impotence had discouraged him more and more. "Now, whenever I see a nice girl, I just tell myself there's no point in trying. Over and over I get to the same point, and then the whole thing falls apart!"

The Treatment Process:
The Relationship between
Suffering and Power

Martin's psychoanalytic treatment lasted for three years. During the first two years there were repeated interruptions. Every now and then Martin cancelled appointments and sometimes stayed away for several days or even several weeks. Then he started drinking again and simply dropped out of sight. However, on occasion he would call me up, drunk, in the middle of the night, and ask whether he might come and talk with me immediately. He paid me on an irregular basis. Indeed there was no form of provocation which he omitted in order (indirectly) to encourage me to break off his treatment. He believed he was hurting me by drinking away all his money over and over, missing appointments without offering any excuse, and not paying me my fee. And in fact I was annoyed by his persistent outrageous behavior and the fact that I never knew when he was or was not going to turn up for an appointment. Again and again, when I hoped that we had made some progress in working on one of his problems, he would suffer a new, severe setback. When Martin was, once again, on a drunk, he generally skipped several appointments in a row, which led to recurrent periods of stagnation in the analytical process. It was for this reason that I forced myself to allow him to come to see me even at two or three o'clock in the morning when, drunk, he called me up from some bar. And indeed, whenever he had a taxi drive him over to my place, half drunk, he usually communicated to me particularly significant and deep-rooted fantasies. I realized that there was only one chance of continuing his therapy with any degree of success: He had to find me ready and waiting to see him whenever he was in one of these states of desperation. For a long time he had seemed to me like a young child of chaotic disposition who was incapable of exercising any measure of control over his instincts. His despair deprived him of all inhibition, so that he was delivered over to his oral cravings and a wide variety of self-destructive impulses, as well as to tendencies to hostility and violence of which I will later speak in some detail. I could not, and indeed did not

wish to, conceal from him the fact that it cost me considerable effort to
tolerate his chaotic behavior. I got frightened, lost my temper, and often
was absolutely exhausted by my efforts to treat him. I found his nocturnal
interruptions of my sleep particularly hard to take, especially as they also
disturbed my family at a time when we were living in very confined
quarters. Yet putting up with these difficulties amounted to more than a
sacrifice, for I felt so close to my patient that I was determined to stick by
him no matter what happened now that I had actually committed myself
to his problems. I wanted to show him that he could depend on me. And
he made amends to me for the many problems he caused by allowing me
to witness the unfolding of an inner psychical development far more
intense and dramatic than those which most people—even psychoanalysts—are normally privileged to observe.

The obverse side of his poorly-developed ego was an extraordinary
susceptibility to the breakthrough of unconscious fantasies. His deep-
rooted anxieties, depressions and instinctual impulses shaped themselves
into a steady stream of dreams which, from the very beginning, Martin
had been quite willing to believe represented the key to understanding his
emotional condition. Gradually he learned to use his dreams as a guide to
his feelings, as a central source of orientation in his quest for some kind
of order in the emotional chaos within him. With fascination he
discovered that the discussion of the contents of his dreams continually
gave rise to new dreams, which always stood in some meaningful relation
to those which preceded them and which at times even pointed towards
the solutions to problems which had always appeared insoluble. Thus,
they awakened genuine hope in him.

Accordingly, in the following account of the course of treatment,
the emphasis is placed on a sampling of the more than one hundred
dreams which Martin and I discussed together, and which make clear
some of the main outlines of Martin's psychological evolution.

Records of Dream Therapy

"For years I have been having the same nightmare over and over. It's like
a voice, a cry, which frightened me long ago. Before I went to sleep. As if a
man goes on and on saying something incessantly. No, no, yes, yes. So
oppressive. Like a hammer. Like a cry repeated over and over. It
completely prevents me from thinking... You keep on hearing a voice
inside that tells you what you should do. Not a voice outside. When I used

to concentrate on something, it was there. Even when I was a child. Before going to sleep. Now I have the feeling that a huge mountain is lying on top of me... I can't express it any more. I can't say it any more... I am destroying myself."

He thought of his father in relation to the dream. But this voice he spoke of was inside himself. An incomprehensible power was holding him down from inside. In fact, it was something he was doing to himself.

*

Two sessions later he recounted the following dream: "It takes place at a railroad station. There is a large, heavy table where people are unloading luggage. There were many boys or girls. A girl. I don't know whether I saw her face first or her legs. Then I saw her from another side. I heard that she was a hermaphrodite. Her legs down below were different from the part of her above the table. Her face, up above, had rather masculine features. That immediately repelled me. At first her legs seemed charming. I fell a bit in love with the girl. Rails on the tracks... Seeing this person without a distinct sex, I think that I am, to some degree, in the same situation. In one of these books I'm reading now, there's an old man, a hermaphrodite. I was really shocked at that."

In conclusion he asked me if I knew for certain that he was a man and not a woman. He did not at all like the fact that he had such plump breasts. He was thinking about taking boxing lessons. He did not want to fight with other people, but simply to work out in the gym and train with a punching-bag. Usually he felt so fat and sluggish. Actually he had been planning for some time to go in for this kind of exercise, but he could not get up the energy. We talked about the fact that he really was not quite sure what his own body was like. He had not yet taken possession of his body, in a sense. But the dream, we decided, also reflected his concern as to whether he wanted to have a relationship with me and whether he could succeed in "working" or "training" himself back to health. Also, he was probably afraid of being dependent on me.

*

Two sessions later he began by telling me a short dream: "It was here with you. I said I had spasms of pain in my abdomen. I asked you to examine my appendix."

It became clear to him that his dream expressed his desire to establish a relationship with me. We spoke of the fact that in the dream his sex still appeared uncertain. The appendix could have stood for the penis. In this case the question would have been whether he had a healthy member or a diseased one which might have to be operated on.

Immediately after that, Martin told me about another dream: "I am invited over to their house by my former wife and my mother-in-law. My father is there too. There is a banquet. Several people are sitting there. A feeling of hostility emanates from my wife and mother-in-law. My wife introduces her new husband to me, and I don't like him. I asked the new husband something—he was a businessman. He showed me some promissory notes. I thought, concerning my wife: 'Now you have what you want.' He said: 'We have lots of these.' Suddenly we were climbing around inside boats. I was looking for my wife. It was on the beach. She was sailing out on the lake in a boat; I couldn't follow her. Then I walked home with my father, a long way. I wanted to turn around and speak with my wife again. I wanted to explain to her that not everything was my fault. Then I actually did go back. I wanted to eat something more. Then my father said, 'No doubt I'm disturbing you two?' At that moment I immediately had the feeling that it would be meaningless to speak with her. In the end I did it all the same, but it didn't do any good."

"I'm still attached to my wife. She was very close to her mother—a very overwhelming woman. My father was always hostile to my wife. One day, when I was first getting to know my wife, she and I were with my father. He considered the idea of our getting married sheer madness. He said to me: 'Do what you have to do! I guarantee you, it'll go wrong. But if you ever need me, come back home.'"

"After my marriage was annulled, I could hardly ever take a girl home with me. If I did, I immediately had the feeling that my father had her completely under his thumb. I always felt inadequate in his presence. When, as a child, I wanted to make something with my hands, he always showed me how to do it first, in such a way that I could not imitate it."

We considered the fact that at home he had always felt like an outsider in relation to his mother and sister, just as, in the dream, he did with his wife and mother-in-law. Then he recalled the bedroom scenes with his sister, when they were often caught in the act by their mother. He had, he said, an uncanny feeling during these sexual games, and even now it frightened him to think that his sister was able to remember them too. His mother wanted to keep him away from his sister. His father always claimed Martin for himself. The businessman in the dream who gave his wife what she needed was no doubt giving her sexual satisfaction, which Martin could not "deliver." He thought of his miserable failure on the beach ten years ago, the first time he was seduced into a sexual adventure, when his penis lay limp in the sand. Even the helpless clambering around in the boats symbolized his impotence. In the end nothing was left but to resign himself and return to his father. But his father would neither grant him access to his wife nor let him partake of the food.

*

Two weeks later Martin recounted a dream which clarified, in the most graphic terms, the fatal way in which he was chained to his father:

"I'm playing tennis with a man. I am standing on the left-hand side of the court. I thought: 'If he's clever now, he'll play the ball into the right-hand court. I couldn't get over that far. I'd never hit it.' It was as if someone were holding me in a vise. I try to serve several balls. Then an older man turns up, the stage-manager L., who strikes me as being like my father. I could not get any of my balls over the net, even though I had practiced my serve several times. It was all for nothing. Then Mr. L. came over and said, 'But it's really so easy! Let me show you how it's done.' He hits the ball but it sails far away to the left, beyond the court.

"In my dream I thought, 'You old know-it-all! Why don't you just leave us alone, you can't do it a lick better than we can! You're trying to put yourself in a godlike position which you can't maintain.' The man really can't have had any notion of how to play tennis. My serve was okay in itself. But the ball was caught in the net."

Now he recalled, he said, that his first analyst, the female one, had often said that he lacked the ability to make the initial breakthrough.

During further discussion of the dream we discovered that he obviously regarded his relationship with his father as an absolutely insuperable obstacle to his ever becoming potent. He could not get over the net—i.e., could not deflower the woman. But his father always drove him into the left-hand corner, into a tight corner. His father kept him on the left, as if Martin were his own left side. The father had occupied the right-hand side. The smart-aleck stage-manager may have expressed Martin's doubts of my ability to make him potent. His skepticism about my power to change anything in his fatal bond with his father would soon become more apparent.

*

A week later he told me about a conversation with his colleagues at the theater. They had been talking about a murder case in the news. When one man had claimed that all murderers ought to be executed, Martin had grown excited and advocated the opposite view, saying that society could not punish murder in this way. The others asked him whether he wanted to protect the murderer. The fact that he was so terribly overwrought revealed to him how painful the conversation had become for him. He had felt that murderous aggressions also existed in him, and he had shown his theatrical colleagues things about himself which he ought never to have revealed. Immediately afterwards he had gone home by streetcar. On the way he had suddenly run into a violent thunderstorm and had felt a terrible dread. During the storm he clung secretly to a wooden handgrip in the streetcar, for he had been afraid that he would be struck by lightning. "After all, there is a power which can wipe you out just like that!"

Thus the scene of the tennis game had been transformed into desires to commit murder and the fear of being struck by lightning; clearly there were life-and-death issues at stake. We can already see indications of Martin's fantasy that only through a murder could he free himself from the paralyzing tie to his father, but that his father's vengeance would in turn annihilate him. Later in the analysis this fantasy would come dangerously close to reality. Now we were arriving at the same point at which Martin fled his first psychoanalysis. At that time the thought that he was capable of wanting to kill his father terrified him so much that he had broken off his treatment. Now it was all the more essential that, by openly discussing this subject, we instilled in him the confidence that we could keep his problem under control.

*

During the next few weeks the dynamics of the psychical process taking place within Martin produced a dramatic climax. Martin visited his father on the latter's birthday. His father drank with him and talked with him, in a sort of secret code, about questions of conscience, the inner voice to which one must always hearken. Nevertheless, without being detected, Martin stole 100 marks from a jacket of his father's that happened to be lying around. Immediately afterward he spent 60 marks of it on liquor.

A week later he visited his father again, on the evening before his mother's birthday. "I wanted to get some money out of him, but he didn't give me any. Then I wanted to get drunk. At home I still had a bottle of cognac I had just started. Gradually I drank it all. Then I suddenly took all thirteen of the asthma pills that I had with me. Then I went on and on masturbating in bed. I was completely done in. It was like a suicide. After sleeping a few hours I read some of Sartre's *La Nausée—Nausea*. Then I began to pray. I believe that I prayed for about two hours. During that time something completely new dawned on me."

Now, greatly excited, he told me that this evening, for the first time, the meaning of the redemption through Christ had become clear to him. Now he knew for a fact that Christ had taken on himself the burden of our sins. "This evening I experienced, in the most personal way, that fact that it is impossible for human beings to live with their sins." While he was praying he had still felt afraid, but it was no longer a completely irremediable fear. In the end he took great joy in the thought of redemption, which gave him a feeling of peace and strength he had seldom known. "Yesterday I filled up with water like a plant which has been standing for a long time in a dry desert."

This morning, he said, he had "taken matters in hand," telephoned several creditors and written to others, promising that he would pay all the debts he owed them by a certain date.

After Martin, crying and in a state of great excitement, had reached this point in his account, he suddenly went limp and fell asleep for several minutes. When he woke up, his feeling of liberation had completely vanished. In a quiet, grim monologue he told me that he thought his father might well have been responsible for his mother's death. Then he fell asleep again for several minutes. Having awakened again, he expressed great gratitude for the treatment he was receiving and for my patience with him. We clearly established how important it was that he learn to effectively communicate his positive feelings so that these feelings would then meet with an affirmative response from others. When he stole from his father or failed to pay me, this not only indicated aggressive feelings but also a masochistic variation on the desire for care and concern from others. He would have liked to participate in his father's potency. Instead, as Martin saw it, for ten years his father had done nothing to encourage him or show him his approval. Indeed, his father had not even spoken to him directly concerning his thefts. In other words, despite this provocative gesture, his father had not considered him worthwhile enough to have it out with him. The dramatic excesses of his behavior clearly betokened, on the one hand, that he was directing against himself those murderous impulses he felt towards his father. He was fleeing, so to speak, from the danger of destroying his father—whom in his fantasies he blamed for having killed his mother—and was taking refuge in a masochistic self-destruction. But at the same time he was sacrificing himself *for his father*. Thus he identified with the propitiatory death of Christ. But in his case the atonement was made not for the sins of all men, but only for the mortal sin committed by his father. He was willing to sacrifice himself for his father, who had murdered his mother. In terms of the structure of his present relationship with his father he would, by sacrificing himself for his father, finally remove from his father the latter's left-hand or sinister side, his repressed negative side, and would maintain his father in that state of godlike perfection with which the latter was inwardly so obsessed.

"If only my father would speak affectionately to me just once, he would have me right where he wanted me. I'd change my tune in a flash. But he's just letting me rot. Since I left home he hasn't once come to visit me. He never asks me what I'm doing. He has never attended a performance of any play I was in." Obviously Martin found a certain sustenance in the fact that he could incorporate into his transference to me some of the positive feelings to which his father failed to respond. But his bond with his father was so overwhelming that it remained doubtful whether the amount of help I could offer would be enough to make the needed difference. This became apparent in a dream which we talked about four sessions later:

"I am taking an unpleasant trip with a companion. Three times very painful things happen, very difficult situations which I could deal with successfully if I only had a tin of cream. But my companion eats up this tin. Of the three events of our journey, I can only remember one clearly. I'm hauling charcoal to an elevator. I ask the caretaker for a poker, for it's still cold. I open the door of the elevator. Suddenly weights press up, and I'm afraid that somehow I'm going to get squeezed between them. Ghastly. Then my companion turns up again. I tell him: 'You rotten dog, why are you eating the cream, I need it!' The cream looked like egg yolk. I've forgotten the plots of the other two dreams. All I know is that in them too, my problem would have been solved by the cream.

"When I was a little boy, my father had some skin cream like the kind in the dream. It used to stand on the table in the bathroom where our toilet articles were kept. It was a particularly fine type of cream, an English brand. It was among the really special things my father had. I never saw anyone else using that brand. I would have liked to use it once, but naturally I didn't dare. If my father had seen me, he would have gotten terribly angry. Actually, in the dream I could have taken the cream away from him. But he ate it up contentedly."

Once again Martin remembered the business involving the washcloth. Why had he wanted his father's washcloth, and why had his father gotten so angry about it? The things his father did in the bathroom seemed mysterious to Martin. We discussed the fact that as a small boy, Martin had clearly believed that his father used to acquire mysterious powers of some sort in the bathroom. The objects he used there may have held a magical significance for the boy. As far as the "egg yolk" idea was concerned, it occurred to Martin that for him an egg yolk was a symbol of power. But the experience with the washcloth had shown Martin that in fact his father did not want to allow his son access to his power, his potency. He wanted Martin to remain small and weak. This was why, in Martin's dream, Martin had no poker of his own, and experienced great sexual anxiety. He needed the caretaker—his father—to become potent. Martin flew into a rage at the fantasy that his father would not give away anything of himself and devoured his energy, the egg yolk, all by himself. "I had no choice but to steal from him a little of what he always wanted to keep exclusively for himself." It was clear to Martin that all his thefts of money were related to his old desire to steal a piece of his father's potency, which his father refused to give him of his own free will. But all the thefts were of no avail as long as they took place in secret and Martin did not dare to confront his father openly about them. "Naturally he knows perfectly well that I have stolen from him at least fifty times. But he says nothing. And by this very fact he reduces me to helplessness." During these weeks Martin spent time with a young woman, a sketch artist. He went to the movies with her several times and also visited her at home. But at her home he once again had an asthma attack and was forced to leave. These states when he found it difficult to breathe had recurred quite frequently, each time he thought about attempting to have sexual intercourse with the girl. This period ended with a two-month vacation, during which therapy was interrupted.

*

During this vacation he paid off a large number of his debts. But he failed—despite the fact that he had the means to do so—to give any money to the most dangerous of all his creditors, who had already placed a writ of attachment on Martin's assets at the theater. At this point, Martin was deeply impressed by a new dream:

"We are sitting, several of us, in a big room. An American general is sitting there at the table. I talk with him. There is a couch in the room.

Female secretaries. Ought I to lie down on this couch? I talk with the secretaries about my apartment. But in the dream, somehow the apartment merges with my father's house. I talk about my driving capabilities. A woman said: 'My room is dark. It gets too hot there in winter.' I have the feeling that I must speak with the general. I ask him: 'Did you come to this country in order to make war on us?' Then he shows me a letter. Is there something about a mother in it? I begin to read the letter. I read about a trial, and I can also see the trial taking place right in front of me. Some English lieutenant has raised the barrel of a cannon beyond a certain angle. There was something wrong about what he did. The lieutenant had a defense attorney, very reliable, who stood up and made his plea for the defense. Suddenly he was asked some questions. Then he licked his lips with his tongue and couldn't say another word. Justice hangs by a thread. But somehow the thread supports it.

"I don't entirely understand what the general with the letter is trying to tell me. I say to him: 'You come here and carry on hanky-panky with thirty people.' I could not establish any connection between the letter and what I had asked him. Then the scene flashed back to the letter. And once again I saw the trial scene in front of me. The defense attorney had to give way. The letter was from a woman. Justice was hanging by a thread. Something was hanging on it. The little tin of cream? Perhaps it was the tin? No. Then I gave the general the letter. As he sat beside me on the couch, I saw that he looked like my father."

Martin was deeply moved by the dream. "A couple of days ago I saw a picture of this same general in the papers. He was in a car, greeting a couple of boys on the street. I thought: 'Just like a Nazi leader. What a damned self-centered turd! That this general guy should let himself be photographed like that."

"Now my father is attacking me again with all his might. I was at his place two days ago. Now he's written a treatise. I read the manuscript. It's in dialogue form. He is using it to vent his feelings. No doubt I'm the only one he'll allow to read it. He's just dying to talk to someone about it. I only read the first half. At the beginning my father describes himself giving another man his manuscript. My father says that he hasn't long to live, and after his death he'd like the other man to publish the manuscript. In the text itself my father analyzes, or tangles with Goethe's *Faust*. He really picks Faust to pieces, this heroic figure." Martin, highly excited, rolled back and forth on the couch. "He's crazy! How could a person write something like that! He's swallowing me up again, down to the last fingernail!" Martin started crying. When he had finally calmed down again, he told me that before reading the treatise, he had once again stolen money from his father.

"The defense attorney in my dream, that's you. And you can't answer the questions I put to you. These are the questions about guilt. I don't believe you completely. Maybe you think you can free me from my guilt. But how could that happen? I haven't got a prayer. After all, my father's still around. And I really stole the money. Do you think that's all going to just vanish into thin air? ... Now I have the same feeling I often have just before going to sleep. This voice ... this cry. It's absolutely crushing me."

Thus once again the dream was linked to the desire for potency. Martin talked with the girls in the dream about his driving capabilities. He was afraid of the dark, hot genitals. Once more he felt that his father must help him. But by presenting him with a sort of "invoice" in the form of the *Faust* treatise, his father showed him that the little English lieutenant was not permitted to raise the barrel of his cannon, i.e., to have an erection. Justice and the little tin hung on the same thread, they hung together—i.e., were related. This was a crucial key to Martin's problem. The father was turned, in the dream, into a belligerent general who resembled Nazi leaders. He held a trial, but in reality his concern was not with justice but with force. The general, Martin felt, ought to have allowed the lieutenant to raise the barrel of his cannon. If he forbade this act and tried to punish the lieutenant for it, he himself would be a criminal. But then came Martin's inner voice, paralyzing all his faculties. And I, as a psychiatrist cast in the role of the defense attorney, was too weak to liberate Martin from the oppression he suffered.

Meanwhile Martin had gotten through several paydays without getting drunk. He had gathered new hope. But his most recent dream had deeply confused him again. He felt that he must confront his father and clarify their unspoken conflict. But he was concerned that he would not be able to tolerate the process of thrashing out their problems, and feared that his father would immediately beat him down again. His next payday was just around the corner. Of his own accord he promised that this time he would not drink away his money. But I noticed that already he had become very restless.

*

On the night following payday he called me up after midnight. He was clearly a bit drunk and scornfully said: "See, you've fallen for it again. I bet you were really counting on me not to drink." I could hear him sobbing. I asked him whether his call meant that he would like to talk with me. "What's the point? What more do you intend to do with me? I'll never get well." He was sobbing. Finally he announced that he was coming.

A quarter of an hour later he came staggering up the stairs to meet me, collapsed onto the couch, and quietly wept for a long time. The evening before payday, he told me, he had read the conclusion of his father's treatise. "I was completely shattered all over again. This feeling of being so defenseless against him! *This feeling of powerlessness!*" Gradually he revealed that in the manuscript his father had torn the character Faust completely to pieces, so that in the end Faust cut a very sorry figure, and somehow his father was soaring high above him. And the really crazy thing was that in a supporting scene, his father had some third party praise him to the skies for his talents as an author. Martin shrieked with fury, in a way I had never seen him do before. Then he started crying again. I told him I had the impression that he was testing out on me the kind of behavior he intended to use on his father. He had, I said, really gloated over having disappointed me. This suggestion made sense to him. We talked about his conflict—the fact that he wanted very much to have my help but felt that he had to guard against the possibility of becoming subservient to me. He had to prove to himself that he was not going to "have it out" with his father at my behest, as we had discussed, but solely because he himself chose to do so. Then he became very tender and said that he thought it was really important that I had not simply left him in the lurch but instead had had him come over to see me in the middle of the night. Suddenly he turned on his side, curled up and peacefully went to sleep. I was somewhat perplexed about what to do next. But then, a quarter of an hour later, he woke up and looked at me shyly. He thanked me again. Then he departed, relatively steady on his feet.

*

Soon afterward, he came down with a throat infection which seemed to drag on and on. He telephoned me twice during the next three weeks. Then he showed up again: "I dreamed that I was sitting on the couch. My father was pacing back and forth across the room. I was howling in the most frightful way; I was having a real crying jag. I cried that same way, with all the stops out, when my mother died. In the dream I said: 'Someone is going to die!' As I said this I suddenly felt certain that my father would die. I cried like mad.

"In the dream I actually had the feeling that my father was going to die. Now I think about the fact that it may well be possible for me to get free of him. Something inside me has changed during my illness."

*

At the second session following this one, he began to drowse or daydream, as sometimes happened, and abandoned himself to a stream of fantasies. He had been to see his father again, twice. "Always thinking to myself: You must pinch some money from him... But now he's resisting it with all his might. During the preceding weeks it was easy for me. He did nothing to prevent my pilfering his cash. He's never said a word about it... Now he doesn't leave his wallet lying around any more... I'm drinking again...

"The thought of myself in prison... Perhaps I'll kill him after all... There's no other solution... What if I kill myself!"

"It's so dark... I'm thinking of my mother. I believe he killed her. She had the most awful pain. I don't understand anything about the situation between my mother and my father. A large, round room. Like a ball. I'm in this room, right in the middle... Did you know that my mother was never buried? Her crematory urn is somewhere in the cellar, I think... Just marked with a number. In the crematorium. She doesn't even have a gravestone. I wanted to visit her just now, at Christmas. But there is no place for me to go. I might just as well put some bottle in my room [and pretend it's her]... " He started crying and fell into a gloomy mood. "I'd really pay my father out that way... That's terrific. It's so ghastly... And he brought her from Finland here to Germany. He knows that I've caught on to the fact that he contributed to her death... But I'll go to him before Christmas and tell him that he must bury my mother's ashes. And I won't let myself be put off the way I usually do!"

We talked in more detail about his mother. It became apparent that Martin needed to achieve an emotional reconciliation with her. If he could make an ally of her, he believed it would give him strength to challenge his father.

But what happened at first was just the opposite of what he had intended. He did not come to see me for several weeks. During this time, as I learned later, he became very close to his father and celebrated Christmas with him. He didn't say a word about burying his mother's ashes. Nevertheless, he resisted the temptation to tell his father about his psychoanalysis. To be sure, his father knew that he was in analysis, and for a time Martin had even told him something about what was going on in our sessions. But now Martin no longer wished to expose this area of his life to his father. When, after a pause, he started seeing me again, he openly confessed tht he had really felt the urge to forget about the analysis altogether. He had been too frightened of what lay ahead of him if he were to continue therapy. But then he realized that now that he had embarked on the course of psychoanalysis, there was no way he could turn back. He had no choice but to continue. But this also meant that his relationship with his father would inevitably fall apart. He had wanted to avoid this, but now nothing could be done to stop it. From then on he continued analysis on a regular basis, despite the fact that his impulsive cravings and instability were waxing rather than waning.

During another drunken orgy he beat up the owner of a bar. He had caught this man of about fifty cheating at cards and had beaten him until he was unconscious. Later he tearfully made peace with the man again.

His employers at the theater, he said, wanted to get rid of him because he was so unreliable. Once again he had failed to turn up for a performance. But up to now he had always been lucky, and his colleagues had often stood up for him. The idea of killing his father was gradually acquiring compulsive features. "Perhaps I ought to leave the country immediately," he thought. "Emigrate to somewhere in South America, clear the jungle for cultivation. Chop wood. Just get away from the old man! Not to have to look at him any more!" We discussed the fact that he had broken off his first analysis when he had reached much the same point that he had reached now. I felt rather uneasy, even though—despite all my patient's wayward behavior—I was counting on his ability to deal successfully with all the perils of his situation.

*

A new dream: "There were two other people there, a woman and a man. We were somewhere beside the ocean. I was lying with the woman in our hotel. I had on a pair of pajamas. I caressed her, but I was not allowed to possess her. I caressed her from a distance. Then we went down to the sea. The sea was turbulent. I had a mad desire to go swimming. Two people were swimming there. We walked along the beach, and the sea was very beautiful. There were also some critical situations in the dream that I can't remember any more.

"In the dream I was absolutely certain that the woman was my mother. My mother always protected my sister, even from my father. I envied Ellen because she was a girl and I wasn't. No doubt my mother was afraid that I was going to turn out exactly like my father. If she knew me now, surely she would treat me differently. Actually I always thought that my mother was very beautiful."

Martin was clearly revealing an incestuous fixation on his mother. He was trying to revise his view of the rejections and disappointments dealt him by his mother. He would have liked to imagine that his mother could love him now if she could only see that he had not been swallowed up by his father, but inside, deep down, was remaining faithful to her.

One week later he was again fantasizing about his impotence and said: "It's my way of doing penance for something." Immediately thereafter it occurred to him: "When I broke off my first analysis, I had told my father about a dream in which I had wanted to kill him." Thus there still persisted in his mind the same old fantasy about the relationship between his father and his impotence: Either he had to remain impotent and surrender himself to his father, or he had to demand to be potent—in which case he must kill his father, for he could not conceive of any other way to acquire potency, over which his father had a monopoly. There was just no other way to break the stranglehold of his father's omnipotence. Martin repeatedly found himself suffering from one problem, an overwhelming problem indeed: It was almost impossible for him to distinguish between his inner fantasies and his actual conduct. He continued to experience himself and his relationship to his father and mother on the primitive, magical level of a three- or four-year-old child. For him his father was still the all-powerful magician, ally of the storm god, who a short time ago had almost struck him dead in order to punish him. And he, Martin, could free himself of the magic spell cast on him only if he committed a magical murder. Martin found it extraordinarily difficult to imagine that it was not his father as a real person who was destroying him, but only an internalized, demonic image of his father. Fantasy and reality formed a magical unity. In Freudian terms this means that Martin had a very limited capacity for engaging in a "therapeutic splitting of the ego." In other words, he had difficulty using a reflective, self-critical, "healthy" part of his ego to observe and investigate what was going on in the "sick" part of his ego. It required an enormous effort for him to observe, think about and work out those emotional impulses which continually plagued him, while still remaining detached from them. Again and again his entire ego was forcibly inundated and "carried away" by the impulses and fantasies rising from the depths of his psyche. His extraordinary ability to understand his dreams with lightning-fast precision, and to accept the fact that they represented the essence of his inner reality, constituted the obverse side of that poorly-developed ego which prevented him from establishing himself as a real, integrated person separate and distinct from all other persons, and from deliberately planning and controlling his own actions. Thus his discriminating intelligence was of little use to him because his limited ability to "split" his ego was continually overwhelmed by a more primitive, magical way of experiencing. Martin could scarcely get his head above water and have a chance to get his bearings, before he was dragged down once more into magical fantasies which took total possession of his mind, and indeed literally turned him into a man "possessed."

Clearly this infantile helplessness was closely related to the overwhelming power of the self-denying father. One might be tempted to regard Martin's chaotic and confused behavior as symptomatic of a purely personal illness, if the objective evidence did not bear witness to the fact that his father did indeed possess an inordinately inflated self-image, and made every effort to hold on to his son so that he could use him as a substitute for the negative side of his own identity. But in reality I could not treat Martin as if he were suffering from a personal illness, for actually he formed a kind of single unit with his father, and his father had managed to shackle his son to himself. As a result I, as a psychoanalyst, could not bring my patient to engage in the kind of patient-to-doctor transference—the basic working relationship—which can usually be established with the average neurotic. In this case such a relationship existed only to a limited degree. In a sense I had to follow Martin's cues and, whenever I could, take advantage of favorable opportunities to help him observe and perceive the structure of his problems. In addition, I had to help him by supplying him with a dependable source of concern and care, so that despite his tempest-tossed existence he might gradually come to trust in a kind of inner continuity in his life, which could develop in a meaningful direction. But before this could happen, a perilous crisis occurred.

*

Martin was harboring thoughts of separating from his father once and for all and not visiting him again. But his father, Martin said, was now so clever that he took care never to irritate Martin or correct his faults. No doubt he suspected that Martin was only waiting for some excuse to have things out with him. Immediately before a crucial battle with his father, Martin had this dream:

"I was tobogganing with my father and my sister. Several boys from my class, whom I haven't seen for years, were also there. I took money from my father and hid it while we were tobogganing. My father came to me and asked what I was thinking of to take his money. It was my sister who had tattled to him about the theft. I saw my sister's malicious expression, and I got furious at her and wanted to hit her. My father held me back. He was absolutely odious. Then he lifted his arm to strike me, but I grabbed his arm and said in a threatening tone: 'Now you won't hit me.' I was in a rage and almost hit him in turn.

"Then the picture in the dream changed. My mother was sick in the hospital. I was terribly ashamed. My conscience was really bothering me. I had done something wrong. Then I visited her in the hospital. Several other people besides myself were going into the hospital. I believe that I had brought something there with me. I saw my mother through a screen. She was very pale. Blonde hair. And then all that changed into photographs which someone was showing me.

"Suddenly I was out tobogganing with my sister again. It was so slushy there. There was a slope, then a path, then another slope. Across the path was a grate, a fence. One had to ride through it." Martin cleared his throat and hesitated for a moment. "The fence made the thing rather dangerous. I rode down there. Then everyone screamed, but I got through. It was pretty hard, for there was only a narrow little gate."

Now, he said, he wanted his father to hit him. He would hit back and then go away. When his father scuffled with him in the dream, Martin had pushed him back with great strength. It was, he said, also important that the money he had stolen did not turn out to be worthless later, as it had in two dreams I have not recorded here. Instead, the money retained its bright shine.

Regarding the interpolated dream sequence involving his mother, it seemed to him that when she was alive he had felt guilty because he had not visited her often enough in the hospital. But now he recalled that shortly before her death his mother had once said to him: "It's you that I'm most concerned about if I die now." This remark had moved him deeply. In fact it had changed everything. By saying this his mother had shown that she accepted and approved of him after all. Martin began to cry with abandon. For several minutes he could not get himself under control. For him it was an overwhelming revelation that his mother had showed him she really did care for him. For she had expressly said to him: "I'm not as worried about Ellen as about you." "That was the first and the last time that I was ever accepted at home. And I had totally forgotten it." He started crying again. Concerning the photographs it occurred to him that his father had kept some photos of his mother in an album, but had never shown them to his son.

We clarified the fact that the stolen potency, the money, did not, in this dream, immediately lose all its value under the pressure of guilt feelings and was not thrown away on something meaningless. The money appeared to give Martin strength to survive the dangerous adventure of the toboggan slide. Perhaps the tobogganing course represented the female genitals. First came a declivity, then a small fence. It was dangerous and difficult to pass this fence. He was afraid, but he was successful. His father was no longer the all-powerful general who condemned him. Instead, Martin took the tin of cream away from him and was suddenly just as strong as his father. But another crucial factor which lent Martin strength was the encouragement he had received from his mother. For him the fantasy of achieving a reconciliation with his mother represented a total transformation of his entire situation. Now he felt that he had the strength to talk with his father.

*

On the following day he finally confronted his father as he had been intending to do for months, but had never dared. Martin described the scene as follows:

"I was not at all easy in my mind about the whole thing. I had drunk a little beforehand and was a bit tight. But I wasn't drunk. I went to my father and said, 'I have to talk to you.' He replied that it was entirely up to him whether or not he wanted to talk with me. I said: 'Now, for the first time, you are going to have to listen to me.' I told him that I had stolen money from him. He answered that he was glad I had come to him about this matter, and that actually he had been waiting for me to do so for a long time. 'Really?' I said. 'But you've never given me the slightest hint that you knew that I had stolen from you.' My father tried to talk his way out of that one by saying that he never knew for certain what had happened to the money. He had not really had any proof. I went on: 'I didn't come here in order to beg your forgiveness. I don't feel guilty about the money. I think it was really a low trick that you never spoke to me about it. Now for once you must break out of that equanimity of yours, that always lets you bounce back like a rubber ball. For the first time in your life I want to really shake you up. For once I want to shake up your existence. For the first time, you must deal with me as your son. I refuse you the right to condemn me from the start.' "

Martin's father had tried to run away, Martin said, but then came back and said: "You are without decency, you're a filthy pig!" "Then I said to him: 'Now I'll tell you what it means to be a filthy pig. First, the way you treated me when I stole money from you. And second, the fact that all these years you haven't arranged for the burial of the urn with my mother's ashes. I haven't come here to confess. For once I demand that you be involved in the trial too.' Thereupon my father said: 'You're drunk.' Then I told him that in a couple of months I would have reached the point of being able to talk to him even when I was sober. 'And that'll be even more unpleasant for you than this.'" In the course of this confrontation his father first adopted a superior and arrogant air. Later he grew excited and angry. He himself, Martin said, had occasionally been pushed into a corner, but he said everything he wanted to say.

*

Two days later there followed a dream directly linked to this confrontation with his father. This dream represented a kind of turning-point in the analysis:

"A Jewish baby is about to be exposed in a basket at sea. A sea captain standing on board a ship wants to do this. I am on another ship with a woman who is crying her heart out. Both of us are horrified by the crime. She says: 'They want to exterminate us.' I console her: 'You'll be the people who survive after all the rest, because everything you have can be moved from place to place. And when the time comes, you will have those places on earth which are burning the least.' We look at this ship with the captain who wants to put the basket in the water. The whole thing is a couple of hundred yards away. We see it only from a distance. Suddenly a thought goes through my head: 'I'll massacre the man who does that!'

"I'm on the sea in a motorboat with someone else, and the boat is moving. I think about what I can do to stop the captain. I look at my companion and say: 'I'll get a pistol and shoot him.' That's an absurd decision. I am having a terrible struggle with myself.

"Then we are racing across the water in the motorboat at breakneck speed. Then a man comes past, a driver from the theater, a man with black hair whom I recognize. My acquaintance calls to him. Then he tosses us a pistol which he is carrying with him. Strange to say, this pistol does not sink in the water. Then suddenly I am in the water and grab hold of the pistol. I sense that now a fearfully dangerous part of the incident is beginning. I swim towards the ship with the pistol and see the captain waiting for me. Naturally the ship is taller than I am. I sense that this man possesses supernatural powers, and that something is awaiting me here which I will probably not survive. I feel surprised that the pistol does not stop working in the water. As I swim towards him, I see that on his ship he has a round thing like a spotlight. Like a mirror. It throws a beam of white light into the air. Actually not like light. The beam was mirror-bright, but compact, not diffuse. With this beam he destroyed an airplane. I was mad with fear. It was clear to me that his man was immune to bullets. This beam was a link to the upper region, to higher forces. He is in league with supernatural powers.

"I am filled with dread in the water with my pistol. But I don't abandon my plan. I sense that I can hit him. He looks down at me. I can't manage to hide the pistol under water. He sees it and guesses my plan. Then he reaches behind him, and suddenly he has a small revolver in his hand. I am terribly afraid. Nevertheless I swim closer to him holding the pistol under the water. I swim back and forth, raging about the crime he has committed. I see that he is laughing at me. Then I aim at him. I perceive that a ray is coming from my pistol. This ray strikes him but goes straight through him. I am half dead with horror. But I don't give up. Suddenly I see: To be sure, he seems invulnerable, but I am stronger than he! I cannot give in now. I go on shooting at him. Then he gives a convulsive twitch. I am hitting him. I swim back and forth in the water. In certain positions I can see how my shots are wounding him. He starts back in terror. I see that I will not kill him, but that nevertheless he will not survive. Suddenly my fear is completely gone. I am absolutely secure. Then I see the captain become furiously angry and afraid. He feels he has to defend himself against me. But as I said, I am completely safe. He comes towards me. I go on shooting. I don't hit him every time, but only sometimes. Then he hurls himself upon me and, despite his wounds, pulls me down and sits on me. My pistol flies a long distance off. For the moment I am defenseless. But I don't give up and tell my companion, who has suddenly reappeared: 'Here, give me the pistol!' I take it in my hand again and fire with the courage of desperation. I hit him again. He is gravely wounded. Finally he says: 'I see that you are stronger than I.' He rises from my body and goes up and away from me."

He immediately thought of me in connection with the driver at the theater, who gives him the pistol. I was, he said, also the companion who at the end gives him the pistol again after he has already dropped it once. In the beginning, when he was racing across the sea, he still felt as if he were doing something unlawful. The pistol he was given did not sink but lay, at first, on the surface of the water. He recalled my once having said to him that water was the symbol of the unconscious. It was a terrific feeling to be in moving water. The pistol filled with water as if it were being loaded with water, not bullets. "You give me the pistol, and there it goes on lying in the water, good for nothing. Thus it is still no use to me. Not until I put it into the water does it become valuable to me. Once I fired a shot under water, and it made a hissing noise. If I could have held the pistol in the water even longer, probably the captain would have been finished off completely . . . Now I feel completely secure. When I woke up after this dream, I thought, I would like to have killed him. But actually it's fine that I didn't kill him."

Never had he had a confrontation of this kind with his father, he said. And if he had ever engaged in such a confrontation in the past, it would undoubtedly have had a much more terrible end. The woman in the dream might have been his mother. As far as the spotlight was concerned, it made him think of his father's ultra-violet lamp, whose glow he had often seen in the morning, when he was a small boy, through the creamy glass pane of a folding-door. The ultra-violet lamp had always made him uneasy. His father had bathed in its rays. We discussed the fact that the ultra-violet light, like the tin of cream, must have been among those objects dispensing magical powers which Martin had suspected his father of employing.

As for the casting adrift of the baby at sea, Martin dimly recalled having studied an illustrated Bible for young people when he was around eleven or twelve, a Bible in which there must have been a depiction of Moses being set adrift on the Nile. He was surprised that this scene was turning up again now, for he could not really claim that it had made much of an impression on him at the time.

In reality the casting adrift of a male child on the water, designed to wipe out the last member of a tribe or race, followed by the miraculous survival of the child and his return to take his revenge, is a primordial mythological motif which has come down to us in numerous variations. In the songs of the Finnish *Kalevala*, for example, we find virtually the same scene as that represented in the Book of Exodus. One can hardly avoid feeling that this picture summed up vividly the emotional dynamics at work in Martin's family. Martin felt helplessly exposed; a part of his psychical constitution still corresponded to that of a child drifting helplessly about on the water. And he experienced his father as the person who wished him to be in this condition, to be incapable of surviving. But now he was capable of fighting back, for during the past few weeks he had gained some stability from his positive relationship with his mother. The reconstruction of the memory that he had in fact received loving acceptance from his mother gave him new strength. His archaic superego was losing power. He no longer felt that he had no choice but to be paralyzed by chaotic feelings of guilt. At last he was able to reverse the terms of the trial scene he had witnessed in the dream about the American general. At last he was certain that his father did not represent the union of might and right. His image of his father was transformed into that of a tyrant whom he set out to punish for the injustice done to his mother and himself. How was he to survive the struggle against the all-powerful magician who had death rays and supernatural forces at his disposal? He made sure that he could count on the support of his analyst. But the crucial thing for him was the fact that once the weapon had been handed him, he himself dipped it under water and, so to speak, made it strong and hard. For he had to feel this was his own battle he was fighting. Yet up until the very end he was always on the brink of passively surrendering to his father, for the captain succeeded in sitting down on top of him. Still, Martin experienced great satisfaction over the end of the dream, which proved his ability to stand fast under pressure.

It was not until he had this dream that the belligerent discussion with his father, which took place just before the dream, became, in a full sense, a psychological reality for Martin. For Martin himself interpreted the dream sequence as the final, ultimate bit of information concerning the psychological stage he had just attained. He was intoxicated by the conviction, which he now experienced as an absolute certitude, that his dream revolt was only the beginning and that he would soon succeed in dealing with the problem of his father in an even more self-assured and independent way. This belief was confirmed by the fact that he had already warned his father during their conversation that soon he, Martin, would be able to confront his father cold sober, without the support of alcohol.

Martin's rebellion threw his father, seemingly so self-assured, into a state of panic. The week after his fight with Martin he sent his son five letters containing a total of eighteen single-spaced typewritten pages. In these letters he fully revealed the sadomasochistic relationship between father and son. The moment Martin departed from the role of the compliant masochist, the father instantly lost his ability to function. His overwrought letters read like one long conjuration intended to compel Martin to return to the role which he was preparing to abandon for good. Moreover, it was also significant that during the weeks that followed this confrontation the father conducted a correspondence with Carl Gustav Jung in which he asked for advice and got Jung to arm him with arguments designed to render ineffectual my influence as Martin's psychoanalyst.

This strategy of Martin's father was based on the principle or the argument that the father had nothing whatever to do with Martin's emotional state. Martin, the father claimed, was fighting a phantom, not his real father, who bore no resemblance whatever to this phantom. But almost all of the father's statements were self-contradictory in that they were nothing but a wild barrage of direct and indirect accusations, primitive curses and derisory remarks. He would not move so much as a single centimeter to meet his son's needs. But often there shone through his armor of self-righteousness the real fear that he would surely fall apart if he lost his dominant position over Martin. A few characteristic excerpts from his letters suffice to show his true state of mind:

1. "An aged father and a young son are two completely different things, and it would be very wrong to forget this fundamental difference. You must always keep this in mind, with all the consequences it entails. This distinction between us is to be expressed, when you are conscious of who and what you are—i.e., when you are sober—in proper and sensible and decent behavior, in a certain shyness and reserve which you exhibit towards me, almost, as it were, as a matter of course. In fact you cannot and dare not speak to me as you would with some drinking buddy your own age, not even if you were sober, and it would be a grave mistake on my part to lend myself to any such notion. The fact that you lose these 'inhibitions,' as you call them, in that state of drunkenness which in you, unfortunately, is far from being a happy state, reveals, once again, that the truth which emerges from wine, like every other truth, must be interpreted rationally if it is not to turn into utter nonsense. And the truth revealed about you through this stuff you drink is quite simply this: In some primitive region inside you, a region which drinking brings to the surface, you are hiding an incredibly wild and tangled snarl, or a huge and mostly undigested lump—or whatever you choose to call it—having to do with your relationship to your father. Just try, why don't you, to write down, in a sober condition, everything that pops out of you when you are drunk, and imagine it all coming out of the mouth of another, sober person; just write it all down honestly, without trying to tone it down or pretty it up—in the form, say, of a dialogue spoken by two persons other than yourself—and then you yourself will see what nonsense is bubbling away in your brain."

2. "There is something strange and evil about your father. He's always coming and disturbing you and demanding that you not do those

things which are the most appealing. He commands and forbids, and usually that is all very unpleasant. Thus the Almighty, the Good, the Giver of All, the all-powerful magician, is also the uncanny one, the evil one, the one who prevents you from doing what you want to do. A lunatic, and an old lunatic at that, resembling me and yet so different, even physically—I must have it out with him, and above all I must really tell him the truth, this fellow who is bad and wicked in so many ways and has done so many wicked things; it's high time that we settled things between us! And then you drink your courage out of a bottle, and then all those feelings and thoughts come out, and then comes the courage too. So, let's have at him, mates! And then you come and start in on me, and then suddenly you find it isn't working, or at least not the way you thought and wished it would. Every time when you're about to get a grip on him, when you think that now you have him good and proper, you find it's not at all what you thought, he eludes your grasp, you can't get hold of him. And naturally, because you are so furious with him you say: There, you see exactly what a scoundrel he is: he won't sit still and keeps slipping through my fingers! And you sit and wag your head and blink your eyes and point your forefinger at me dramatically, but none of it helps; this whole scene which you have been building up in your mind simply never comes to pass—or at most, it amounts to your uttering, in a tremulous voice, a few dubious monologues with a lot of long words in them, which you yourself know are nothing but trash, badly performed."

3. "The powers which are making themselves felt in you are your God, your Devil, your conscience. Particularly when you are drunk, you get mixed up and confuse all these things with your Papa. Then you go to him and decide to attack him. And then, naturally, it turns out that what you were seeking isn't really there. There sits a little old man, and when you reach out to grab him, you find nothing there to grab. That is all quite accurate; only the words you use to describe all this are not quite accurate. It is not 'he' who eludes you, or even 'it,' for the simple reason that what you are looking for doesn't exist. You can't grasp hold of anything and really get your hands on it, because there is nothing there in the place where you are reaching out—or at least not the thing you are looking for. Your God, your Devil, and your conscience—the most powerful and overwhelming of forces—are speaking to you, and you run to your Papa and attack him, an old man who has already grown weak. *That is blasphemy against the Lord!*"

4. "Aha, grunts the great big drunken pig, look at how he's defending himself! There we have it all down in black and white! Ha-ha-

ha! My reply to this trash is that one can speak of 'defense' only in relation to some authority *against* which one can be said to be defending oneself. A great big drunken pig does not represent any such authority, and so this old tune about 'defense' is nonsense! But here we have a young man who is suffering from growing pains and is unaware of the import of his acts, and who presumably, let us dare to hope, will not always be ridden by the great drunken pig. Perhaps it will help him and those swine who supposedly share his views for someone to write down these obvious facts both for him and for them!"

5. "My dear Mr. Pig, it is not I who am terrifying you so. I am merely making it clear to you that it is your own God and your own Devil and your own conscience which have caught you in their pincers. I am also pointing out that your swinishness and its destructive consequences in turn result from the fact that your kind of swinish actions make life hard and, indeed, crushing and destructive for the person who commits them, and to whom they happen. It's a well-known fact that people must deal with their own burden of sin, not with the sins of other people. So please, do not add complete idiocy to the swinish behavior you are already displaying!"

6. "Solomon had many wives, allegedly six hundred. Most of them probably had children, so that it is by no means an exaggeration to suggest that, for example, Solomon must have had at least 365 sons. Now, if each one of them had behaved in the manner devised by Martin and had a row with his father every night after he had gone out and gotten himself good and drunk, then Solomon wouldn't have had a free evening or night the whole year round. But perhaps the sons got together and talked the matter over and decided to come in groups. This somewhat reduced the risk involved in facing the old man. And there are writers who pity Solomon because of his many wives, because they must really have worn him out. But in reality it was most probably his sons who really stirred up all the commotion, on an average of one son a night. Poor Solomon."

*

Thus Martin's father was towering high above him, completely out of reach. He perceived nothing more in Martin's explosion than fantasizing, projection, drunkenness, swinish and filthy behavior, rank stupidity. He did not make the slightest offer of help or sympathy. He could not and would not share with his son the experiences which caused Martin's suffering. Martin was supposed to suffer alone and leave the high and mighty Solomon in peace.

But behind the irate preaching and polemics lurked a grisly fear. The father's repeated assurances that he had not been hurt and was totally out of reach failed to conceal the fact that he had been cut to the quick and in fact was afraid for his very life. Thus, in one of his letters he implored Martin not to kill him—although of course he gave even this plea the appearance of a reprimand delivered by someone in total control of the situation:

"I would like to clear up one more thing with you. You were already on the point of getting physical with me—not much of a trick for a great hulking brute like you. You were very drunk. I think the conclusion is obvious. You know as well as I do that there's nothing new and unusual about all this and that there have been many cases in which mental disorder has led to the ultimate in physical violence. To my knowledge, the results were always highly unsatisfactory for the survivor. For either he immediately perceived his mistake, in which case he could not stand himself and took his own life (and after all, what use is a dead Papa if one is no longer alive oneself?), or he stayed alive, and then, as a rule, other people take care of the matter and do something to the person in question, like locking him up or executing him, which I consider an unpleasant and senseless fate and which one really ought to try to avoid. Or he might stay alive and make himself scarce, but then he would realize that he had not really changed anything and that he had killed the wrong person: For in reality, in order to solve his problem he would have had to kill his God, his Devil and his conscience, which is impossible, so now the situation is worse than ever. My position is more or less this: I do not cling to life much any more, but I would dislike being abused—or worse—by my son (or naturally by anyone else either). I don't know exactly what I'd do if I found myself in this kind of situation, because I have never experienced it before. I suspect that I wouldn't do much of anything, for I have always been opposed to attempting things which one possesses inadequate means to carry out, and my physical resources would prove woefully inadequate against some kind of colossal beast, whether drunk or sober. Perhaps I could try to run away and find safety, and given your recent mood, you would probably take advantage of this opportunity to compose and perform the 'Ballad of the Cowardly Papa,' with some theme like 'The cowardly bastard! He won't even let me kill him! Ha-ha-ha!'—In my opinion one ought not to do anything of this sort!"

*

Martin removed the rest of his belongings from his father's home and stopped visiting him. But the letters from his father gave him a lot of trouble. He came down with influenza. When he reappeared at my office after his recovery, he seemed depressed. Actually he would still have liked to be able to lean on his father. On the other hand, he also hated him. He experienced more and more tender feelings for his mother, as well as for his sister. But as a rule these feelings were linked with rage at his father. He was absolutely certain that his father had never helped his mother to feel at home in this, to her, alien country. Martin said that his father isolated his mother and let her shrivel up and die. Moreover, he had also systematically prevented Martin's sister from leading an independent life. She was as afraid of their father as he was. As soon as their father appeared on the scene, his sister lost her ability to play the violin, even though she could play wonderfully under other circumstances.

Martin recounted a dream which made him angry: "The Federal Chancellor is visiting an island. I was something like his secretary or volunteer assistant. We were flying in an airplane. After landing we were given a spectacular welcome on the island. Actually I quite dislike the Federal Chancellor. But it's clear to me what the dream means: The pistol slipped out of my hand again. My father sits on me. The thing is that all my life I never managed to be independent. I always found it easier to let someone else lead me around and tell me what to do, to be in a subordinate position as I had always been at home. I was always humble and submissive. But now I recall again that aggressive boy who wanted to enslave me when I was a child, and whom I hit on the head with a spade. He really bled quite a lot." Then he thought of another dream: "There are some cliffs. I hold on tightly to the edge up above. I have climbed onto the cliffs and am just on the point of pulling myself over the top. But someone up above hits me on the hand with a hoe or a spade so that I have to let go."

He remembered that at the time he had been roundly scolded and severely punished for his own childish attack with a spade. We discussed the fact that after this act of violent protest at the age of three or four, he had always played the role of the passive slave, and that now he was obviously trying to get back in touch with this earlier, rebellious phase. The fit of rage which Martin had provoked from his father when he was a child and they were out buying shoes must also be viewed in this context.

During this time Martin became acquainted with a new young girl, Marianne, whom he liked enormously because she was so natural and candid. But he claimed to experience great problems in making any sexual advances to her. All the same, he found her very alluring.

At our next session he paid me, right at the beginning, some of the outstanding debt he owed me for my services. He told me: "Actually I wanted to tell you just to go to hell. Today I got some money. I wanted, once again, to ruin everything: my chances with analysis and also with Marianne. But then I remembered again the last conversation I had with my mother in the hospital. Now everything seems different again. It's really changed my whole life." Once more he sobbed quietly. "If I can tell myself that my mother really loved me after all, then I'll be facing a completely different situation. I think that's why I couldn't just chuck the money out the window any more. In general I feel much more capable of standing up for my rights. If someone were to give me a disapproving look now, I would not simply go away the way I did before. I'd take him to task for it right on the spot." He felt certain that he would experience no further setbacks in his analysis. He felt that he could become a freer person if he followed his analysis through to the end.

*

During the next few weeks he adopted a more critical and remote attitude towards me. I was experiencing, in a modified form, some of that growing spirit of resistance which he first tried out on his father. In addition, ever since their confrontation, he had been paying his father regular installments on the money he stole.

*

During the following weeks Martin spent most of his time talking about his new girl friend Marianne. Martin was glad that Marianne was completely different from his former wife and the other women he had known in the past. There was nothing cold and virginal about her; she was just a completely natural and uncomplicated young woman. She was a student, but was also domestic and practical. He liked the fact that she enjoyed doing needlework.

*

One day he was deeply impressed by the following dream: "I'm on the street where I live. But strangely enough, it's not our house but the building, the institute where my father works. Marianne and my parents are there. I've been away and am coming back. The house has disappeared without a trace, so that I can't find it again. I'm absolutely desperate and start crying. But I don't call for my parents, I call Marianne. Then along comes a waitress. I ask her: 'What happened to it all?' The houses are burning all around. I embrace her. She says that she must go on and has no time. Then I notice that she is telling someone else what I said to her and is laughing. Then some man or other arrived. A driver from the theater. I was crying like mad. All the same he was friendly to me. In the dream I had the feeling that I would see Marianne again. And suddenly there she was coming towards me, while I was still talking with the driver. It was really great, it was so marvellous." He began to sob.

"Yesterday evening I was at the movies with Marianne. Before that I was working out at the gym. I wanted to drink a soda at a refreshment stand. Suddenly the stand was no longer there. It had been torn down overnight. That really scared me." In 1944 the house in which he and his family had been living had burned down during an air raid. He had sat in the garden with his father and sister and the belongings they had saved, watching the conflagration. At that time he had felt more excited than sad. But in his dream, he felt at first that everyone was dead. His home was gone, lost to him forever. It amazed him that, although he was looking for his parents' former home, he found himself on the street where his father was employed. Thus he was really looking for his father. The waitress, he thought, must surely be a prostitute. However, she could just as easily be his former wife. Prostitutes, when they leave him, go on to the next man, and his wife too had married another man since the annulment. In any case this person was a woman who had gotten rid of him. Up until now this was what had always happened to him. He had been rejected and ridiculed. It occurred to him: "Yesterday I told Marianne that I would have problems sleeping with her. She laughed and said: 'No one's asking you to.'" This reply pleased him very much. Two days ago, at two o'clock in the morning, he had gone to see her and brought her flowers. Although he had drunk something beforehand, she did not take offense. He thought that the driver from the theater who appeared in his dream might have been myself.

We discovered that the dream described Martin's situation, both pros and cons. Now that he had broken with his father, he really no longer had any home; but he still felt attached to his father. This was why, in his dream, his burning home was connected in his mind with the place where his father worked. At that time he was seeking the support of

a woman. But he was uncertain whether he could rely on a woman after
having been rejected so often by his mother and later having such
disappointing experiences with his wife, his mother-in-law, and many
other women. The prostitutes, who in a sense "served" him sexual gratification, could not provide a solid, dependable relationship. It was
conceivable that Marianne would not ditch him even though he had
confessed to her that he was impotent. And in this dream it looked as if
his relationship with his psychoanalyst was not disrupting, but rather
contributing to, his relationship with Marianne. At this point Martin
repeated once again how happy he felt at the end of the dream, when he
was holding Marianne in his arms.

*

During the next few weeks, in which his friendship with Marianne grew
more intense, Martin continued to contribute supplementary data which
helped to fill in the picture of his father. It dawned on him that from time
to time his father had committed petty thefts and actually felt proud of
doing so. During the years immediately following the war, his father had
often been invited to visit high-ranking Allied army officers and had
repeatedly carried off something when he left. One time it was a cigarette
lighter, and once a gold fountain pen. Sometimes he even took things
from hotels. But obviously no one had ever taken notice of these thefts,
and Martin's father had always gotten away with them. Martin was very
excited when he realized the relationship that existed between his
pilfering and his father's thefts. Incidentally, Martin had never stolen
anything from anyone but his father. But while his thefts had always
represented a terrible problem for him, and still did, his father had never
given a second thought to his petty pilfering. Stealing meant nothing to
him whatever. "It's really incredible that I never realized that before!"
Moreover, his father drank quite a bit, but never in such a way as to
publicly compromise himself. The father always conducted himself so
that he never completely lost his self-control. Actually, Martin said, his
father drank all the time, whereas he himself drank excessively only at
certain times, namely in the periods following his paydays. But now he
had his drinking well under control, and he felt that his relationship with
Marianne was very important to him in this respect.

*

Three weeks later he was extraordinarily fascinated by two dreams which,
once again, presaged a change in his mode of life.

"I was with somebody I know in a bar. At first it was closed. We knocked on the door. Then a rather old woman opened up. We went to the rear of the bar, where this woman slept. In front the bar was very small. A miserable room. She used to sleep there in order to guard the place. There was a window. Suddenly I was terribly startled. I heard someone opening the window. I said, 'Now we must be very quiet. There's a burglar breaking in.' Then a man came in holding a pistol. We had to put our hands up. Then he rummaged around the room. For a moment he laid the pistol down on the table. I grabbed the pistol and made the man put his hands up as he had done to us. The others grabbed him. I said, 'So, my good lad, now the game's up.' Then we led him away. I twisted his arm around onto his back and led him into the street. Then I turned him over to the police."

The second dream: "The dream took place on a ship. A man was there. He had a jar of cream, it may even have been the kind of cream you whip. My sister was there too. He wanted to give my sister some of this cream stuff in a spoon. I knew that it contained poison. Suddenly the scene changed into a sort of courtroom trial. I put some of the creamy stuff in the spoon and behaved as if I were going to feed it to my sister. At the same time I watched him closely. I told him to his face that the stuff was poisoned, and in this way forced him into a confession. He was sentenced to death. They led him down a staircase. Down below I comforted him and felt sorry for him. But I told him that nothing could be done to change things. It would only take a moment, I said. Then they led him out. He was going to be beheaded."

Martin recounted these two dreams, one right after the other. We compared the two, noting that in both of them Martin prevented a male criminal from carrying out his evil plan. In both cases the criminal act was directed against a woman. The older woman in the first dream suggested Martin's mother. The second dream clearly referred to his sister. In both dreams Martin took an instrument of some kind away from the criminal: the pistol and the spoon. Martin castrated his father and broke the spell of his father's magical potency, which once again was symbolized by the cream. For the first time Martin had the police on his side. In the past, in the dream about the general, both might and right were against him just as both might and right were—symbolically— hanging from the same thread. Now both might and right were on his side. He overcame his father by lawful means, as one does an evil man. And it seemed important that in the first dream he appropriated the tool

of his father's potency—the pistol—and twisted his father's arm behind
his back.

*

Reality made good on the promise of the two dreams. The day after the
two of us discussed the underlying theme of the dreams, Martin suddenly
became sexually potent for the first time. He was even able to have
intercourse with Marianne several times on the same day, and each time
experienced a full orgasm. He was blissfully happy and could scarcely
believe that this symptom, from which he had suffered so much pain,
could actually be cured. He told me that he no longer felt any fear of
the female genitals, and described how much he enjoyed caressing
Marianne's genitals and how good it felt to be inside her vagina. With the
elimination of his sexual problems, his relationship with Marianne
became even closer. They took excursions together. He was able to speak
openly to her about all his problems.

It was a great relief to him that despite his many problems,
Marianne accepted him. He could see that she was dependable and was
standing by him. He was happy about their relationship. At the same
time, he understood that this relationship was not purely accidental, but
that the changes in his emotional attitude also played a role in it. He
could relate to Marianne in a different way than he had to other women
in the past now that he had achieved an emotional reconciliation with his
mother.

In a circumspect but positive way, Marianne was supporting him in
his conflict with his father. She put up with the fact that strong
ambivalent feelings still attached him to his father. She felt that she had
nothing to fear from any competition with the father. Martin indirectly
confirmed to her how much she meant to him by remaining fully potent
in their intensive sexual relationship.

*

The change in Martin's situation was reflected in a dream which,
although brief, made a deep impression on him:

"Our old place in Tegel. My father is sitting in the room on the sofa.
I go and lower the roll-down window blinds. He says: 'Don't forget to
wake me up!' 'No,' I say. 'I've set the alarm clock. And besides,' I say,
'Marianne is coming tomorrow morning!' I saw my father looking as I
had often seen him when I was a child, when he got up in the morning.
In pajamas. We often had disagreeable conversations at that time of day.

Above all about school. That was around the time I was thirteen or fourteen, and was beginning to steal from him. My father always distrusted me. He always wanted to keep me impotent; that's quite clear to me now."

After a pause he went on softly: "I don't want to kill him at all. I only intend to put him to sleep. Marianne is giving me the chance to wake him up the right way. After all, she showed me that I'm potent. So I don't need to kill him any more."

*

Henceforth he maintained the separation from his father. In the course of a year they had no contact except a few telephone calls which did not arouse any particularly strong feelings in Martin. He finished paying off the money he owed his father. His drinking problem also improved. Only once did he suffer a relapse, when Marianne went away on a lengthy trip to the Orient. After two and a half weeks had passed without his hearing from her, he reverted to his old ways and squandered most of his pay in various bars. After Marianne's return he quickly regained his sense of security in their relationship, and his stability was renewed. He continued to attend our sessions faithfully and stopped trying to break off his analysis. A year later we jointly terminated his treatment.

Soon afterwards he married Marianne and invited me to witness their marriage. On this occasion I also met Martin's father, who impressed me as a man who was summoning all his strength to control himself and was finding it difficult to conceal his deep depression. Marianne appeared to be an unaffected, quite independent young woman. Obviously she loved Martin very much.

After some time Martin followed through on his old plan to emigrate and left for South America with Marianne. In the final phase of his analysis he had often discussed the fact that he would feel safer if he were far away from his father. Later, I heard that from time to time he used to start drinking again. Apparently serious crises occurred in his marriage, but he and his wife were able to reconcile. They now have two children.

Even before Martin's emigration, his father's condition had steadily deteriorated. He became depressed and confused and was taken to a hospital. There his psychological deterioration continued. I was told that he was losing touch with reality more and more. Up until the end he continued to exhibit the same proud and imperious behavior he always had, which now appeared quite incongruous in view of his progressive psychical disintegration. Then he died alone in the hospital. The doctors could find no satisfactory explanation for the rapid deterioration of his health. They cited, as one of the principal factors contributing to the abrupt decline in his brain functioning, damage stemming from the chronic intake of alcohol.

Conclusion

There are many indications that his father's breakdown represented the inevitable consequences of the change in Martin. For more than twenty years the father had managed to consistently maintain an image of himself as a powerful and exalted being, because he had under his thumb a son who could serve as the embodiment of the negative side of himself, which he had repressed. The other members of his family as well—his wife and his daughter—were forced to renounce any opportunity for self-development so that the father could become a sort of archetypal, textbook example of the type of the "top dog," who corresponded to the prevailing sociocultural ideal of the super-macho male. But Martin was of central importance to him. He needed Martin to serve as the representative of all suffering, masochism, absolute dependency and impotence, so that he himself could identify with just the opposite traits—with a self-confidence devoid of suffering, with total independence, with inflated omnipotence. He could be—as in Martin's dream—the "right-hand side," because his son bore for him the burden of being the "left-hand side." Martin experienced as his own an isolation which his father was able to repress as long as he kept his son under his thumb. Martin broke down under the pressure of alcoholism—a problem which afflicted his father as much as it did him, but which his father—at least until his breakdown—was able to conceal. Martin experienced the thefts he committed as a shameful self-degradation. His father enjoyed playing the role of the gentleman thief who assumes sovereign rights when he places himself above petty bourgeois morality. The father was able to portray himself as a modern, but superior and purer type of Super-Faust because Martin relieved him of the burden of contemplating the other aspect of his nature, pathetic, primitive, disgusting "swinishness." But these two sides of a person belong together. Moreover, it was in fact profoundly impressive when, in the final phase of his analysis, Martin came to understand that his increase in strength would inevitably lead to his father's collapse. "When he doesn't have me any more, he'll suffocate!" Incidentally, this motif of suffocation found its counterpart in both men, and its character altered in accordance with the polar reversal in their respective positions: when the son finally became able to breathe freely (those attacks, resembling asthma, in which he found it hard to breathe, disappeared completely during his psychoanalysis), the father began to suffer acutely from difficulties in breathing. To judge by Martin's observations and by photographs of his father, the latter constantly found himself compelled to clutch at his throat.

*

My formal psychoanalytic training had been restricted to instruction in the methodology of individual analysis, and thus at the time I first met Martin, I was not yet capable of recognizing at once that Martin's emotional illness represented a joint problem shared by both father and son, which called for the kind of treatment now employed in family therapy. At that time family therapy was something psychoanalysts simply did not recognize the need of. But my experience with Martin and my discovery that emotional dynamics involving the entire family lay at the root of his problems constituted for me a kind of revelation which inevitably led me in the direction of family therapy. The things I have learned since that time make me realize the shortcomings of the treatment I gave Martin, which I have outlined here. The comparative improvement in Martin's condition was achieved at the cost of upsetting his father's emotional balance. To be sure, the father was not my patient, and for decades psychoanalysts and psychotherapists, like all other physicians, had been trained to accept responsibility for treating only that person who directly exhibited pathological symptoms. Not until quite recently have we learned that many psychological disorders are essentially *group disorders* involving families as a whole, and that they should be treated as such by including all the affected members of the family in the therapy.

Of course, the principal reason why for a long time therapists had such difficulty achieving a comprehensive understanding of the kinds of problems found in Martin's family has to do with deep-seated conflicts, rooted in our world-view and in the sociocultural phenomena which we all share. It has long been a part of our intellectual heritage to split psychological health and psychological disease into two separate categories. It will take time to undo this error and come to understand that strength and weakness, like freedom from suffering and despair, power and impotence, are inseparably bound together from the very outset, and that they influence and interpenetrate each other in all facets of human society as well as in all facets of the psyche. For the interdependency of power and suffering, graphically illustrated here in the case of Martin and his father, does not represent a unique clinical phenomenon, but rather a universal psychological reality in which we all partake. The only unusual factor in this case history is the extreme degree of polarization attained by the two principles. In more conventional relationships we find the psychological aspects of the problem less clearly-defined, which makes it more difficult for us to understand the underlying dynamics.

Psychoanalysis evolved almost a century ago, and we are only now beginning to grasp the fact that the emotionally "ill" in fact represent the obverse, the hidden side, of the emotionally "healthy." In other words, those persons in our society who function smoothly within it and who on the surface appear to be free of pathological symptoms are, invisibly, carrying around the same unmastered problems as their obvious victims, that ever-increasing host of people exhibiting behavioral difficulties and symptoms of psychopathology, who are now clamoring for counselling and other forms of treatment. Accustomed though we are to equate psychological health with self-confidence, social success and freedom from physical symptoms, we are now finding every reason to doubt the validity of those traditional ideals of health and disease which we have taken for granted for so long. People who, like Martin's father, develop inflated ideas of their own magnificence reflect not only intrapsychic phenomena but social functioning in general in that their behavior always accompanies repressed feelings of misery and insignificance. The two phenomena, the inflated and the deflated ego, are invariably connected. Therapists authorized by society to cure only the visible suffering of the individual, without reference to that invisible disease in others which directly relates to the individual's malady, must, in the end, fail to perform their healing task. Thus it is only logical that ever-increasing numbers of professional therapists, confronted with the insoluble difficulties of the task society expects them to perform, are calling for a revision of the self-image of Western man, and ultimately of the structure of Western society itself.

We are living in a phase of history in which the Martins of this world—i.e., the representatives of traits repressed by society at large—are increasingly protesting against the oppression they suffer. Movements to achieve emancipation are being organized wherever there is divisive oppression or imperialism in any form: in the relations between the generations, the sexes, the social classes, the have and have-not nations. Those who are at the moment the more powerful—those who occupy the position of Martin's father—have every reason to treat this wave of emancipation as an incentive to voluntarily surrender the dubious privileges of power. For what happened to Martin's father on the microcosmic scale threatens all individuals and groups who engage in a blind struggle to defend themselves against the numerous liberation movements which are springing up among the ranks of the needy, the weak and the underprivileged. In the long run, human society will flourish only if we discover a new basis for this society in the involvement of all humans in the problems of all others and if the awareness of this involvement leads, both on the public and the individual level, to a steady elimination of self-destructive human relationships based on the concept of "inferior" and "superior."

Bibliography

1 Agrippa von Nettesheim, Cornelius, *De anima humane, et per quae media iungatur corpori*, ch. XXXVI of Book III, *De occulta philosophia*, in Henrici Cornelii Agrippae ab Nettesheym, *Opera in duos tomos*, Lugduni per Bernigos Fratres (n.d.).

2 Agrippa, *De occulta philosophia*, Book II.

3 Aristotle, *De anima* [English *On the Soul*].

4 Augustine, Saint, *Confessions* [*Confessionum*].

5 Augustine, Saint, *The City of God* [*De Civitate Dei*].

6 Bacon, Francis, *Essays*, Essay 40, "Of Fortune," from *The Essays or Counsels, Civill and Morall, of Francis Lord Verulam, Viscount St. Albans*, London, Haviland, 1625.

7 Beckmann, Dieter, E. Brähler and H.E. Richter, *Neustandardisierung des Giessen-Test* (GT), *Diagnostica* 23, 287, 1977.

8 Bernfeld, Siegfried, "Sozialismus und Psychoanalyse," in *Psychoanalyse und Marxismus*, Bernfeld et al., Frankfurt, Suhrkamp Verlag, 1970.

9 Boehme, Jakob, *Theosophische Sendbriefe* in *Vom Geheimnis des Geistes*, ed. by Schmid-Noerr, Leipzig, Reclam Verlag, 1940.

10 Cf. Bonatti, Walter, *On the Heights*, London, R. Hart-Davis, 1964 [translation of *Le mie montagne*].

11 Bruno, Giordano, *Cause, Principle and Unity* [translation of *De la causa, principio e uno*].

12 Carus, Carl Gustav, *Psyche: Zur Entwicklungsgeschichte der Seele*, Stuttgart, Scheitlin's Verlagsbuchhandlung, 1851.

13 Daschner, F. in *Medical Tribune* 13, No. 29, 1978, "Mangelhafte Krankenhaushygiene." [Article on poor hospital hygiene].

14 Descartes, René, *Principles of Philosophy*, "Of the Principles of Human Knowledge" [translation of *Principes de la Philosophie*].

15 Descartes, René, *On the Passions of the Soul* [translation of *Traité des passions de l'âme*].

16 Cf. Elias, Norbert, *The Civilizing Process: The History of Manners*, New York, Urizen Books, 1978 [translation of *Über den Prozess der Zivilisation*].

17 Empedocles, *The Fragments*.

18 Epictetus, *The Discourses*.

19 Erdmann, J.E., *Grundriss der Geschichte der Philosophie*, Vol. 1, Berlin, Hertz Verlag, 4th ed., 1896.

20 Erikson, Erick Homburger, "Eight Ages of Man" and "Youth and the Evolution of Identity," in *Childhood and Society*, New York, W.W. Norton, 1950, 2nd ed., 1963.

21 Fenichel, Otto, "Über die Psychoanlayse als Keim einer zukünftigen dialektisch-materialistischen Psychologie" (1934), in *Marxismus, Psychoanalyse, Sexpol*, Vol. I, ed. H.P. Gente, Frankfurt, Fischer Bücherei, 1970.

22 Fichte, Johann Gottlieb, *Patriotism and Its Opposite* (1807).

23 Fichte, Johann Gottlieb, *Addresses to the German Nation* (1808).

24 Fichte, Johann Gottlieb, *The Closed Commercial State* (1800).

25 Cf. Freud, Sigmund, *On Narcissism: An Introduction* (1914), vol. 14 of the Standard Edition of the Complete Psychological Works of Sigmund Freud, edited by James Strachey with the assistance of Anna Freud et al., London, The Hogarth Press and the Psycho-analytic Institute, 1953–1966.

26 Cf. Freud, Sigmund, *Instincts and Their Vicissitudes* (1915), vol. 14 of the Standard Edition.

27 Cf. Freud, Sigmund, *Beyond the Pleasure Principle* (1920), vol. 18 of the Standard Edition.

28 Cf. Freud, Sigmund, *The Ego and the Id* (1923), vol. 19 of the Standard Edition.

29 Cf. Freud, Sigmund, *Negation* (1925), vol. 19 of the Standard Edition.

30 Cf. Freud, Sigmund, *Civilization and Its Discontents* (1930), vol. 21 of the Standard Edition.

31 Cf. Freud, Sigmund, *Female Sexuality* (1931), vol. 21 of the Standard Edition, and *Femininity*, v. 33, ibid.

32 Cf. Freud, Sigmund, *New Introductory Lectures on Psychoanalysis* (1932), vol. 22 of the Standard Edition.

33 Fromm, Erich, *The Art of Loving*, New York, Harper, 1956.

34 Fromm, Erich, *The Anatomy of Human Destructiveness*, New York, Holt, Rinehart and Winston, 1973.

35 Funcke, O., *Vademekum für junge und alte Eheleute*, Geibel Verlag, Altenburg, 1908.

36 Grossarth-Maticek, R., *"Der kurze Weg von der Ausstossung zur Radikalität,"* *Frankfurter Rundschau* No. 217, September 30, 1978.

37 Hammes, M., *Hexenwahn und Hexenprozesse*, Frankfurt, Fischer Taschenbuchverlag, 1977.

38 Hobbes, Thomas, *Leviathan*, B. Blackwell, Oxford, 1960.

39 Hoffer, W., Oral Communication.

40 Holmsten, G., *Jean-Jacques Rousseau*, Rowohlt Taschenbuch Verlag, Reinbek, 1972.

41 Cf. Jaspers, Karl, *Reason and Anti-Reason in Our Time*, New Haven, Yale University Press, 1952 [translation of *Vernunft und Wiedervernunft in unserer Zeit*].

42 Jungk, R., *Der Atomstaat*, Kindler Verlag, Munich, 1977.

43 Jurinetz, W., "Psychoanalyse und Marxismus," in *Psychoanalyse und Marxismus*, Bernfeld et al., Frankfurt, Suhrkamp Verlag, 1970.

44 Kant, Immanuel, *Critique of Practical Reason*.

45 Cf. Kant, Immanuel, "Idea for a Universal History with a Cosmopolitan Purpose," in *Kant's Political Writings*, Cambridge (England) University Press, 1970.

46 Krauch, H., ed., *Erfassungsschutz*, Stuttgart, Deutsche Verlags-Anstalt, 1975.

47 Leibniz, G.W., Dr. Clarke's First Reply (26 Nov. 1715), in *The Leibniz-Clarke Correspondence*, ed. H.G. Alexander, Frome and London, Manchester University Press, 1956.

48 Leibniz, G.W., *Monadology*.

49 Cf. Lorenz, Konrad, *Civilized Man's Eight Deadly Sins*, London, 1974 [translation of *Die acht Todsünden der zivilisierten Menschheit*].

50 Maier, A., *An der Grenze von Scholastik und Naturwissenschaft*, Essen, Essener Verlagsanstalt, 1943.

51 Malebranche, Nicolas, *Investigation of Truth*, vol. I [translation of *Recherche de la vérité*].

52 Marcus Aurelius, *Meditations*.

53 Marcuse, Herbert, *Eros and Civilization: A Philosophical Inquiry into Freud*, Boston, Beacon Press, 1971.

54 Marx, Karl, "Private Property and Labor," in the *Economic and Philosophical Manuscripts*.

55 Marx, Karl, *German Ideology* (1845–46).

56 Mitscherlich, Alexander, and F. Mielke, *Medizin ohne Menschlichlichkeit*, Frankfurt, Fischer Bücherei, 1960.

57 Moeller, M.L., *Selbsthilfegruppen*, Reinbek, Rowohlt Verlag, 1978.

58 Moser, T., *Gottesvergiftung*, Frankfurt, Suhrkamp Verlag, 1976.

59 Mumford, Lewis, *Technics and Civilization*, New York, Harcourt, Brace, Jovanovich, 1963.

60 Narr, W.D., "Die Generation der Ausgeschlossenen," *Die Zeit* No. 4, January 20, 1978.

61 Nietzsche, Friedrich, *Thus Spake Zarathustra*.

62 Nietzsche, Friedrich, *Beyond Good and Evil*.

63 Nietzsche, Friedrich, *The Genealogy of Morals*.

64 Nietzsche, Friedrich, *Dionysos-Dithyramben* ["Dionysian Dithyrambs"].

65 Nietzsche, Friedrich, *Aus dem Nachlass der Achzigerjahre* ["Posthumous Papers"], in *Werke* in drei Bänden, vol. 3.

66 Paracelsus, *Philosophia Sagax* in *Werke*. ed. W.E. Peuckert, Darmstadt, Wissenschaftliche Buchgesellschaft, 1967.

67 Parin, P., "Der ängstliche Deutsche: Kleinbürger ohne Selbstbewusstsein," in *Psychologie heute*, No. 10, 14, 1978.

68 Pascal, Blaise, *Pensées*. [Numbering of paragraphs follows that of *Pascal's Pensées*, New York, E.P. Dutton, 1958].

69 Plato, *Symposium*.

70 Plato, *Timaeus*.

71 Cf. Reich, Wilhelm, *The Mass Psychology of Fascism*, New York, Farrar, Straus & Giroux, 1970 [translation of *Die Massenpsychologie des Faschismus*].

72 Richter, Horst Eberhard, *Flüchten oder Standhalten*, Rowohlt Verlag, Reinbek, 1976.

73 Richter, Horst Eberhard, "Freiheit oder Sozialismus?" in *Worte machen keine Politik*, ed. I. Fetscher and H.E. Richter, Reinbek, Rowohlt Taschenbuch Verlag, 1976.

74 Richter, Horst Eberhard, *Engagierte Analysen*, Preface, Reinbek, Rowohlt Verlag, 1978.

75 Richter, Horst Eberhard, "Beide Geschlechter können sich nur gemeinsam befreien," in *Enagierte Analysen*, Reinbek, Rowohlt Verlag, 1978.

76 Rousseau, Jean-Jacques, *The Social Contract* [translation of *Du Contrat Social*].

77 Rousseau, ibid.

78 Sandkühler, Hans Jörg, "Psychoanalyse und Marxismus: Dokumentation einer Kontroverse." in *Psychoanalyse und Marxismus*, Bernfeld et al., Frankfurt, Suhrkamp Verlag, 1970.

79 Sapir, J., "Freudismus, Soziologie, Psychologie," in *Psychoanalyse und Marxismus*, Bernfeld et al., Frankfurt, Suhrkamp Verlag, 1970.

80 Cf. Scheler, Max Ferdinand, *Ressentiment*, New York, Free Press at Glencoe, 1961 [translation of essay, "Das Ressentiment im Aufbau der Moralen"].

81 Cf. Scheler, Max Ferdinand, *The Nature of Sympathy*, Connecticut, Archon Books, 1970 [translation of *Wesen und Formen der Sympathie*].

82 Cf. Scheler, Max Ferdinand, *Formalism in Ethics and the Non-Formal Ethics of Value: A New Attempt towards the Foundation of an Ethical Personalism*, Evanston, Northwestern University Press, 1973 [translation of *Der Formalismus in der Ethik und die materiale Wertethik*].

83 Schelsky, H., *Der selbständige und der betreute Mensch*, Stuttgart, Seewald Verlag, 1976.

84 Schmidt, G., *Selektion in der Heilanstalt 1939–1945*. Stuttgart, Evangelisehes Verlagswerk, 1965.

85 Schopenhauer, Arthur, *Über das Fundament der Moral* (1840), in *Die beiden Grundprobleme der Ethik*, 2nd ed., Berlin, Deutsche Buch-Gemeinschaft, 1860.

86-87 Schopenhauer, *The World as Will and Idea* [translation of *Die Welt als Wille und Vorstellung*].

88 Schopenhauer, Arthur, "Über die Weiher," from *Parerga und Paralipomena, Sämtliche Werke*, vol. 5.

89 Schumacher, Ernst Friedrich, *Small Is Beautiful: A Study of Economics as if People Mattered*, London, Blond and Briggs, 1973, and Schumacher, *A Guide for the Perplexed*, New York, Harper & Row, 1977.

90 Schumacher, Ernst Friedrich, "Ein anderer 'Way of Life'—Ist der Fortschritt noch ein Fortschritt?" in *Bergedorfer Gesprächskreis*, No. 56. 1977, with the permission of W. Nordmann, Hamburg.

91 Seneca, "On the Happy Life," in *The Moral Essays*.

92 Cf. Sève, Lucien, *Marxist Theory and the Psychology of Personality*, New Jersey, Humanities Press, 1978 [translation of *Marxisme et théorie de la personnalité*, 1969].

93 Simmel, Georg, *Schopenhauer und Nietzsche*, Munich-Leipzig, Duncker & Humbolt Verlag, 3rd ed., 1923.

94 Skinner, Burrhus Frederick, *About Behaviorism*, New York, Random House, 1974.

95 *Der Spiegel*, "Wie verzaubert, betäubt, berauscht," 32, No. 29, 36, 1978.

96 Spinoza, Baruch or Benedict, Part V of *The Ethics*.

97 Stettner, L., *Das philosophische System Shaftesburys und Wielands Agathon*, Tübingen, Niemeyer Verlag, 1974.

98 Tilton, H., " 'Das grosse Buch vom Laufen' führt Bestsellerlisten," *Frankfurter Rundschau* No. 180, August 18, 1978. [Review of James F. Fixx, *The Complete Book of Running*, New York, Random House, 1977.]

98a Troeller, G., and C. Deffarge, *Die grauen Panther*, German television film presented August 28, 1978.

99 Watson, John B., "Psychology as the Behaviorist Views It," *Psychological Review*, 1913, vol. 20, 15.

100 Watzlawick, Paul, Janet H. Beavin and Don D. Jackson, *Pragmatics of Human Communication: A Study of Interactional Patterns, Pathologies, and Paradoxes*, New York, W.W. Norton, 1967.

101 Weizenbaum, J., *Die Macht der Computer und die Ohnmacht der Vernunft*, Frankfurt, Suhrkamp Verlag, 1977.

102 Weizsäcker, Carl Friedrich von, "Das moralische Problem der Linken und das moralische Problem der Moral," *Merkur* 31, 611, 1977.

103 Weizsäcker, Viktor von, *Der Gestaltkreis*, Stuttgart, Thieme Verlag, 3rd ed., 1947.

104 Windelband, W., *Lehrbuch der Geschichte der Philosophie*, ed. H. Heimsoeth, Tübingen, Mohr Verlag, 1935.

105 Windhoff-Héritier, Adrienne, *Sind Frauen so, wie Freud sie sah?*, Reinbek, Rowohlt Verlag, 1976.

106 Wundt, M., *Fichte*, Stuttgart, Frommanns Verlag, 1927.

APPENDIX

Translator's Notes to Part One

Part I of this book treats intellectual history from a European point of view. The purpose of this appendix is to supplement Dr. Richter's European data with brief examples from the Anglo-American culture sphere, in the hope of suggesting further areas of study to American readers.

Notes to Part I. ALL MIGHTY as psychohistory and the history of psychohistorical inquiry in the United States

Part I of ALL MIGHTY belongs to a study commonly referred to as psychohistory or psychohistorical inquiry, which has had a varied career in the United States. The thesis of ALL MIGHTY, as a work of psychohistory, is that at the close of the Middle Ages man's repressed insecurity at the loss of divine parental care led to an attempt to fill the vacuum by an assumption of divine prerogatives. The diagnosis of mass societal phenomena in terms of mental disorder has been challenged by some clinicians and cultural historians who feel that it makes sense to speak of such disorder only within a clinical context and in relation to an individual psyche. For example, in one of Dr. Richter's source works, *The Civilizing Process,* [1]   social psychologist Norbert Elias points out the questionable nature, to modern historical thinkers, of the premise that a psychical process can extend over many generations, and he stresses that not all the phases of a society's history are reproduced in the psychic history of every civilized individual; thus at any one time there will be many persons who do not fit the theoretical psychic profile of the age. Moreover, in psychohistorical inquiry a divergence in the selection of data can lead to a divergence in conclusions. So, in his classic text *The Waning of the Middle Ages,* Johan Huizinga concludes that the Middle Ages, not the Renaissance and the modern era, was the representative epoch of overweening pride; [2]   and psychoanalytically-oriented comparative mythologist Joseph Campbell, in his compendium of world mythology *The Masks of God,* refers to the various phenomena of ego absorption in God and absorption of God(s) into the human ego ("mythic identification" and "mythic inflation") as perennial psychic data regularly manifesting themselves during periods prior to that of Dr. Richter's study, and outside a European setting. [3]

However, Freud himself set the precedent for the concept of cultural analysis as the legitimate extension of psychoanalytic procedure with *Totem and Taboo* (1913) and *Moses and Monotheism* (1939). The latter work, originally conceived as a historical novel, contains a disarming, more or less overt confession that analysts who engage in such procedure unconsciously repress data contrary to the thrust of their argument, but that Freud intends to go them one better and suppress this data *consciously.* The human mind is inadequate to the phenomena it studies because in the real world all phenomena involve multiple causation, or are "overdetermined"; and human beings react to this bewildering multiplicity by reducing reality to a single mental pattern. Nevertheless, Freud states, he intends to uphold the tradition in Western thought, both inside and outside of science, of discovering connections to which there is nothing corresponding in reality. [4]

Later figures who followed in the psychohistorical tradition include Erik Erikson, a German who spent much of his active working life in the United States. Erikson tried to reconstruct the religious, societal and psychological context of an era through the analysis of a key figure of the time, such as Luther or Gandhi, from whom he could extrapolate to other data. [5]   Psychohistorical inquiry then branched off in other directions which have received greater or lesser degrees of sanction from clinicians and scholars. Jung's concept of the collective unconscious, and Freud's of the historical return of repressed primal events and archaic fantasies, in effect opened the way to the idea of a collective psyche, and in the 1960's, the era of the New Frontier, the Great Society, the Greening of America, civil rights activism and campus revolt, when Americans were particularly prone to Utopian expectations, some theorists proceeded on the assumption that the nation suffered from a collective cultural neurosis and that realization of this could alleviate many woes. Exemplary of this school of thought was Norman Oliver Brown, whose books earned great popular acclaim despite criticisms from more sober academic minds. [6]

What is regarded as a more solid and clinical approach has been adopted in the mass psychological studies of Robert Jay Lipton, based on the examination of large numbers of persons who have shared the same experience, with a view to arriving at more generalized conclusions concerning the psychological aspects of delimited phenomena such as atomic warfare, brainwashing, and other trauma. [7]

Notes to Part I, Chapter Two: Man's suffering self-image in the Enlightenment

The figure of the shape-shifter predominates not only in shamanistic and totemistic cultures: Swift's Gulliver sees possible shapes of the human race in pygmies, giants and horse-like beings. In the eighteenth-century United States, while the Enlightenment set the dominant mode of critical thought in Europe, New England theologian Jonathan Edwards (1703–1758) reflected man's ambivalence about his self-image. Profoundly influenced by Lockean empiricism and a scrupulous scientist from his earliest years, Edwards was nevertheless the motive power behind the Great Awakening, a highly emotion-charged religious revival in the style then being set by pietistic groups in Europe. Among his posthumous writings the mystical essay "Concerning the End for Which God Created the World," [8]   uses different geometric metaphors—the vertical line and the circle—to express man's ambiguous relationship with God. By nature man is part of God and designed for strict union with Him; yet God is an infinite height man cannot scale, the center of a circle where man is confined to the circumference. It is the nature of the separation between them that is problematic. In their eternal motion towards the center of the circle, men are moving at the behest of God: "And if God be the centre, then God aimed at himself." But the lingering distinction between man and God means that not just man's but God's will is eternally thwarted: for although God aims "at an infinitely perfect union of the creature with himself," yet "there will never come the moment when it can be said, that *now* this infinitely valuable good has actually been bestowed." The contrasting geometric metaphors—vertical line and circle—each point up a traditional and ongoing tension between immanent and transcendent concepts of divinity.

Notes to Part I, Chapter Six: Intrapsychic schism and the repression of woman in England and America

This is not the place for a history of feminism from the vantage point of the English-language reader. The only purpose of this appendix is to mention a few examples of the abundant philosophical and literary material from Britain and America which testifies to the ubiquity of themes touched on by Dr. Richter.

For example, the prevalence of the Doppelgänger motif in the nineteenth century seems to reflect that intensification of the sense of intrapsychic schism alluded to in Chapter 6. Dr. Jekyll and Mr. Hyde, Poe's William Wilson and Frankenstein are examples: the Monster is really Frankenstein himself during moments of sleep or self-forgetfulness, when the scientist is enslaved by unconscious urges. It seems no accident that *Frankenstein* was written by the daughter of a feminist and an anarchist: for libertarian trends in Britain and North America were linked with some degree of awareness of the crucial importance of sexual relations in achieving psychic unification. Mary Shelley was the child of English feminist Mary Wollstonecraft and anarchist social reformer William Godwin. Godwin's ideas became the model for concepts expressed by his son-in-law Shelley in *Prometheus Unbound,* in which the emancipation of man—the unchaining of Prometheus—is effected through the "feminine" traits of compassion and understanding, which Prometheus exhibits towards his divine captor. In *Frankenstein, or the New Prometheus* (1818), by Shelley's wife Mary, the revolt of nature and emotion against the godlike presumption of the rationalistic male scientist is embodied in a monster who destroys his creator for the arrogation of divine prerogatives.

William Blake too perceived the relationship between sexual emancipation, the liberation of human imagination, and the renewal of society. The male mythic figures in Blake's later poems have female counterparts with whom they must live in union if man is not to be split into various warring members and bring about his own fall. [9]

John Stuart Mill's influential treatise on the *Subjection of Women* was not published until 1869; but liberation was already in the air in the theories of Hume, Adam Smith, Mary Wollstonecraft and the English Romantics. The right of women's suffrage was first proposed in the United States in 1848.

The Gothic novel, as a warning against the male's godlike propensities and suppression of the Id or the feminine sphere, was just one of the subterranean rumblings from the female domain. The tales of Edgar Allan Poe are saturated with the revolt of the vampire-woman, the image of Victorian repression of emotion, nature and the unconscious, who rises up, often from the dead, to destroy the man for his failure to love her or for his literal attempt to murder or bury her. Just as Oscar Wilde's Salome will rise up and slay the unresponsive male principle Jokanaan in 1893, Poe's women of the 1840's—Madeline Usher, Ligeia, Morella, Berenice and the murdered wife of "The Black Cat"—all rise from male-imposed death. Cf. Poe's "Berenice," which reveals the psychological process behind the male's intellectual murder of the woman and her subsequent overthrow of the rational principle.

A striking modern illustration of Dr. Richter's discussion of the psychic disintegration which attends male oppression of female attributes can be found in the 1937 novel *Descent into Hell* by Anglican writer-theologian Charles Williams. The protagonist, archetypal narcissist Lawrence Wentworth, decides that he prefers to live with a fantasy-image of the woman he loves because he can exercise more complete dominion over this "image without incarnation" than over the real woman. To his horror he finds that the image with which he is living tends to decompose whenever he is not actively exerting control over it; and in the end, overtaken by madness, he loses that intellectual faculty which was his greatest pride. Wentworth parallels, to a degree, the famous Continental type of the dehumanized intellectual, Paul Valery's Monsieur Teste (from the French *teste* or *tête*, "head"), who relates to his wife by analyzing her prayers and is led to his death by the "funeral march of thought."

Footnotes to Appendix

1   N. Elias, *The Civilizing Process* [Über den Prozess der Zivilisation], New York, Urizen Books, 1978.

2   J. Huizinga, Chapter I, "The Violent Tenor of Life," p. 18 ff., *The Waning of the Middle Ages* [Herfsttij der Middeleuwen: Studie over Levens- en Gedachten-vormen der Veertiende en Vijftiende Eeuw in Frankrijk en de Nederlanden], London, E. Arnold & Co., 1937.

3   J. Campbell, *The Masks of God: Oriental Mythology*, Part I, Chapter 2, "The Cities of God," VI., "Mythic Inflation," pp. 72-83 et al. in *The Masks of God*, New York, Viking Press, 1959-68.

4   Sigmund Freud, Essay III, Parts A and B, *Moses and Monotheism*.

5   Erik Erikson, *Young Man Luther: A Study in the Psychoanalysis of History*, New York, Norton, 1958; *Gandhi's Truth: On the Origins of Militant Nonviolence*, New York, Norton, 1967.

6   Norman O. Brown, *Life against Death: The Psychoanalytic Meaning of History*, Middletown, Conn., Wesleyan University Press, 1959; *Love's Body*, New York, Random House, 1966.

7   Robert J. Lifton, *Death in Life: Survivors of Hiroshima*, New York, Random House, 1967-68; *Thought Reform and the Psychology of Totalism: A Study of "Brainwashing" in China*, New York, Norton, 1961; *Home from the War: Vietnam Veterans, Neither Victims nor Executioners*, New York, Simon and Schuster, 1973; *History and Human Survival: Essays on the Young and Old, Survivors and the Dead, Peace and War, and on Contemporary Psychohistory*, New York, Random House, 1976.

8   Jonathan Edwards, *Basic Writings*, New York, London and Ontario, The New American Library, 1966.

9   For example, cf. Urizen's speeches in Night III of *Vala, or the Four Zoas*.

Use This Handy Order Form
for Your *SPECIAL DISCOUNT*
on Hunter House
Psychology & Health Books

ALL MIGHTY: A Study of the God Complex in Western Man
by Horst Richter, Ph.D.
    A ground-breaking examination of the two forces that have shaped western philosophy and culture: the will to power, and a fear of suffering. The non-fiction bestseller in Germany in 1979.
    First Edition   320pp   Hard Cover $19.95

INTRANCE: Fundamental Psychological Patterns of the Inner and Outer World by C.J. Schuurman, Ph.D.
    An introspective journey through the psyche that illuminates the gap between our inner and outer worlds and discusses the true meaning of individuation.
    First Edition   160pp   Soft Cover $7.50

LSD PSYCHOTHERAPY by Stanislav Grof, M.D.
    The first scientifically complete and balanced source of information on the subject. "His writings offer a new cartography of the human mind which moves psychology far beyond the limited notions of Freud. . . ." *New Age Magazine*
    First Edition   352pp   Hard Cover $24.95
    52 Full-color Illustrations

COUPLES IN COLLUSION: The Unconscious Dimension in Partner Relationships by Jürg Willi, M.D.
    Explores the secret and unconscious agreement between partners in a marriage to avoid the real areas of conflict between them. Awarded the Prix Dubois of the Swiss Society of Medical Psychotherapy. To be followed by DYNAMICS OF COUPLES THERAPY.
    First Edition   288pp   Soft Cover $9.95

QUESTIONING TECHNIQUES by Arthur Kaiser
    A practical handbook of techniques for effective goal-oriented conversation and interview. With models for counselors, teachers, students and salespeople.
    First Edition   128pp   Soft Cover $3.95

See over for ordering & discounts

Add postage and handling at $1.50 for one book and $0.50 for every additional book. Please allow 6 to 8 weeks for delivery.

PLEASE PRINT:

Name _____

Street/Number_____

City/State _____ Zip _____

PLEASE SEND ME:

ALL MIGHTY: .... _____ @ $19.95 _____

INTRANCE .... _____ @ $ 7.50 _____

LSD PSYCHOTHERAPY .... _____ @ $24.95 _____

COUPLES IN COLLUSION ..... _____ @ $ 9.95 _____

QUESTIONING TECHNIQUES _____ @ $ 3.95 _____

TOTAL _____

DISCOUNT AT _____ % **LESS** $ (_____)

TOTAL COST OF BOOKS $_____

Shipping & Handling $_____

California Residents add Sales Tax $_____

TOTAL AMOUNT ENCLOSED $_____

☐ Cash ☐ Check ☐ Money Order

☐ Check here to receive our catalog of books

Please complete and mail to:
HUNTER HOUSE INC., PUBLISHERS
PO Box 1302, Claremont, CA 91711, USA

If you don't use this offer – give it to a friend!